The Natural History of

OTTERS

The Natural History of
OTTERS

PAUL CHANIN

Facts On File Publications
New York, New York ● Oxford, England

First published in the United States by
Facts On File, Inc.
460 Park Avenue South
New York, New York 10016

Library of Congress Cataloging in Publication Data

Chanin, Paul
   The natural history of otters.

   Bibliography: p. 168.
   Includes index.
   1. Otters.   I. Title.
QL737.C25C43   1985   599.74'447   85-6858
ISBN 0-8160-1288-1

Typeset by Columns of Reading
Printed in Great Britain
10 9 8 7 6 5 4 3 2 1

Contents

To Brian and Janet Chanin

Colour plates

Figures

LIST OF FIGURES

Tables

Acknowledgements

I am extremely grateful to Ernest Neal for suggesting that I write a book on otters and for his help and encouragement over a lengthy gestation period. I would also like to acknowledge a longer standing debt as it was his book *The Badger* which first focussed my attention on mammals in general and carnivores in particular. My thanks also to Vincent Weir who persuaded me to take a deeper interest in otters and who encouraged and supported my early research on them.

Over the past ten years I have had help, information and advice about otters from many people, particularly those involved in otter surveying, otter hunting and otter conservation. I have also had fruitful discussions with many friends and colleagues. All these have contributed in their various ways to this book. I could not possibly name all of them and it would be invidious to select a few but my sincere thanks are due to them all. One name does stand out however and I would particularly like to express my gratitude to Sam Erlinge whose friendship and advice from the time I first worked on otters is greatly valued. His abilities as a field worker and ecologist have had a long lasting influence.

Frank Ansell, Ian Coghill, Jim and Rosemary Green, Don Jefferies, Tony Mitchell-Jones and Jane Twelves very kindly made available material that was unpublished or in press for which I am most grateful.

My thanks to Donald Bligh for access to word-processing facilities and to Lynn Spiller whose patient and friendly help enabled me to make good use of them.

Michael Clark's illustrations speak for themselves. The care and attention to detail he has put into them is deeply appreciated. I am also Very grateful to the photographers: Don Jefferies (17), Will Lewis (7, 8), Pat Morris (jacket, 1, 3, 6), Ernest Neal (4, 11, 14) and Mary Pearson (2).

I would especially like to thank Libby Andrews and Chris Buckingham who read the book in draft at very short notice. Their comments and suggestions for improvements were invaluable and made the final editing much easier. Any deficiencies or errors are of my own making, probably where I failed to take their advice.

Finally I must thank Sarah and Victoria for tolerating an absent or pre-occupied husband and father over many months and for giving encouragement when it was most needed.

Paul Chanin

1 Introduction

I first saw a wild otter in Devon, probably in 1974. I cannot remember the details of that first sighting, or indeed of most of the succeeding ones but I do have several impressions engraved on my memory. I particularly remember a knotted-up feeling, part anticipation and part anxiety, giving way to excitement when I realised that the vague lump on the bank opposite really was an otter.

In contrast, my memories of where I went otter-watching are very clear indeed, probably because I had plenty of time to develop them. I do not know how many hours I spent with my back to the small stone bridge peering into the darkness, several dozen I should think. Usually I stayed for an hour before dusk and a few hours after, even, on a few occasions, right through the night. I would sit on the right-hand bank facing upstream. To my left, on the opposite bank, was a clump of willows and brambles, ahead the water ran straight towards me through tall reeds for a hundred yards and disappeared from view round a sharp bend.

Many impressions remain from those watches: ducks and moorhens clucking and squawking in the reeds; smaller birds twittering; glow worms in the grass beside me. Then there were the otters: splashing along the path on the opposite bank; making scraping noises under the willows; the appearance of a dark, humpbacked shape on the path, pausing briefly before slipping silently into the water and vanishing; the strong V-shaped ripple of an otter swimming towards me; best of all — the sight of an otter swimming past in the half dark and then diving so that for a few brief seconds I could see it below the water before it passed under the bridge and out of sight.

In all those long hours of waiting I saw otters perhaps a dozen times, usually for no more than brief glimpses. Five or ten minutes observation for several hundred times as many minutes watching. Was it worth it? Certainly! Not for any scientific observations I made, all I learned was how difficult it is to watch otters, but for the reassurance of knowing that the elusive animal really did exist and for the excitement of seeing a wild otter.

If I had been studying otters 50 years ago when they were more common in Britain I would certainly have had more success, although less excitement. Even today it is much easier to see otters in some parts of Britain than others. On the coasts and islands of western Scotland and in the Orkney and Shetland isles, otters are not only common but also active during the day, because they suffer little disturbance.

In 1977 I spent four days on a remote part of the Scottish coast where I knew that otters were common. Signs were abundant but although I spent most of the daylight hours walking along the coast I only saw an otter once. I had a good view, intermittently, for about five minutes but it spent much of that time under water so I added little to the sum of human knowledge. My failure as an otter watcher was not made easier by the comments of various friends and acquaintances who had had good

INTRODUCTION

views of otters without even trying, while on holiday. I was very comforted recently to find that Hugh Miles who made a superb film about the otters of Shetland had many days of disappointment when he first went to look for them. You need to spend a great deal of time getting to know the animals before you can expect to see them regularly, even in the best places for watching.

If it is so difficult to watch otters, how can they be studied? One answer is to use expensive and sophisticated equipment such as miniature radios to follow them from a distance. A major problem with this technique is that you must first catch an otter in order to attach the radio. There are now ways of doing this safely and, in the last ten years, radio-tracking has contributed greatly to our knowledge of the habits of otters. Simpler methods are also available, of course, and some information has been gained by studying captive or tame otters. Much has also been learned by studying the signs of otters such as footprints and droppings. For example, the bridge at which I watched otters was selected with some care. There was a well-worn path leading to the willows and I often found otter footprints along it. Under the trees I found between 20 and 30 otter droppings each month which confirmed that otters visited frequently. It was obviously a potentially good place for watching.

Otter faeces have played a major part in the study of the animal and are referred to in practically every chapter in this book. In Britain there is even a special name for them, 'spraints'. Originally a hunting term, it has now been adopted by many naturalists and ecologists in Britain and Europe. Americans prefer to use the word 'scat' which is a more general term for the droppings of animals. When dealing with otters, the two words are interchangeable and I use both but tend to refer to the faeces of European otters as spraints and of other otters as scats.

Fortunately, otter scats are inoffensive and consist almost entirely of the undigested hard parts of prey such as shells, bones, scales, fur or feathers. These remains are virtually odourless and the characteristic smell of spraint is added by the otter from its scent glands. It is not unpleasant and has been described as sweet or spicy. Otter scats have been of great value to ecologists studying various aspects of otter biology including distribution, density, movements, diet and parasites.

My own interest in otters came through studying mink. Research on the diet of mink in Devon led to a comparison with that of the otter. Later I became involved in studies of the distribution of otters and factors leading to their decline. Where appropriate I have used examples from my own experience and research to illustrate aspects of otter biology but, inevitably, most of the work described in this book has been carried out by other people. There may appear to be a bias towards research done in western Europe and North America and this is not because I am more interested in otters in these countries but because much more work has been done there. Recent studies in Africa and South America have begun to redress the balance but there is much ground to be made up and research in Europe and America continues apace. A consequence of this is that when seeking examples the choice may be rather limited. Sometimes, for example, I have had to refer to two observations made in Devon and none in the rest of the world.

INTRODUCTION

Torn between cluttering up the text with the scientific name of every animal and plant mentioned or leaving them out altogether I have adopted a middle course. The scientific and common names of otters are set out in Chapter 2 and in the rest of the book only their common names are used. Other species which have common names are referred to by them. The equivalent scientific name is also given the first time the name is used if I felt that it was necessary in order to avoid ambiguity or would be helpful to an interested biologist. In practice this has meant that scientific names occur most frequently in the chapter on diet, mainly because there are many types of fish and invertebrates for which common names are not sufficiently precise to describe a species unambiguously.

2 What is an otter?

Otters are members of the weasel family, the *Mustelidae*, small to medium sized carnivores which have short legs and rather long bodies. Most mustelids feed mainly on vertebrate animals although a few including some species of otters are adapted to feeding on invertebrates. They are the characteristic small carnivore of the northern hemisphere but with the exception of Antarctica are found on all continents including Australasia where they have been introduced by man. Most species are adapted to life at ground level but some have taken to hunting below ground, some in trees and some, of course, in water. There are five sub-families which contain a total of about 60 species:

(a) *Mustelinae* — weasels, martens, polecats and mink.
(b) *Melinae* — badgers.
(c) *Mellivorinae* — the honey badger.
(d) *Mephitinae* — skunks.
(e) *Lutrinae* — otters.

Today, all otters seek most or all of their food in water and the first recognisably aquatic otter in the fossil record lived 30 million years ago. Another species, known as *Paralutra jaegeri*, lived in Europe 25 million years ago and may have been ancestral to modern river otters (van Zyll de Jong, 1972). Otters have, therefore, had a long time to adapt to an aquatic way of life but, despite this, they are still unmistakably weasels. The body is long and torpedo shaped, the legs are short and on land they move with the humpbacked gait typical of the family.

Although otters are superbly designed for life in water, they have no unique adaptations to cope with this way of life. Nature rarely invents new structures but is adept at improving old ones and most of the aquatic adaptations of otters can be seen as modifications of the basic design of

Figure 2.1   Skeleton of a river otter

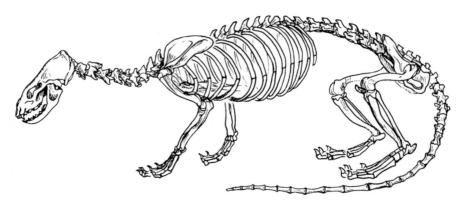

carnivores in general and mustelids in particular. Dogs, for example, have webbed feet, and some are powerful swimmers, but otters have bigger webs. Many dogs also have a waterproof coat and still have a dry skin after long periods of swimming or frolicking in and out of water. Otter coats are similar in structure but have relatively longer and denser fur.

There are, of course, a number of different species of otters, each adapted to a particular environment and way of life and before describing their adaptations in more detail it will help if the names and relationships of the various species are explained.

CLASSIFYING OTTERS

Until recently, relationships within the otter sub-family were not clear. In his book *Otters: a Study of the Recent Lutrinae*, C.J. Harris said that the taxonomy of otters was in 'a state of very considerable confusion', and it is hard to disagree with this. He made no attempt to simplify the chaos but listed 19 species and 63 sub-species of otters, commenting: 'It may occur to readers ... that there are far too many sub-species.'

Part of the confusion was due to the fact that some sub-species had been identified on the basis of single or very small numbers of specimens and part to the enthusiasm of nineteenth-century (and some twentieth-century) taxonomists for naming new sub-species. Add to this the fact that some species were named several times over by different people and it is hardly surprising that Harris included a list of synonyms 15 pages long. While none but the enthusiast would wish to wade through all these, Harris's comments on some of the names are revealing. For example: 'His *felina* is a composite and it is now impossible to determine what he thought he was describing' and of *Lutra montana*, described in 1844 but not rediscovered since, he said: 'There is considerable doubt whether this animal is an otter at all.'

In view of this, a recent review of the *Lutrinae* by Davis (1978) is very welcome. He pointed out that some of the characters used to separate species in the past are much more variable within species than had been realised, particularly tooth size and the proportion of bare skin on the nose. These characters form clines which means that as you examine successive populations along, for example, a North-South or East-West axis, the size of the teeth or degree of hairiness of the nose changes. Thus, otters nearer the equator have hairier noses. Davis made use of characteristics of behaviour as well as structure and appearance in his classification. This has yet to stand the test of time but its simplicity does make it possible to undertake a brief but comprehensible survey of the sub-family.

Davis used three main characters to classify otters: their vocalisations, the shape of the baculum (penis bone) and the appearance of the male external genitalia. On the basis of these characters he recognised nine species of otters which he placed in three tribes: the *Lutrini*, the *Aonychini* and the *Hydrictini* (Table 2.1).

Lutrini

This group consists of a single genus and three species of otters: the Eurasian otter *Lutra lutra*, the American river otter *Lutra canadensis*

Table 2.1 The names of otters and their classification according to Davis (1978)

Tribe	Species	Previous names
Lutrini	Lutra lutra (Eurasian otter)	L. lutra L. sumatrensis
	Lutra canadensis (American river otter)	L. canadensis L. enudris L. provocax L. annectens L. platensis L. incarum L. mesopetes
	Lutra felina (Sea cat)	L. felina
Aonychini	Aonyx capensis (African clawless otter)	A. capensis A. microdon A. congica A. philippsi
	Aonyx cinerea (Asian small-clawed otter)	Amblonyx cinerea
	Enhydra lutris (Sea otter)	E. lutris
	Lutrogale perspicillata (Smooth-coated otter)	Lutra perspicillata
	Pteronura brasiliensis (Giant otter)	P. brasiliensis
Hydrictini	Hydrictis maculicollis (Spotted-necked otter)	Lutra maculicollis

Notes: a. Previous names are those used by Harris (1968).

b. The names in parentheses are used throughout this book.

and the sea cat or marine otter of South America, *Lutra felina*. These replaced a total of ten species recognised by Harris, most of which were Central and South American and which Davis included in the species *L. canadensis*. The other species to be lost in this way was the charmingly named hairy-nosed otter of South-east Asia which Davis considered to be the same species as the Eurasian otter.

On the basis of this scheme the American river otter can be considered to range over virtually the whole of the New World (Figure 2.2) where it is an ecological equivalent of the Eurasian otter. The range of the latter species extends from the west coast of Ireland to Japan and from Arctic Finland to North Africa and to Indonesia. These two species are referred to as 'the river otters' a convenient, if inaccurate, term. Both species can live on the coast and all but two of the other species of otters usually live in rivers.

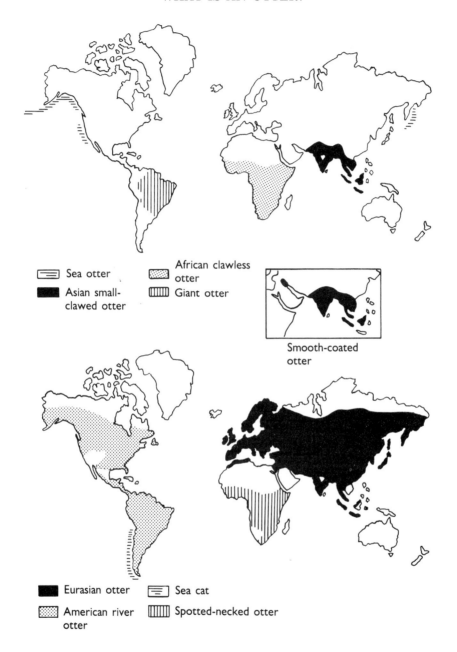

Figure 2.2 Distribution of otters (after Duplaix-Hall, 1975)

The sea cat is very rare and confined to the coastal strip of western South America, mainly Peru and Chile. Very little is known of its biology and, owing to its rarity, Davis was unable to collect all the data he needed on its habits and structure. He believed that it is very similar to river otters but a little smaller.

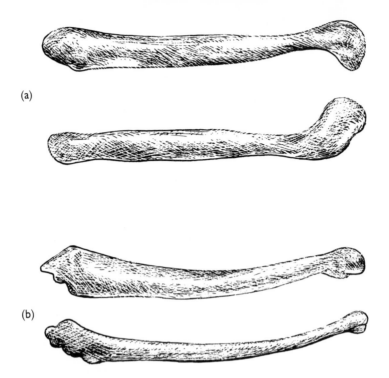

Figure 2.3   Otter bacula. (a) River otter — hockey stick type; (b) aonychin otter — baseball bat type

The features uniting these species and distinguishing them from others include an affection call which Davis described as a chuckle and a single syllable contact call. In males, the baculum is shaped like a hockey stick (Figure 2.3a) and the penis is entirely covered by the skin of the abdomen. Although, like most otters they take a wide range of prey, they tend to concentrate on fish. Family groups of river otters do not usually include an adult male.

Aonychini

This group is more disparate than the *Lutrini* mainly because its members have adapted to a wider range of habitats. They are united by the shape of the baculum (like a baseball bat, Figure 2.3b), and in all species but sea otters the penis extends just beyond the abdominal skin to form a preputial button. They lack an affection call and have a disyllabic contact call. These otters tend to be more sociable than the *Lutrini*, sometimes living in family groups which include the male and even a previous litter of young. The group includes African clawless and Asian small-clawed otters, the giant otter, the smooth-coated otter and the sea otter.

Davis included all species of African clawless otters in the single species *Aonyx capensis* and abandoned the genus *Amblonyx* which had previously been used for the Asian small-clawed otter (see Table 2.1). The common names of these otters come from the fact that, in the adults, the claws are much reduced. Their dexterity is remarkable and I have watched a tame small-clawed otter remove a key-ring from a handbag and even juggle with hazel nuts.

African clawless otters are found in central and southern Africa while the Asian species (*Aonyx cinerea*) occurs in India and neighbouring countries, its range extending eastwards to Borneo and Java.

The range of the smooth-coated otter (*Lutrogale perspicillata*) covers much of southern Asia from India eastwards but there is also an isolated population 2,000 km to the west in the marshes of Iraq. This suggests that the species was once much more widespread. Virtually nothing is known of its ecology except that it eats a higher proportion of fish than the small-clawed otter. An expedition to Asia by Wayre (1976) showed that its preferred habitat there is large rivers, mangrove swamps and coastal areas. Gavin Maxwell's first otter, Mijbil, was of this species and was collected from the western population in Iraq (Maxwell, 1960).

The giant otter (*Pteronura brasiliensis*) is the largest of the non-marine otters and is confined to South America, occurring in all the major river systems from Buenos Aires northwards. A distinctive feature of this species is the broad flattened tail which is relatively larger than in river otters.

The largest otter of all, however, is the sea otter (*Enhydra lutris*) which has been studied in far more detail than any other species. This is partly because it was nearly hunted to extinction for its valuable fur but also because a number of populations are found off the west coast of America where they can easily be watched and are readily accessible to American zoologists. Sea otters are more aquatic than other species rarely, if ever, venturing onto land. This, together with a diet consisting largely of marine invertebrates, has resulted in some extreme modifications to their behaviour and structure.

Originally the sea otter was found on the coasts and islands round much of the north Pacific from Hokkaido (northern Japan) in the west to the islands off Santa Barbara and Los Angeles in the east. The population was drastically reduced by exploitation in the eighteenth and nineteenth centuries so that by the early twentieth century only a few scattered populations remained (see Figure 7.2).

Hydrictini

There is only one species within this group, the spotted-necked otter, *Hydrictis maculicollis*. It was previously included in the genus *Lutra* but although it shares some characters with the river otters, it also has some of the characters of the aonychin otters together with some unique features of its own, so Davis isolated it in its own sub-family.

In behaviour and general appearance, it is similar to river otters, with a high proportion of fish in the diet and the female rearing the young on her own. Males lack a preputial button, like the river otters, but the baculum is of the baseball bat type like aonychin otters. Many of the vocalisations are similar to the river otters but the anxiety call is unlike the 'Hah!' sound used by all other species of otters. Davis described it as 'F!'.

Spotted-necked otters are nowhere common but are not considered to be threatened. Their range extends over much of Africa south of the Sahara, throughout much of which they occur together with clawless otters. They seem to occupy a niche similar to river otters in the northern hemisphere.

SIZE AND GENERAL APPEARANCE

The ancestors of otters were probably weasel-like animals which increased the variety of their diet by taking aquatic prey as well as birds and mammals, much as mink do today. The earliest otters had sharp cutting teeth which suggests that it was fish rather than hard-shelled invertebrates such as crabs and crayfish which first attracted them into the water. Having taken to the aquatic way of life, otters discovered that it was possible to feed on the invertebrates there as well and the fossil record shows that adaptations to doing so have evolved more than once (van Zyll de Jong, 1972). During the course of evolution the teeth of the invertebrate eaters became modified and so did their feet (see below) so although river otters are very specialised fish predators, they are probably closer in structure to their early ancestors than the other species of living otters. For this reason river otters are described first and then other species compared with them. This is followed by a comparison of feet, tails and teeth amongst the otters.

River Otters

Many people, in Britain at least, mistake mink for otters and since mink are typical mustelids in appearance a comparison of the two helps to illustrate the general characteristics of river otters (Figure 2.4). Mink and river otters have the same general body form and, at first glance, the most obvious difference is in size. Male mink measure about 60 cm from nose to tip of tail while both male and female otters are over a metre long when adult, nearly twice the length of the mink. The disparity is even greater when weight is considered and in each sex the otter is close to ten times heavier than the mink. Even a large male mink, weighing perhaps

Figure 2.4 (a) River otter compared with (b) American mink

Table 2.2 Average weights and lengths of river otters

	Sex	Weight (kg)	N	Total length (m)	Tail length (m)
Eurasian otter					
Denmark	M	8.3	32	1.09	—
Ireland	M	9.1	15	1.16	0.45
Britain	M	10.1	433	—	—
Denmark	F	6.2	35	1.02	—
Ireland	F	6.2	12	1.03	0.40
Britain	F	7.0	220	—	—
American otter					
Idaho	M	9.2	4	1.18	0.46
Ontario	M	7.3	111	1.09	—
Idaho	F	7.9	6	1.11	0.44
Ontario	F	5.9	84	1.05	—

Notes: a. N = number of otters weighed.
b. Some otters from Denmark, Ireland and Idaho were weighed as skinned carcasses. These were corrected to whole body weights using data from Stephenson (1977) which showed that skinned weight is 80 per cent of whole body weight.

Sources: Denmark, Jensen (1964); Ireland, Fairley (1972); Britain, personal records; Idaho, Melquist and Hornocker (1983); Ontario, Stephenson (1977).

1.6 kg is very much lighter than a small female otter of 4–5 kg. A closer look reveals other differences. Where mink have a thin but bushy, cylindrical tail, the otter's tail is stout and oval at the base becoming flat and tapering throughout its length. Mink have pointed faces, like weasels, while otters have broad muzzles.

Table 2.2 sets out examples of the average lengths and weights of otters from various areas. It shows that males normally weigh rather more than females which is common in mustelids and probably occurs in all species of otters. It has been said that American river otters are larger than those in Europe (Duplaix, 1972) but this is evidently not so. The few otters trapped in Idaho were close to the weights of the Eurasian species but those caught in Ontario were 20–25 per cent lighter. This may appear surprising but it is not unusual for animals at different latitudes to vary in weight. Animals living nearer polar regions tend to be heavier than those in temperate or warmer zones but in the weasel family this phenomenon is reversed.

Sea Otters

These are the heaviest of the otters, reaching a maximum weight of 45 kg although the average is somewhat below this (Table 2.3). The skeleton of

11

Table 2.3 Average weights and lengths of sea otters in Alaska

	Weight (kg)	N	Total length (m)
Male	28.3	79	1.35
Female	21.1	254	1.25

Note: Tail length is approximately 25 per cent of total body length.

Source: Kenyon (1969).

a sea otter when mounted for a museum looks not unlike that of a well-built, conventional mustelid (Figure 2.5) but live sea otters spend most of their time lying on their backs, only turning over when they dive. The conventional upright quadrupedal posture is no more a part of daily life for them than doing the breaststroke is for us.

Sea otters have improved their swimming ability at the expense of being somewhat slow and clumsy on land. They have large, flipper-like hind feet much bigger than those of other otters, shorter legs and also a shorter tail. When moving on land the characteristic, humpbacked gait is exaggerated compared to other otters and they move rather like sea lions. Notice also that the sea otter has a relatively large rib cage and short tail compared to river otters (see Figure 2.1).

Sea otters spend virtually all their time in the sea so the insulating properties of their fur need to be exceptionally good and this is why the coat is so thick and luxuriant. All otters have dense fur and, like other mammals, otters have two sets of hair, long stout guard hairs which form the outer layer and the finer but more dense underfur. The guard hairs form a waterproof barrier and this covers and protects the underfur which traps a layer of air to provide the insulation. Sea otters have guard hairs which are 30 mm long, half as long again as those of river otters. The density of hairs on a sea otter's skin is about twice as great as river otters with a maximum of 125,000 hairs per cm^2 (Tarasoff, 1974).

Unlike seals and whales, which rely on blubber for insulation, sea otters have very little subcutaneous fat, possibly even less than river

Figure 2.5   Skeleton of a sea otter

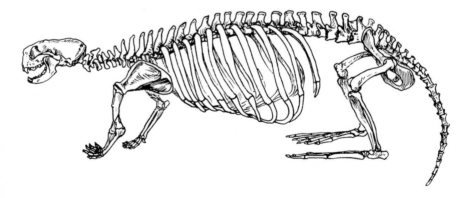

otters (Tarasoff, 1974). The advantage of air over fat is that it is a more efficient insulator and 1 cm of air is as effective as 4 cm of fat. Seals and whales have a very thick layer of fat which is advantageous when diving deeply. In deep water air is compressed and the insulating layer reduced in thickness but fat is virtually incompressible and equally effective at any depth. However, seals and whales as well as diving deeper are much larger than sea otters. A sea otter which had a layer of blubber equivalent to its fur would look like a barrel.

Sea otters are well known as tool users (see Chapter 3) and in addition to being able to hold and carry items in their paws, they have a loose flap of skin under each foreleg which extends onto the chest to form a pouch. Small rocks which are used as tools are sometimes carried in these or the otter may place several small items of food in the pouch before carrying them to the surface for consumption.

Other Otters

The other species, while differing in detail, tend to be closer in appearance to river otters than the sea otter. They vary somewhat in size but there are few reliable data and only estimates of the ranges of sizes are available (Table 2.4). Notice, for example, that although sea otters are supposed to be the heaviest species the range of weights for giant otters extends well beyond the average for sea otters of both sexes.

The colouring of otters consists of variations on a theme of brown, often darker above and lighter below. In some species the change from dark brown on the back to a more greyish brown below is quite gradual but in others it is more distinct, particularly on the face. Small-clawed and clawless otters, for example, have a tide-mark running from below the eye to below the ear while in spotted-necked and giant otters, although the belly is dark, there are areas of pale fur on the chin and throat. In

Table 2.4 The range of weights and lengths of other species of otters

	Sex	Weight (kg)	Total length (m)	Tail length (m)
Sea cat	B	4	0.91 – 1.15	0.3 – 0.36
Giant otter	M	26 – 32	1.5 – 1.8	0.5 – 0.7
	F	22 – 26	1.5 – 1.7	0.5 – 0.7
African clawless otter	B	16 – 20	1.15 – 1.5	0.4 – 0.6
Asian small-clawed otter	B	2.7 – 5.4	0.65 – 0.95	0.24 – 0.30
Smooth-coated otter	B	7 – 11	1.1 – 1.3	0.4 – 0.5
Spotted-necked otter	B	4 – 6.5	0.95 – 1.07	0.33 – 0.45

Notes: a. M = male, F = female, B = both.
b. One (male) sea cat only weighed.

Sources: Giant otter, Duplaix (1980); spotted-necked otter, Ansell (in press); other species, Harris (1968).

Figure 2.6 Otter feet: forefeet on the left, hind feet on the right. (a) River otter; (b) Asian small-clawed otter; (c) sea otter

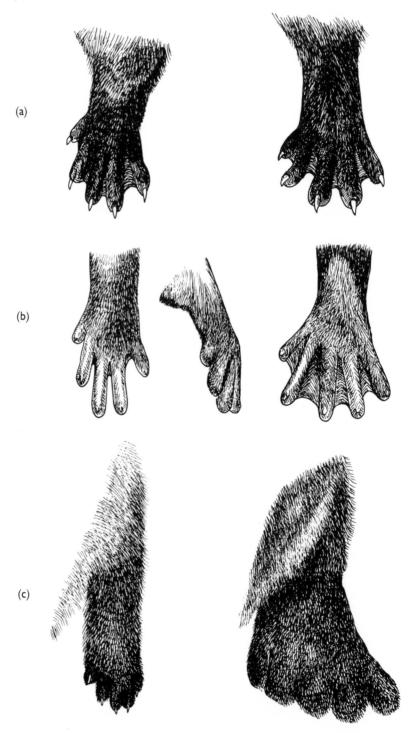

(a)

(b)

(c)

giant otters these may be no more than irregular patches of off-white or yellow on the chin or the patches may merge, sometimes forming a large bib. Spotted-necked otters tend to have a large pale area spotted with patches of brown fur. The Eurasian otter may also have pale patches under the chin although these are less distinct against its paler underside. The smooth-coated otter is rather uniform in colour though darker above than below but really does have a smooth coat and when dry seems to be wearing velvet.

Another feature which varies is the length of the face. Some species, especially small-clawed and giant otters, have their eyes set a long way forward and very short, almost puglike faces. Others such as the river otters have rather longer muzzles with the eyes nearer to the midpoint between the nose and the ears.

Feet and Tails

Although all otters have webbed feet, the extent of webbing varies between species and tends to be greater on the hind feet which are usually larger than the forefeet.

River otters have well developed webs on all feet and these extend at least to the base of the last bone on each digit. The hind feet are not markedly larger than the fore feet and all the toes have well developed claws. In clawless and small-clawed otters on the other hand the webbing is reduced, especially on the front feet and the claws are also very small, sometimes absent or reduced to vestigial flattened structures not unlike human nails. The fingers are very sensitive and used for feeling for prey in muddy water or under stones.

Sea otter fingers are not easily distinguished (Figure 2.6) and the front feet have tough pads which help to grip slippery or spiny prey. The paws are very sensitive, however, and sea otters are adept at feeling for and handling small items of prey. If a sea otter grips a human finger, the digits can be felt moving inside the paw as if they were in mittens. The claws are retractile like those of a cat and may also be important in holding prey. On the hind foot the pads are much reduced and may be absent, except for the tips of the toes. The sole is covered with fur and the foot is broad, flipper-like and webbed right to the tip. Unlike other mammals, the fifth digit (little toe) is longer than all the others and this enables the sea otter to spread its web more widely when swimming. When spread, the surface area of a sea otter's hind foot is five times greater than that of a river otter.

Tails as well as feet are used in swimming (see below) and in most species they are similar to river otters. The two largest otters have distinctive tails (Figure 2.7) which taper less than in other species and are flattened, rather like stretched out beaver tails. In the sea otter, the tail is comparatively short and this is probably connected with the fact that the species has been able to develop large flippers to provide the thrust in swimming. Giant otters spend more of their time out of the water and have had to compromise, enlarging and broadening the tail rather than the feet in order to maintain their mobility on land. Instead, the tail has wide flanges along the margins so that it is broad almost throughout its length, only tapering within the last few centimetres.

Figure 2.7 *Tails of: (a) river otter; (b) sea otter; (c) giant otter*

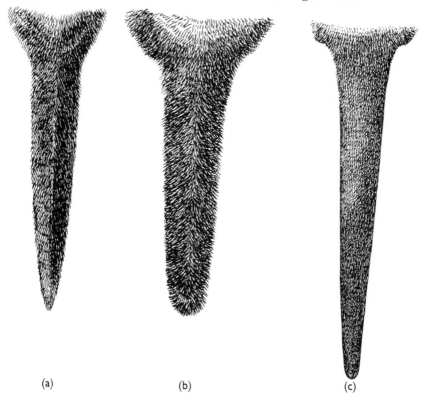

(a)   (b)   (c)

Teeth

Crushing the shells of crabs and molluscs requires different tools to those needed for gripping slippery fish and slicing up their flesh, so it is not surprising that the teeth of otters vary considerably. Also, whereas otters which eat invertebrates pick up their food with the paws, piscivorous species usually use the mouth and need sharp teeth to hold wriggling fish. River otters and sea otters represent the extremes of the spectrum (Figure 2.8), river otters using their teeth mainly for gripping and slicing and sea otters using theirs mainly for crushing.

Most carnivores have one upper and one lower molar tooth modified for slicing and these 'carnassial' teeth have sharp cutting edges which slide past each other as the jaws close. In river otters they are well developed but in sea otters and African clawless otters although the cusps which normally form the shearing edges can be recognised, the teeth are rounded and lumpy in appearance. In Asian small-clawed otters the cusps are pointed and the shearing edges present but the teeth are very broad. Indeed all otters, including river otters, have fairly wide molar teeth, compared to weasels for example. This reflects a compromise between crushing and slicing, enabling the otters to exploit a wider range of prey than would be possible with extremely specialised teeth.

Most otters, like other carnivores, have three pairs of incisor teeth and one pair of canines in each jaw. The canine teeth are larger than those

Figure 2.8   Skulls and teeth of: (a, c) river otter and (b, d) sea otter

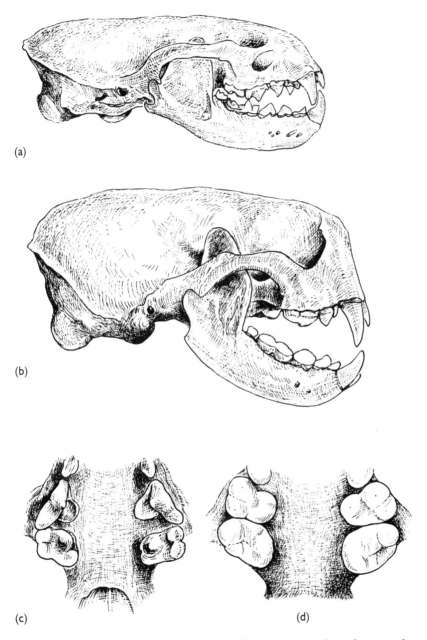

(a)

(b)

(c)   (d)

around them and are conspicuous when the jaws open but they are by no means massive in otters. In some species they help to grip struggling prey but are probably also used in aggressive behaviour either for display or as weapons. The incisor teeth of most otters are small and may be slightly notched, at least when unworn. Their main function is for grooming, when they are used like small combs to remove particles and tangles from the fur. Sea otters are unique amongst carnivores in only having two pairs of incisors on the lower jaw. They protrude fowards and are spadelike for scooping the remains of prey such as sea urchins from their shells.

AQUATIC ADAPTATIONS

No matter how much time an otter may spend on land, it has to seek most of its food under water and for some otters this involves chasing and catching the prey as well as finding it. This means that otters, whose ancestors lived on land, need adaptations to enable them to move rapidly through the water and to detect their prey. This is not as simple as it sounds since most mustelids rely heavily on scent for prey detection and the mammalian nose is not designed to work in water. A related problem for aquatic mammals is that they are normally unable to breathe while hunting so the length of time they can spend searching or chasing prey is limited. Finally, aquatic mammals face the problem of keeping warm.

Swimming

When swimming slowly or at the surface, river otters dog paddle using all four legs (Figure 2.9). There does not seem to be a fixed sequence of limb movements, the animal sometimes kicks with its hind feet together, sometimes both left feet or sometimes all four at the same time (Tarasoff *et al.*, 1972). The limbs are moved fore and aft, parallel to the midline of the body very much as in walking except when the forelimbs are used for turning and are pushed out sideways to force the body round into a turn. This may be aided by vigorous paddling of the appropriate hind foot.

For fast swimming the feet, tail and hind end of the body are used together, undulating up and down. When swimming like this, the flattened tail provides a significant proportion of the thrust, especially in giant otters and the legs are held to the side of the tail, sole upwards, to increase the area used in propulsion. The forelegs are tucked into the chest except when steering. Such rapid swimming is only kept up for

Figure 2.9   River otter swimming at the surface

short periods and may be followed by the otter gliding for a stretch or by paddling.

The sea otter's normal method of swimming under water is very similar except that during acceleration the legs are not held rigidly alongside the body but provide added thrust by kicking upwards at the end of the stroke, finishing above the level of the back. Sea otters also have an intermediate technique in which just the feet and tail are swept up and down. As the hind feet are so large they are swung out sideways from the tail by about thirty degrees in order to give room for the web to expand. Sea otters also swim like this on the surface, but only do so face down. When moving slowly, they lie on their backs and propel themselves by sculling the tail from side to side or by using the flippers, either in synchrony, as if rowing or alternately, as if paddling a kayak.

Sea otters appear to be the only species which use the faster, undulating type of swimming at the surface but no one has managed to measure their speed when doing so. Kenyon (1969) timed sea otters swimming on their backs on the surface over known distances and found that the maximum speed they could sustain was about half a metre per second. Other otters at the surface probably swim no faster than this but all otters seem capable of higher speeds under water. Following sea otters in a boat, Kenyon found that the maximum sustainable speed was 2.5 m/sec. although they were able to attain higher speeds briefly.

There are few measurements of the speeds of other species but Kruuk (pers. comm.) estimated that Eurasian otters swim at about 1 m/sec. while under water, the same as the maximum speed recorded by Mortimer (1963) for the spotted-necked otter. The highest speed of all was reported by Duplaix (1980) who timed a young male giant otter which, when alarmed, dived and swam a hundred metres in 26 seconds, an average speed of 4 m/sec.

Senses

Although otters have rather small external ears, perhaps for stream-lining, their hearing is very good and Wayre (1979) believed that it is more important than smell for detecting danger. The sense of smell is also acute, however, and is particularly important in some forms of communication (see Chapter 5). Under water, smell cannot be used and although sound travels well, without special adaptations, which otters do not have, it is very difficult to judge direction. For otters, therefore, the senses of touch and sight are particularly important in hunting.

Tests of the visual acuity of Asian small-clawed otters showed that in bright light they could resolve fine detail (narrow black and white stripes) as well in water as in air, but in dim light their vision in water was poorer than in air (Schusterman and Barrett, 1973). Human eyes are not adapted for vision under water and we can only see clearly when the surface of the cornea is separated from the water by a layer of air. Otters achieve their adaptation by modifying the shape of the lens to make it more spherical so that they can compensate for the different refractive index of water. In the dark or in turbid water, however, other senses play a greater role.

The sensitivity of the hands of the African clawless, Asian small-clawed and sea otters has already been mentioned and all these use their sense of touch when foraging. The importance of this sense is reflected in their brain structure and in all three species the part of the brain which deals with sensory information from the forelimbs is enlarged (Radinsky, 1968). In giant and river otters, on the other hand, this part of the brain is similar to other mustelids but the area of the brain which handles information from the facial area is larger than expected. This matches the fine spread of whiskers (vibrissae) which may be observed in these otters (see Figure 2.10).

A series of simple experiments showed the importance of this sense (Green, 1977). Powdered charcoal was added to water until a bright metal object 10 cm below the surface could not be detected by the human eye. In this darkened water otters took four times as long to catch fish as in clear water. One otter was then anaesthetised and its vibrissae trimmed away. After this it was able to catch fish as easily in clear water as before but when given fish in darkened water it took twenty times longer than in clear. It seems then that when it cannot use its sight, the otter is able to detect the presence of fish by using its whiskers.

It has been shown that, although the vibrissae of the common seal (*Phoca vitulina*) are no more sensitive than those of a cat, they are well adapted for detecting the beat of a fish's tail, but only at fairly close range (about 40 cm for a fish the size of a large herring). It is probable that otters' whiskers behave in the same way, although no detailed studies have been carried out on their sensitivity.

Heat Balance

Water conducts heat much more rapidly than air so without their thick fur coats, otters would cool down very quickly indeed. Even with this efficient insulation otters in water lose heat more rapidly than in air and

Figure 2.10   Head of a river otter

to compensate for this they have a high metabolic rate. The sea otter, spending virtually all its time in the water, has a metabolic rate $2\frac{1}{2}$ times higher than terrestrial animals of a similar size and in river otters it is about 50 per cent greater than expected. On the other hand, after vigorous exercise, particularly in warmer water, the reverse problem could occur, the thick coat might cause the otter to overheat and so means of heat dissipation have evolved alongside conservation measures.

The hind feet and tails of sea otters present a relatively large surface area through which heat could be lost and this is undoubtedly why the feet are held out of the water when resting. The fur on the tail is thicker than elsewhere and the soles of the flippers are covered with hair which also helps to reduce heat loss.

Many birds and mammals, including man, have countercurrent heat exchangers in their limbs which help to reduce the amount of heat lost. In these, the veins which return blood to the body pass so close to the arteries carrying it out that heat is transferred from one to the other. In some species the veins enclose the arteries completely and the exchange is so efficient that blood leaving the body is cooled almost to the temperature of the outside air or water and blood returning is warmed to body temperature again. This ensures that the heat is retained inside the body and not lost to the environment. When the animal is overheated, bypass vessels open up and warm blood passes out to the limb. The blood vessels supplying and draining the hind limbs of sea otters and river otters do run close to each other and such a system may well be present in otters.

On the upper surface of the sea otter's foot, just below the skin, is a network of blood vessels which are not found in river otters. Blood can be diverted into these superficial vessels to increase the rate of cooling by the water. It has been calculated that sea otters could lose as much as 80 per cent of their surplus heat in this way. At very high temperatures (28°C) water penetrates the fur to permit even faster dissipation of heat. When this happens the otters sink lower in the water because they are less buoyant (Morrison *et al.*, 1974).

Sea otter feet are dark in colour making them very suitable for both absorption and dissipation of heat. Captive and wild sea otters hold their flippers out of the water and expand them at intervals when resting at the surface. This happens more frequently as the air temperature increases and not at all when the air is cooler than the water, suggesting that the flippers are being used as solar panels rather than as radiators. Adjustments such as these enable sea otters to live in water ranging from twenty degrees above to twenty degrees below freezing point without altering their metabolic rate.

Oxygen Supply

As otters cannot breathe while foraging there are severe limitations on how much time they can spend seeking or chasing their prey without having to surface and one might expect them to have evolved adaptations to enable them to stay submerged longer.

Like seals, sea otters have a higher concentration of haemoglobin than terrestrial mammals (and river otters) which enables them to carry more oxygen in their blood. They also have relatively large lungs which, compared to other marine mammals, are twice as large as expected and are the reason for the sea otter's large rib cage. The lungs may form an important oxygen store but it has been suggested that their importance is in providing buoyancy rather than an air supply. This is very necessary in an animal which has little or no fat to give buoyancy and which often carries large stones with it when feeding and foraging (see Chapter 3).

It is not clear to what extent these adaptations increase the length of sea otter dives, or are available to other species of otters but most dives by otters of all species are of relatively short duration. There is one record of a sea otter staying under water for four and a half minutes but most dives last between 50 and 90 seconds (Estes, 1980). Contrary to popular opinion, the other species of otters dive for even shorter periods. Harris (1968) suggested that river otters could dive for three or four minutes but there seem to be no reliable records of this actually happening. Gavin Maxwell (1960) estimated that one of his otters dived for six minutes but this is much greater than all other timed observations and I suspect that he missed some surfacings.

Similar problems were experienced by Duplaix (1980) when studying giant otters. These would often surface under overhanging vegetation where she did not notice them. At the start of her study she recorded a number of dives lasting longer than two minutes but once she had learned to predict where the otters would come up she never recorded a dive longer than 72 seconds. During one period when she watched otters fishing, she recorded 47 dives which averaged 11.8 seconds in length with a maximum of 25 seconds. On another occasion a party of otters which were travelling averaged 22.5 seconds per dive over 39 dives. Similarly, Eurasian otters have been timed by several people and averages vary between 10 and 30 seconds for series of dives (Hewson, 1973; Kruuk and Hewson, 1978; Watson, 1978). Dive times in excess of 45 seconds seem to be very unusual.

BEHAVIOUR

Some aspects of otter behaviour such as foraging, courtship and communication are dealt with in later chapters but two aspects are covered here, grooming and play.

Grooming

All furred animals spend time grooming in order to keep their coats in good condition and, sometimes, to remove parasites. It is essential that otters should maintain the integrity of the waterproof barrier provided by their fur since if they did not they would risk wetting the skin and chilling the body.

The importance of this was emphasised by Duplaix-Hall (1975) who pointed out that captive otters need substantial areas of land in their enclosures in order to give them plenty of room for drying the fur. Post mortem reports of 88 otters of various species which died in zoos showed that 35 per cent had pneumonia and she believed that this was a consequence of poor coat condition leading to increased susceptibility to infection.

Grooming in otters does not just consist of licking and nibbling at the fur, most species vigorously dry themselves by rolling and squirming on the ground and rubbing against logs or vegetation. In some areas they have well worn rolling places often close to sprainting sites (see Chapter 5) but elsewhere they probably make use of the nearest patch of suitable ground.

The problem of keeping fur clean and well groomed is even more acute for sea otters which do not usually go onto land and yet must ensure that their coats are fully waterproof 24 hours a day throughout their lives. A wild female that was observed by Kenyon (1969) spent 11 per cent of her time in grooming and observations by other people suggest that this is a very time-consuming occupation in sea otters. Loss of condition of the coat seems to occur very quickly in captivity, even when the otters are kept dry. A number of sea otters which were transported in crates containing dry straw failed to survive because when released into the sea their coats were no longer waterproof. They quickly became soaked to the skin and consequently chilled. Those that were not recaptured died of hypothermia.

Various methods of grooming are used by sea otters. The fur may be rubbed with the feet, especially the fore feet which squeeze the water out of the coat. The otter twists round in its loose fitting skin and undergoes various contortions in order to get at the parts of the body which are hard to reach, such as the mid-back. The amount of air trapped in the fur is increased by blowing into it, sometimes aided by a frenzied beating with the feet which whips the water into a foam (Kenyon, 1969). To aerate the fur on its back, the otter turns onto its front and pleats the skin of the back into folds along the length of the body. This increases the buoyancy and when the otter turns over again it floats higher in the water (Tarasoff, 1974).

Some people have suggested that the vigour with which grooming is carried out indicates that sea otters suffer from lice or other parasites but they are remarkably free from such problems (see Chapter 6) and the frenzied activity has nothing to do with pest control.

Play

The popular view of otters as playful animals is not borne out by observations of animals in the wild. Certainly captive otters indulge in play but captive otters do not have to find and catch their next meal. Not that play never occurs in wild otters but it happens far less frequently than people usually think. For example, out of 294 observations of otter behaviour over four years, Melquist and Hornocker (1983) saw otters playing only 17 times and in each case immature animals were involved. Usually the play consisted of wrestling or chasing but occasionally single cubs were seen playing with prey.

Many people also believe that otters enjoy sliding games but this too seems to be based more on fancy than fact. Again, otters do slide, in fact sliding may be a common method of locomotion in some conditions. Beckel-Kratz (1977) found that otters often travelled in this way over snow and ice and made use of natural slopes in order to extend the length of the slides. They did not return to the top for another go, however, as they would do in play. It must be easier for a short-legged animal to slide over snow than to wade through it and the reasons for sliding seemed to be purely practical.

WHAT IS AN OTTER?

People often say that they have seen otter slides on river banks and many of them believe that the otters play sliding games down these. I have only seen a few such slides and they were on a small winding stream with steep banks less than a metre high. There were several otter paths, cutting across loops in the river and at the end of some of these, where the bank was very steep, were well worn slides down into the water. It was clear that these were simply places where otters entered and left the stream and, on some, there were ledges and footholds which the otters used to haul themselves out of the water and up the bank. Any otter trying to enter the water down such a steep slope would inevitably slide down, it could hardly help doing so. The slides reminded me very much of runs made by badgers across the high hedge banks found on country roads in Devon. I have no doubt that badgers skid down these too but they use them as roadways, not playgrounds.

3 Food and feeding behaviour

In her book on the Carnivores, Ewer (1973) answered the question: 'What do the Carnivora eat?' with 'what they can get' and this is as true for otters as it is for any of the other species. It also explains why the Eurasian otter, despite being primarily adapted for catching fish, has been recorded as eating an astonishing variety of food. Pitt (1927) said: 'there are few things that swim, fly, run or crawl that it will not devour', and there are records of these otters eating a range of prey spanning the animal kingdom, from beetles to beavers and from mussels to mink (Harris, 1968). Despite this, when asked what otters usually eat, most people reply 'fish' and, of course, they are right. Similarly, although sea otters and small-clawed otters feed primarily on invertebrates, they also eat a wide range of other prey.

Otters are beautifully designed as aquatic predators but, like most carnivores, they are opportunists and other types of prey form a variable proportion of the total diet. To understand completely the diet of otters, it is necessary to find out not only what they eat but also how much of each type of food is consumed. If this can be measured or estimated it is then possible to compare the diets of otters in different places or at different seasons, with those of other predators and in some cases to assess the likely impact of otter predation on populations of prey. The first consideration must, therefore, be the ways in which the diet can be quantitatively analysed.

SOURCES OF INFORMATION

Sea otters are one of the few species of carnivorous mammals whose diet can be determined accurately from direct observation. They forage close to the shore and have to come to the surface to eat, so their prey can usually be identified with the aid of a telescope. The length of dives, the proportion that are successful and the sequence in which prey is captured may also be recorded. This makes it possible to determine the ease of capture of various types of prey, the consistency of otters (do they concentrate on one type of prey?) and differences between adults and juveniles, males and females, and so on. Where otters have been marked it is even possible to compare the diets of individuals. For these reasons the sea otter is an ideal predatory mammal on which to test current ideas on foraging strategies. Similar, though less detailed observations have been made on coastal Eurasian otters (Watson, 1978) but generally these otters are less obliging. Nocturnal, secretive and living in places where direct observation is difficult, their diet has to be studied indirectly.

It is rarely possible to watch river otters feeding (Figure 3.1) but in some areas the remains of prey may be found although there are considerable problems in interpreting these. For example, it is unlikely that the remains of small items will be left by the otter as, although large

Figure 3.1   River otter eating an eel

fish are taken to the bank and the bigger bones left uneaten, small fish are eaten in the water. A further problem with finding prey remains is that other predators may have been responsible for the kill.

An alternative source of information about food habits is the gut contents of dead animals. Examining the contents of stomachs is a very good method of studying diet since digestion will not have proceeded far. Recognition of the food is fairly easy and it is not too difficult to assess the proportions of each type of food eaten, either by weight or by volume. However, as food proceeds down the gut and digestion removes all but the hard parts, both identification and quantitative assessment become more difficult. By the time the rectum is reached all the digestible material will have been removed and identification of most items will be based on fragments of skeleton, feathers, fur or scales. Soft-bodied animals such as worms or lampreys will have virtually disappeared leaving only microscopic bristles and small horny teeth respectively. On the other hand, prey with a high proportion of indigestible parts such as crayfish will be easily recognised but will form a disproportionately large part of the remains. For example, in otters which were trapped in Michigan, crayfish formed 5 per cent of the volume of remains in the stomachs but 35 per cent of the remains in the intestine (Lagler and Ostenson, 1942).

The greatest difficulty with this method is obtaining supplies of dead otters, particularly now that they are very scarce in many countries. Only when otters are caught in large numbers for the fur trade is it possible to obtain large samples and these are usually only caught during the winter, when the fur is at its best. In addition, a large sample of otters must inevitably come from a very wide area and so it is rarely possible to relate the diet of the otters to the prey available.

A much more abundant source of information on the otter's diet is spraint. As otters tend to leave spraint in conspicuous places and it is a renewable resource it is not too difficult to collect considerable quantities in a reasonable length of time. In two years, Erlinge (1967b) collected 14,600 spraints from twelve locations in Sweden, 70 per cent of them from only two of the areas. In fact, in my experience, it is much quicker and easier to collect otter spraint than it is to analyse it.

There are two main problems in the analysis of spraint: how to identify the remains and how to estimate the amount of each type of prey eaten. Where there are no guides available it is usually possible to make a reference collection of the likely prey to compare with scales, bones or other fragments in the scats. In Britain a booklet specifically designed to aid spraint analysis in freshwater habitats covers fish and amphibia (Webb, 1976), while fur and feathers can be identified with the aid of keys prepared by Day (1966). Other prey can often be easily recognised, the elytra (wing cases) of beetles, for example, or fragments of crab or crayfish skeletons, but in any analysis there is always a proportion of items which remain unidentified.

Estimates of the proportions of each type of food consumed can be made in three ways. Quickest and simplest is to record the number of times each type of prey appears in the spraints. Unfortunately, this method tends to overestimate small and infrequent items and underestimate those which are only important at some seasons. The other methods depend on measuring either the weight or the volume of each type of food and although more laborious, they can be more accurate, particularly if used with 'correction factors' (see below).

As every particle has to be identified for weighing or measuring its volume, these methods can be extremely time-consuming and Wise (1978) combined weight and volume by weighing the whole spraint and estimating the proportions of each type of prey in it. Multiplying the two figures gave an 'estimate of bulk' of remains in the scats which was converted to an estimate of prey intake by multiplying by a correction factor. This was determined by carrying out feeding experiments on mink. She found that when a mink ate 40 g of eel, on average 1 g of eel remains were found in the scats but after eating 40 g of trout 2 g of remains were found. In other words, trout have about twice as much indigestible material in their bodies so the correction factor for eels is 40 and for trout is 20. As the digestion of a mink is as thorough as that of an otter these correction factors can be used with confidence for both species. Other people have devised similar methods using various combinations of frequency, volume, weight and correction factors to estimate the proportions of different items in the diet.

FOOD SELECTION

The items which make up the otter's diet vary according to the species of otter involved, time of year and place. They depend on what species are available, and it is also possible that otters have preferences for certain types of prey. Food selection and preferences cannot always manifest themselves in the otter's diet. For example, in a mountain or moorland stream there may be no choice for the otter if only trout and salmon parr are present. At the other extreme, in a slow-moving lowland river with up to a dozen common species of fish, the otter may pick and choose if it wishes and coastal otters may have an even wider choice of prey.

There are considerable problems in detecting such preferences in the diet of wild otters. Even if considerable care is taken to determine the otter's diet it is rarely possible to obtain more than a rough indication of the relative abundance of the prey species available. For this reason most evidence for selection comes from studying captive otters and in the wild it is rarely possible to show whether otters are selective or merely catching whatever prey they can get.

The effects of food preferences are most likely to be observed when prey is abundant, or an otter has already fed. In feeding experiments on captive Eurasian otters Erlinge (1968b) found that they were much less particular when hungry than when partially or completely replete. He noticed that large fish, fish with spines or large scales, frogs and crayfish were more likely to be caught and then not eaten by replete otters than smaller fish or those with few or small scales (such as trout or eel). Erlinge suggested that 'ease of eating' was the reason for this selection. Captive African clawless otters, when given a choice of fish, frogs or crabs, showed distinct preferences taking crabs before frogs and frogs before fish. This may be a consequence of the design of the otters' teeth which are flattened for crushing and rather poor at slicing (Rowe-Rowe, 1977b).

It is difficult to define availability. In addition to the relative numbers of each type of prey, it may depend on the behaviour of the prey including migration, whether or not it forms shoals and on swimming speed. The last may in turn be modified by the time of year, water temperature as well as the health and size of individuals within the population.

Erlinge found that captive otters would often chase the most active fish in the tank first, because they were attracted by the movement, but they tended to catch the slower-moving ones sooner because the faster fish escaped more often. Rowe-Rowe's experiments with clawless otters yielded similar results. When an otter was presented with a tank containing five *Tilapia* and five trout of the same size, it caught and ate all five *Tilapia* before any of the swifter trout were captured.

The speed of fish varies from one species to another, many of the fastest freshwater fish belonging to the family *Salmonidae* (salmon, trout and their relatives). They are adapted to life in rapid streams needing to swim quickly to make headway against the current and to be able to negotiate weirs and waterfalls in their upstream travels to spawn. Coarse fish are better adapted to life in lakes and slow-moving rivers and have less need to swim at high speed. The maximum power output of a carp, for example, is little more than half that of a trout. The long body of the eel is designed for moving amongst thick aquatic vegetation rather than fast movement.

Within one species, the speed of swimming depends mainly on size. The fastest fish can attain speeds of up to ten body lengths per second for short periods, so the larger a fish is, the faster it swims. This means that an otter will find it easier to catch the smaller members of a species (see Table 3.1) and since these are usually more abundant than their larger

Table 3.1 The average time and number of dives taken by an African clawless otter to catch specimens of *Tilapia rendalli* in a tank

Fish size (mm)	Dives/capture	Seconds/capture
100–130	2.6	54.0
140–180	4.2	75.4
200–250	5.4	91.4

Source: Rowe-Rowe (1977b).

relatives, the otter frequently preys mostly on them. On the other hand there is much more meat on a larger fish and in theory it would be possible for the otter to decide whether to expend its energy in chasing fewer faster fish or more slower ones. No one has been able to demonstrate a foraging strategy of this sort in river otters but sea otters do seem to make decisions of this nature (see below).

Fish are 'cold-blooded' animals which means that their body temperature varies and is usually close to that of the surrounding water. Since their metabolic rate is determined by temperature, as the water temperature rises their swimming speed increases. Captive clawless otters took four times as long to catch *Tilapia* of the same length at 27°C as they did at 17°C (Rowe-Rowe, 1977b). This sometimes seems to be reflected in the diet of wild otters and a number of studies have shown that otters take proportionately less fish in the summer, particularly of the faster-moving species.

Erlinge found that captive otters caught fish with damaged fins sooner than healthy ones of the same size and species, and Clapham (1922) claimed that: 'The otter must, therefore do considerable good by ridding the streams of weak and sickly fish.' Whether this really happens in the wild is open to question but otters may catch a disproportionate number of diseased fish and no doubt fish that are 'spent' after spawning are particularly vulnerable.

The behaviour of fish is also important in determining their vulnerability to otter predation. Pike, for example, normally hide in vegetation, waiting to pounce on their prey and, being inactive, may remain unnoticed by an otter while more mobile fish may attract its attention. Indeed, any fish which spends its time in dense vegetation is likely to be more difficult for the otter to catch. The effect of shoaling is more difficult to determine. An otter may more easily detect a shoal of fish than single individuals and there will be a wide choice of prey but these advantages may be lost if the otter is confused by fish darting in all directions as the shoal breaks up. Conversely, a single fish may escape the notice of the otter more easily but once found the otter can pursue it until it is exhausted and easily caught. Seasonal movements of fish into shallow water or vegetation to spawn or into deeper water for the winter may also alter the susceptibility of a species to predation.

Finally, the availability of one species of prey can affect the level of otter predation on another. If a species is particularly easily preyed on during one season, for example, the otter may temporarily abandon other sources of food in order to exploit the more readily obtained prey.

THE DIET

General Patterns of Predation

Otters can be divided into two groups on the basis of their diets: (a) fish specialists, including river otters, smooth-coated, spotted-necked and giant otters; (b) the invertebrate specialists, clawless and small-clawed otters in freshwater and sea otters, in the sea.

Of course, neither group feeds solely on one type of prey, sea otters eat fish and Eurasian otters eat crabs and crayfish. Indeed sometimes the alternative prey can assume a greater importance than the principal food. One year on a river in Sweden, for example, fish formed only 30 per cent of the Eurasian otter's diet, the remainder being made up by frogs and crayfish. Conversely, at Amchitka Island in the Aleutians, 50 per cent or more of the sea otter's diet consists of fish. In other words, although the division into fish-eaters and invertebrate-eaters generally

Figure 3.2   Typical diets of the Eurasian otter: (A, B, C) Sweden; (D) Russia; (E, F) Britain

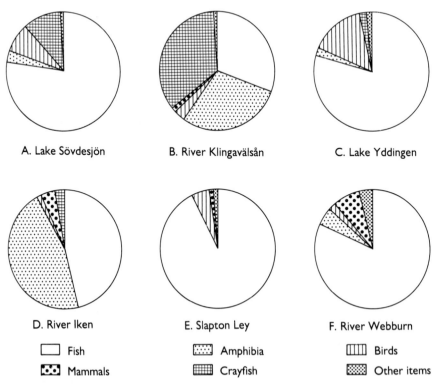

Sources: A, B, C — Erlinge (1967b); D — Grigor'ev and Egorov (1969); E, F – Wise et al. (1981).

holds good the adaptability of otters means that there are occasional exceptions. This adaptability, together with the variety of habitats in which otters have been studied, make it very difficult to summarise the diet of individual species.

The Eurasian Otter

It is only since the end of the 1960s that there has been much published information available on the diet of the Eurasian otter. Early studies include the observations of Elmhirst (1938) on Scottish coastal otters and those of Stephens (1957) based on corpses sent from all over Britain together with a small collection of spraints from rivers in Wales. These, together with a large number of isolated observations on the feeding of otters, have been adequately summarised by Harris (1968). The studies described here have been carried out since that time and most of them involved larger samples and material from one or a few relatively small areas.

Long-term investigations (covering at least a year) have been carried out in several parts of Britain and Sweden and there have also been a number of shorter studies elsewhere. In most of these, fish formed three-quarters or more of the overall diet (see Figure 3.2) but in three areas, one in Sweden, one in Ireland and one in Russia, fish formed less than half the items identified. In these areas, crayfish or frogs were the most frequent items in the diet although elsewhere they were generally of secondary importance. Rabbits and waterfowl may also be of secondary importance as in some areas they are taken quite frequently at certain times of the year.

Fish. Figure 3.3 illustrates predation on fish at Slapton Ley, a productive freshwater lake in Devon where roach (*Rutilus rutilus*), eel (*Anguilla anguilla*) and perch (*Perca fluviatilis*) are particularly abundant. Here,

Figure 3.3   Seasonal variation in predation on fish at Slapton Ley

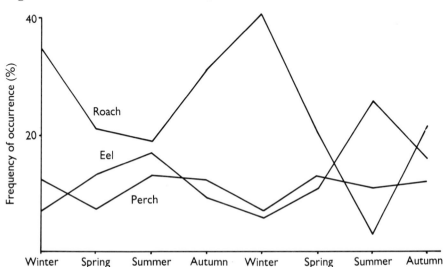

Source: Wise et al. (1981).

otters took eels mostly in the summer and roach mainly in the winter. The low level of eel predation in winter can be attributed to their habit of lying up in the bottom mud at this time, in spring, when they become active again, predation increased markedly. Roach on the other hand are active throughout the year but during the summer may be more difficult to catch because of higher water temperatures and consequent high swimming speed, or because of changes in behaviour such as migration and shoaling.

The proportion of perch to roach in the diet was much lower than expected from the abundance of the two species (Wise *et al.*, 1981), possibly because otters are less keen to eat perch than the other species as they have sharp spiny dorsal fins and opercula.

Predation on pike (*Esox lucius*) took place at a fairly low rate through the year and then increased during the spawning season. Whether this was due to greater activity, movements to spawning areas or the fact that they are more easily caught when spent is difficult to determine. The first two factors seem most likely since although pike are capable of rapid acceleration, they are not designed for sustained high speed swimming and would soon be caught by an otter whether they were in good condition or not.

Slapton Ley is a productive lake and three species of fish are abundant so the otter has a choice of prey available. By contrast, the Dartmoor streams of central Devon have a much lower density of fish and only salmonids are common. In these rivers there are resident brown trout (*Salmo trutta*), parr stages of salmon (*S. salar*) and trout and, at certain times of year, adult salmon and migratory trout returning from the sea to spawn. Eels are present but they are few in number and small in size. Electric fishing on one river produced ten times as many salmonids as eels, most of which were less than 30 cm long. Nevertheless, otters only took trout three times as often as eels on this river, presumably because they are easier to catch. Seasonal changes in eel predation were similar to those at Slapton Ley while predation on salmonids decreased as eel predation increased and vice versa (Figure 3.4).

A number of people have tried to estimate the size of the fish eaten by otters, usually by comparing the vertebrae in spraints with prepared specimens of known size. Wise (1980) refined this technique so that she was able to calculate with considerable accuracy the size of all the main species of fish eaten by otters in her study area at Slapton Ley and on the River Webburn. Since she also measured the fish caught during her sampling programme she was able to compare the sizes of fish taken by otters with those available to them in the wild.

In fact, there was very little evidence for otters selecting fish of a particular size in either study area and in the main, otters took different sizes of fish in proportion to their abundance. In most species there was no significant seasonal variation but on the rivers salmonid fish greater than 21 cm were taken much more frequently in the autumn and early winter than through the rest of the year. This coincided with an increase in the availability of adult salmon and sea trout as they returned from the sea and migrated upstream to spawn. The only evidence for changes in the size selection of non-migratory fish was at Slapton where pike greater than 40 cm long were taken more frequently in spring than

Figure 3.4   Seasonal variation in predation on fish in the River Webburn

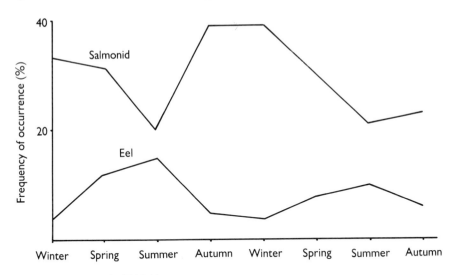

Source: Wise et al. (1981).

during the rest of the year. This is probably because only large pike spawn and they do so at this time.

Otters are capable of taking quite large fish and Harris recorded four instances of otters killing pike of 9 kg or more, very close to the average weight of a male otter. Such occurrences are not common, however, and Table 3.2 shows that in Devon, large fish were taken rather infrequently. At the other extreme, and in the same study, fish less than 6 cm long occurred in many spraints and more than 10 per cent of the salmonid and perch remains were of fish between 3 cm and 6 cm long. In some areas sticklebacks, despite their small size, form a substantial proportion of the diet. On the Somerset Levels, 19 per cent of the items identified from spraints were sticklebacks (*Gasterosteus aculeatus*) (Webb, 1975) and in Norfolk collections of spraint in April 1969 and March 1970 consisted

Table 3.2   The proportions of fish of different sizes taken by otters on the River Webburn (salmonids) and at Slapton Ley (roach and perch)

Size range (cm)	Salmonid (%)	Roach (%)	Perch (%)
< 6	13	2	13
7–12	61	67	61
13–18	15	29	23
19–24	3	2	2
> 25	8	0	1

Source: Wise *et al.* (1981).

entirely of stickleback remains (Weir and Bannister, 1973). Evidently otters find it worthwhile to catch such small prey, perhaps because of their abundance but as they weigh only a few grammes each, it must take a large number of sticklebacks to satisfy one otter. The importance of sticklebacks in Norfolk and on the Somerset Levels shows that otters can take considerable numbers of very small fish.

Lake Sövdesjön where Erlinge carried out much of his detailed work on otter diets seems similar in some respects to Slapton Ley. It is productive, with sandy shores, fringed, in part, with reeds. Perch, pike, eel and three species of cyprinid fish (roach, bream (*Abramis brama*) and bleak (*Abramis blicca*)), were the most common species present and all featured prominently in the otters' diet (Figure 3.5). However, cyprinids and perch were taken far more frequently than the other species. Pike fulfilled a secondary role and eels, together with sticklebacks and burbot (*Lota lota*), were only taken occasionally.

The outflowing stream, the Klingavälsån, meanders through pasture land and marshy meadows and in spring overflows its banks flooding adjacent fields. Here, fish predation was lower than in the lake, largely on account of the high proportion of crayfish in the otter's diet (see Figure 3.1) but it was also spread more evenly between the species. Pike, the most frequently recorded item in the spraints, occurred most often in March and April when the fish moved into the river to spawn, and all species of fish seem to have declined in importance during the summer when crayfish dominated the diet.

Figure 3.5   Predation on fish by otters in Sweden: (A) Lake Sövdesjön; (B) River Klingavälsån

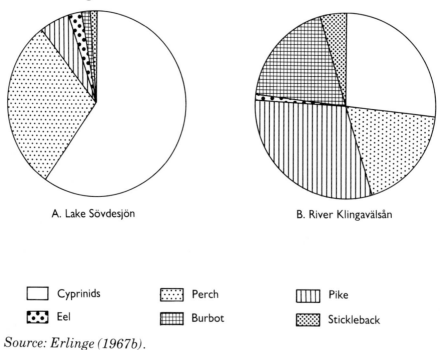

A. Lake Sövdesjön   B. River Klingavälsån

	Cyprinids		Perch		Pike
	Eel		Burbot		Stickleback

Source: Erlinge (1967b).

Figure 3.6   Seasonal variation in large cyprinids (> 15 cm) and small cyprinids (< 15 cm) in the diet of otters at Lake Sövdesjön

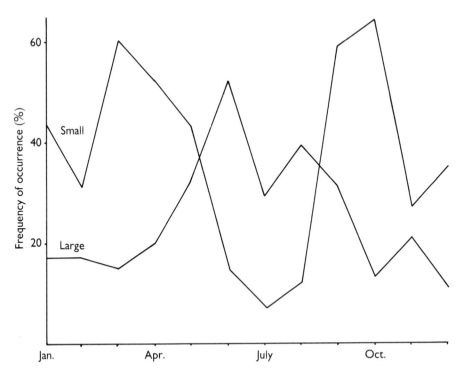

Source: Erlinge (1967b).

On the whole, seasonal patterns of predation revealed by Erlinge's work were similar to those found elsewhere but predation on cyprinids in Lake Sövdesjön was particularly interesting. Small cyprinids (< 15 cm) were taken least often during the summer but large specimens (mainly bream) were taken more frequently at this time than through the rest of the year (Figure 3.6). If swimming speed was a factor limiting otter predation during the summer, one would expect the largest fish to be particularly difficult to catch since they can generally swim faster. The fact that they were taken more frequently during the summer months suggests strongly that in this case it is fish migration or behaviour which determined their frequency in the diet rather than swimming ability. Similarly, the peaks of predation on small cyprinids coincided with times when they swarmed in the shallower parts of the lake.

These examples show that while it is possible to demonstrate unequivocally how fish behaviour, water temperature and so on influence the ability of captive otters to catch fish, it is much more difficult to do so in the wild. The differences between lakes and rivers in Sweden and those in Britain include size, topography, average water temperature and the species of fish present all of which can influence the balance of the otter's diet.

Amphibia. W.P. Collier (1908) writing in *The Zoologist* stated that 'there are no creatures of which otters are fonder than frogs' and at that time frogs and eels were generally considered to be the favourite food of the otter. Collier (an otter hunter) was writing in defence of the otter and went on to say that frogs 'devour more fish in the ova stage in a few months than an otter would kill in a year'. Even allowing for changes that have taken place in the past 75 years there seems to be an element of exaggeration in his arguments, and certainly in most areas that have been studied recently, frogs do not form an important part of the otter's diet.

Amphibia usually form no more than 10 per cent of the diet but in two areas they were found to be much more important. In a study carried out in Russia, Grigor'ev and Egorov (1969) found that for most of the year frogs formed 45 per cent or more of the diet although during the summer they were taken less frequently. In Sweden, on the River Klingavälsån, Erlinge found that predation on frogs increased during November as they congregated for hibernation on the bottom of small streams and ditches, and from December to February formed 45 per cent to 50 per cent of the prey identified. Later the crayfish population was devastated by disease and the otters increased their predation on frogs (and fish) during the summer. This shows that the otters were choosing which prey to hunt, the frog population was obviously available in summer but was not normally exploited while crayfish were readily available.

Most people refer either to 'amphibian remains' or 'frogs' when describing the otter's diet but they could also eat toads. Webb (1975) was able to differentiate between frogs (*Rana temporaria*) and toads (*Bufo bufo*) when jaw bones were found in the sprains. Only a third of the sprains containing amphibian remains had jaws in them but all of these came from frogs.

Frogs are more aquatic than toads and possibly more vulnerable to predation by otters but, in addition, the glands in toad skins make them unpalatable to many creatures. In Scotland, Jenkins *et al.* (1979) found that toads were sometimes killed by otters but not eaten, perhaps for this reason. Other types of amphibia such as newts and salamanders have not been recorded in the Eurasian otter's diet probably because they are small, uncommon and rarely eaten but also perhaps because no one has looked for them.

Birds. Birds form an important secondary item in the otter's diet in some areas and waterfowl are usually the most important species. Unfortunately, since birds as a group are rarely more than about 10 per cent of the diet over the year, many samples are too small to illustrate seasonal changes or preferences by otters. In more than 250 sprains collected from a river in Devon I only found four with bird remains. Even at Slapton Ley where more sprains were collected and birds were eaten more frequently, they were only found 42 times.

In studies at Slapton Ley and in Somerset, ducks, coots (*Fulica atra*) and moorhens (*Gallinula chloropus*) formed the main part of the bird prey and other groups were taken rarely if at all. At Slapton Ley ducks were taken nearly twice as frequently as coots, whereas on the Somerset levels moorhens were taken more often than ducks reflecting the relative abundance of the species in each area.

FOOD AND FEEDING BEHAVIOUR

The studies in south-west Britain revealed a very small number of instances of otters preying on other groups of birds but elsewhere otters have been shown to do so more frequently. For example, 8 per cent of the bird remains in spraints collected in Jenkins' study area in Scotland were of waders. This is perhaps to be expected since such birds might well feed and roost in the wetland areas nearby, but even more interesting was the fact that passerine (song) birds comprised nearly a quarter of the bird remains. Erlinge found that passerines formed over a third of the bird remains in his collection of spraints and identified these as being mainly starlings (*Sturnus vulgaris*) and swallows (*Hirundo rustica*). Although one would not normally expect to find passerine birds forming a significant part of the diet of an aquatic predator, both starlings and swallows have one particular habit which would make them vulnerable. They roost communally at certain times of the year and sometimes congregate in reedbeds in vast numbers. In one reedbed in Devon, nearly a quarter of a million starlings have been recorded. Swallows also gather in reedbeds prior to migration, when they may be numbered in tens of thousands. With such large numbers of birds accumulating, it is likely that many will die in the roosts. I have found dead starlings in reedbeds during the winter and I suspect that otters, and other predators such as mink, take advantage of this windfall and eat dead and dying birds when they find them.

Seasonal variation in bird predation depends on the species involved. I found that bird remains occurred in scats most frequently in May and June and that a high proportion of the birds preyed upon were juvenile. Other people have found that bird predation was highest during the breeding season and the moulting period while elsewhere high levels of bird predation during the winter reflect the importance of starlings at this time of year.

Mammals. Otters are not sufficiently agile to catch many species of mammals which do not, therefore, feature prominently in the diet. Many instances of mammal predation reflect accidental encounters by otters rather than deliberate hunting. Two species which do seem to be taken rather more frequently than others are rabbits (*Oryctolagus cuniculus*) and water voles (*Arvicola terrestris*). About a quarter of the mammalian remains identified in Sweden and Scotland were of water voles and it is obvious that the waterside habits of these creatures make them vulnerable to otter predation. Nearly half the mammal remains identified in Scotland were of rabbits and Wise found that three-quarters of the mammal intake of otters on a river in Devon was in the form of rabbits. Rabbits certainly can be found close to water but this level of predation suggests that the otters were deliberately hunting them from time to time. Rabbit holes are also used, occasionally, for otter dens. Predation on rabbits was highest in summer when juveniles are particularly vulnerable because, shortly after independence, they are less wary than adults.

Other species of mammals such as shrews, moles, rats, mice and voles are taken from time to time and even other carnivores such as weasels and mink. This happens rarely but the remains of six mink were found in spraints collected on the River Iken in Russia and I found weasel fur in a spraint from Slapton Ley.

Invertebrates. When analysing otter spraints the remains of small invertebrates are often found and it is usually assumed that these have been eaten by the fish and ingested incidentally by the otter. However, from time to time larger specimens are found which the otter has eaten deliberately.

Earthworms and *Dytiscus* (diving) beetles occasionally occur but the only invertebrates which are eaten regularly are crayfish (Figure 3.7). It is also possible that otters eat freshwater mussels in some areas although the evidence is circumstantial. Tame otters do not eat mussels unless they are already opened and seem incapable of learning how to open the shells even after they have been shown the edible contents (Wayre, 1979).

The only documented account of Eurasian otters feeding on mussels comes from North Holland where Veen (1975) found large numbers of mussel shells (*Anodonta cygnea*). He compared tooth marks on the shells with the gap between the canine teeth of otters and other possible predators and concluded from this that it was otters that had been eating the mussels.

Crayfish are not found in any of the areas where the otter's diet has been studied in Britain but since the otter's decline, there are few places in Britain where the two species still co-exist. In Ireland, however, otters are still abundant and widespread and a study of their diet on the Clare river system showed that crayfish (*Austropotamobius pallipes*) were of major importance (McFadden and Fairley, 1984). All the rivers studied flowed over limestone and, excluding one site where fish predominated, crayfish occurred in 80 per cent of the spraints and formed 76 per cent of their bulk. Even allowing for the bulkiness of crayfish remains, this indicates a very high rate of predation. Spraints were only collected between July and September but there was some evidence that fewer crayfish were caught in the winter when they are less active.

Figure 3.7   Crayfish

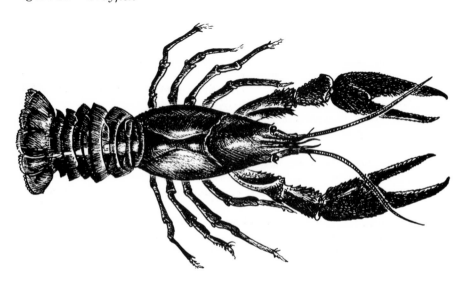

Crayfish (*Astacus astacus*) were also present on all of Erlinge's study areas but not common except on the River Klingavälsån. Elsewhere they formed up to 10 per cent of the diet but on this river they constituted 36 per cent of the items identified in spraints throughout the year and, during the summer, formed the staple diet. Seasonal variation in predation depended on the activity of the crayfish which were most active and, therefore, most frequently eaten during the warm summer months (Figure 3.8).

Figure 3.8   Seasonal variation in predation on crayfish on the River Klingavälsån

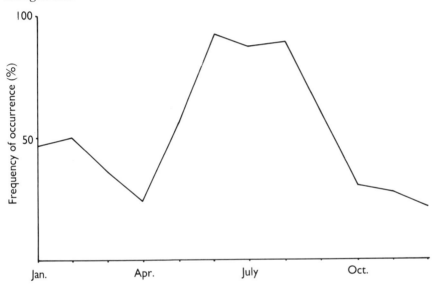

Source: Erlinge (1967b).

Carrion. It is usually assumed that otters do not eat carrion, and despite his comprehensive approach to reporting the otter literature, Harris did not mention it at all. Wayre (1979) also expressed his doubts about carrion feeding and points out the difficulties a number of people have had in trying to mark otter spraint by leaving bait containing dyes or small pieces of plastic. So far no one has succeeded in persuading otters to take any.

Cuthbert (1973) studied carrion feeding on the River Tweed over a period of two months when he was able to visit a 4 km stretch of river two or three times a week. On each trip he observed at least 20 salmon carcasses in various stages of decay and either saw or found signs of ten species feeding on them. Signs of otters were found on four occasions suggesting that otters may eat carrion, but otters are known to leave spraints beside novel objects such as sheep carcasses, without feeding on them (E.M. Andrews, pers. comm.).

Summary. The Eurasian otter has clearly specialised as a fish-eating carnivore which in some areas may temporarily feed mainly on other types of aquatic prey such as crayfish. It is opportunistic and frogs, waterside birds and mammals may be important secondary items. The pattern of predation varies, depending on the availability of species. Where food is plentiful the otter may hunt selectively and easily caught food tends to be taken more readily than that which requires more effort to catch.

The American River Otter

Several people have studied the diet of this species, some using the guts of trapped otters while others have collected scats. Trapped animals were only obtained during the winter months when the fur is at its best and the samples were generally smaller.

The overall picture revealed by these studies suggests that the American river otter is very similar in its feeding habits to the Eurasian species (Figure 3.9). Fish dominated the diet in every case while important secondary items included crayfish, amphibia and birds. Mammals were recorded rarely, the greatest number being in Canada where they were found in 16 per cent of the scats collected by Gilbert and Nancekivell (1982). Half of these were of muskrat (*Ondatra zibethica*, a large rodent) and muskrats were the most frequently eaten mammals elsewhere which, in view of their size (up to 2 kg) and semi-aquatic habits, is hardly surprising. Bird predation was also generally low but in the lakeland habitats studied in Canada, birds were present in 22 per cent of the scats and consisted mainly of ducks and divers. In other areas, grebes and rails were recorded but there were no examples of large numbers of passerine or other 'terrestrial' birds, as in Europe.

Amphibia were not recorded from all areas but remains were found in 18 per cent of the scats collected from a series of lakes in Montana (Greer, 1955). Frogs were the most frequently eaten species but salamanders, mud-puppies (*Necturus*, an aquatic salamander) and newts were occasionally taken by the otters.

The variety of fish available in many of these North American study areas was much greater than in Britain, for example in one reservoir that was studied 20 species were found. This gives the otter greater scope for selecting preferred prey and avoiding food it does not like, but makes it more difficult to show that this is happening because numbers of each species in the scats tend to be small. However, by sampling fish in the Quabbin reservoir in Massachusetts, Sheldon and Toll (1964) showed that otters tended to prey on those species which stayed near the shore. Fyke nets which were set in deeper water caught fish which did not feature so prominently in the otter's diet.

A study of otter predation on trout was carried out in response to complaints by game fishermen which showed that, as in Britain, otters preyed on other species when they were readily available (Knudsen and Hale, 1968). In Idaho on the other hand, it was found that salmonids, particularly one species, the kokanee (*Oncorhyncus nerka*) were taken very frequently during late summer (Melquist and Hornocker, 1983).

This coincided with the spawning run of the fish and, at this time, otters concentrated their foraging in areas where kokanee congregated to

Figure 3.9   Typical diets of the American river otter: (A) North Fork River, Idaho; (B) Thompson Lakes region, Montana; (C) Quabbin Reservoir, Massachusetts

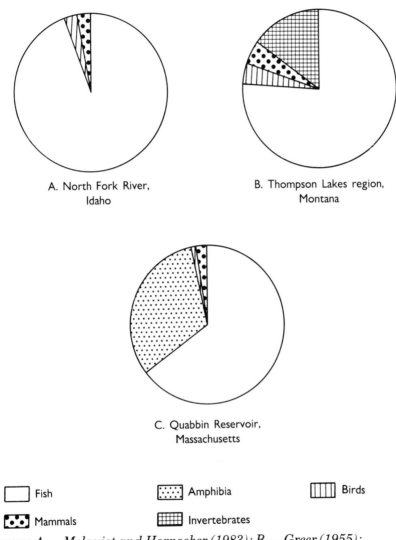

A. North Fork River,
Idaho

B. Thompson Lakes region,
Montana

C. Quabbin Reservoir,
Massachusetts

☐ Fish   ⊡ Amphibia   ⊞ Birds

⊡ Mammals   ⊞ Invertebrates

Sources: A — Melquist and Hornocker (1983); B — Greer (1955); C — Sheldon and Toll (1964).

spawn. It has often been suggested that otters follow the spawning runs of salmon in Britain and one has the impression of otters moving up to the spawning beds with the fish. In Idaho, the otters did not move out of their normal ranges to follow the kokanee but instead concentrated their activities around the spawning beds within their normal ranges during the spawning season (see Chapter 5).

River otters also eat crayfish and freshwater crabs when available, the highest proportion in the diet was in Massachusetts where crayfish were caught throughout the year and found in 46 per cent of the scats.

In California evidence of river otters eating mussels has been found although, as in Holland, the otters were not seen to do so but the pattern of marks on the shell matched with otters' teeth (Morejohn, 1969).

Other 'Freshwater Otters'

Giant otters are confirmed piscivores although Duplaix (1980) did find the remains of crabs in 40 per cent of the 190 scats she collected in Surinam. However, fish remains were found in 86 per cent of the scats and of 202 observations of otters catching and eating prey, all that could be identified were fish. Unidentified prey consisted of items that were eaten out of sight of the observer. Eleven species of fish were recognised in the scats but only one was taken more than a few times, a characin (*Hoplias malabaricus*) which formed 51 per cent of the items identified. Observations of otters catching this species showed that they caught fish ranging in length from 100 to 280 mm and that the most frequently eaten size was between 170 and 220 mm. The largest species taken was the tiger catfish (*Pseudoplatystoma fasciatus*) of which only two specimens were caught, measuring between 500 and 600 mm in length.

In Guyana, Laidler (1980) found that the lazy man patois fish (species unknown) was an important part of the giant otter's diet as were catfish, both of which were slow-moving species which stayed immobile for long periods. Remains of the local game fish, known as lukanani, were not found in otter's spraints. Other types of prey seemed to be unimportant in both areas, Duplaix found the remains of one mammal and one amphibian and in neither area were birds recorded in the diet.

Figure 3.10 illustrates the results of a study carried out in Natal to compare the diets of clawless and spotted-necked otters in two areas, one with trout and one without (Rowe-Rowe, 1977c).

Clawless otters tended to spurn fish, particularly on the trout stream and concentrated on various species of frogs and crabs (*Potamonautes* sp.). Crabs were also frequent items in scats of spotted-necked otters and this was particularly so in spring and summer. Rowe-Rowe concluded that the spotted-necked otters were really fish specialists but that in the face of an impoverished fish fauna and an abundant supply of crabs, they were able to adapt. Certainly other authors indicate that these otters normally prefer fish and a captive spotted-necked otter would willingly catch and eat fish from its pool but given live crabs would play with them but not eat them (Mortimer, 1963).

Coastal Otters

There is no reason why otters which are adapted for life in fresh water should not be able to exploit coastal habitats and at least four species do. Rivers flow down to the sea, often with an intervening estuary which may afford suitable otter habitat even if the open coast is not ideal. One would also expect otters to travel along coasts while travelling between river systems. Since the coastal waters of continents are often very productive and may support dense populations of fish and invertebrates, it is not surprising that species of otters which are normally associated with inland waterways should also be found living along the coasts.

Figure 3.10   The diets of African clawless otters (A, C) and spotted-necked otters (B, D) in Natal. Spraints were collected from the Kamberg Nature Reserve (A, B) where trout were present and the River Mpofana (C, D) where they were absent

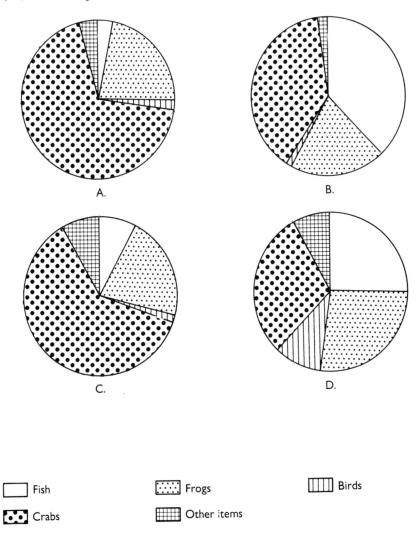

A.

B.

C.

D.

☐ Fish   ⬚ Frogs   ▦ Birds

▨ Crabs   ▦ Other items

Source: Rowe-Rowe (1977c).

In Britain the otter occurs mainly on undisturbed rocky shores, particularly on the west coast of Scotland and the Orkney and Shetland Islands although small numbers also use the coastal mudflats of East Anglia. Otters used to be found on the coasts of south-west England also but seem to have largely abandoned these areas as pressure from the holiday industry has increased. American river otters are found on the east and west coasts of North America, and there are coastal populations of smooth-coated otters in Malaysia and clawless otters in Africa. There are also of course two marine species of otter around the shores of the Pacific. The sea cat (*Lutra felina*) in South America and the sea otter on the coasts of the north Pacific.

Little is known of the diet of the sea cat other than that it eats fish, crustacea and molluscs (Brownell, 1978; Cabello, 1978) and nothing of the diet of coastal smooth-coated otters. However, there have been detailed studies of the diets of coastal Eurasian otters in Scotland, African clawless otters in South Africa and sea otters in Alaska and California. These three species are particularly interesting to compare since one is entirely marine, one a freshwater fish specialist and one a freshwater invertebrate specialist.

Coastal clawless otters were studied by van der Zee (1981) who collected 1,129 scats from the Tsitsikama Coastal National Park on the east coast of South Africa. He devised his own method for assessing the diet based partly on the weight of remains and partly on frequency of occurrence. By using appropriate correction factors and knowing the average weight of different species in the diet, he was able to estimate not only how many individuals of each species were eaten but also the proportion of the total intake made up by each species in terms of live weight. Although his method was very time-consuming he found that it was essential in his study area where prey ranged from crabs, which left a very high proportion of indigestible remains in the scats, to octopus which could be entirely digested except for the horny beak.

Altogether he identified over 30 species of prey in the otter scats, but only four of these were particularly important: red rock crabs (*Plagusia chabrus*), brown rock crabs (*Cyclograpsus punctatus*), sucker fish (*Chorisochismus dentex*) and octopus (*Octopus granulatus*), which between them made up 61 per cent of the items identified and 86 per cent of the weight of prey consumed. Red rock crabs were the most frequently

Table 3.3 The diet of clawless otters in the Tsitsikama Coastal National Park, South Africa

Species	Per cent of scats containing each type of prey	Estimated number in scats	Per cent of the total number of items in scats	Mean weight of each prey item (g)	Estimated weight of prey consumed (g)	Per cent of the total weight of prey
Red rock crab	28	3,413	42	12.4	43,346	36
Brown rock crab	10	2,069	26	3.4	7,033	6
Sucker fish	16	743	9	17.3	12,849	14
Octopus	7	295	4	138.0	40,769	34

Source: van der Zee (1981).

caught prey (Table 3.3) and were taken nearly twice as frequently as brown rock crabs. However, their greater size meant that they were six times as important to the otter in terms of flesh consumed. Of the four items, octopus were taken least often but were still a very important contribution to the diet because of their greater average weight. Indeed the weight values given tend to underestimate the importance of octopus. van der Zee showed that the indigestible exoskeleton formed 20 per cent of a crab's weight while in fish the skeleton was only 5 per cent of the live weight. If this is taken into account, the importance of crabs is reduced relative to other prey and octopus becomes the most important single item despite being less than one in twenty of the items caught.

Van der Zee estimated the availability of food in rock pools and found that nearly half the animals he obtained were kelp fish (*Clinidae*, relatives of blennies and gobies) although the otters took them relatively infrequently. The ratio of kelp fish to suckers in samples was 6:1 but in the otter's diet the ratio was reversed with suckers being taken $4\frac{1}{2}$ times as often. Van der Zee also noted that sea bream (*Sparidae*) were taken less frequently by otters than expected. Evidently the otters preferred to prey on suckers and van der Zee concluded that this was because they were easier to catch. Clawless otters catch their food primarily by feeling for prey with their sensitive forepaws. Crabs and octopus hiding under rocks and in crevices would be readily caught by this technique. More mobile or active fish would attempt to escape and the otter would then have to chase them through the shallow water when it would be at a disadvantage. It would also have to use more energy and time which, like other otters, it seems disinclined to do. Suckers which cling to the undersides of rocks do not respond by fleeing and are, therefore, more vulnerable to the otters.

Apart from octopus all the species eaten by otters averaged under 20 g in weight indicating that food on the shore is generally of small size. Otters tended to take the larger specimens of most prey species but they seemed to select medium-sized specimens of red rock crabs. Van der Zee suggested that this might be to avoid being caught by the crabs chelae although they seem to be less particular with freshwater crabs (see below).

So, on the seashore, the clawless otter is able to indulge its preference for feeding on invertebrates. Although fish were present and abundant the otter took few of them except for the relatively immobile suckers. What then does the Eurasian otter do when faced with a littoral larder?

On South Uist, in the Outer Hebrides, the Eurasian otter eats fish. In two collections of spraints, one taken in February, one in June, 97 per cent of the items identified were fish. The rest were rabbits and shore crabs (Twelves, unpubl.). Working on the mainland of Scotland, Mason and Macdonald (1980) collected 50 spraints from the shores of Loch Broom, a sheltered sea loch, during January. They found 130 items of which the most common were crustacea (mainly shore crabs — *Carcinus maenas*) which were found 25 times. No other invertebrates were found and there were bird remains in only three spraints. All the remaining items were fish belonging to 14 different groups. Bearing in mind that the bulk of crab shells may lead to over-representation in spraints it is reasonable to conclude that in this area otters were concentrating their predation on fish (80 per cent of the items identified). No single species of fish predominated but the two most frequently recorded species were butterfish (*Pholis gunnellus*) and Yarrel's blenny (*Chirolophis ascanii*).

Further north, in Shetland, Watson (1978) also found that crabs formed a relatively small proportion of the diet, 8 per cent of items identified from 437 spraints. Shore crabs were the most frequent species, taken about three times as often as velvet crabs (*Portunus puber*) which were caught mainly in January. Watson described differences in predation between individual otters because he was able to observe a female feeding with her cub. Thirteen of the 61 prey items caught by the cub were crabs while its mother caught none.

In Shetland a variety of fish were taken and 14 groups were identified none of which dominated the diet. To shed further light on the pattern of predation the groups of fish were divided into four categories according to body shape and habits: long-bodied fish, slow demersal (bottom-living) fish, open water fish and flatfish. Otters took mainly long-bodied fish

Figure 3.11   The diet of coastal otters in Shetland as revealed by spraint analysis

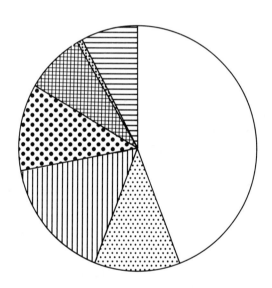

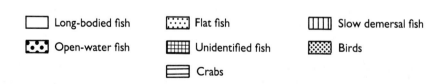

Source: Watson (1978).

(eels, butterfish and blennies) followed by demersal species (sea scorpions — *Cottus* sp. and lumpsuckers *Cyclopterus lumpus*) (Figure 3.11). Flatfish were taken infrequently and open water fish hardly at all. Again, the juvenile otter differed from its parent and also from other otters in that it took a smaller proportion of long-bodied fish. Although none of these studies covered a full year, or was as detailed as van der Zee's study, the overall pattern is clear. The otters were feeding mainly on fish but taking a wide range of species while invertebrates formed a significant but relatively small proportion of the diet.

This raises the question as to whether the differences in diets between Eurasian and clawless otters living on the coast is a reflection of differences in their behaviour or the abundance of food. There is no information on prey availability in the Scottish study area but it is clear that in the clawless otters at least selection is an important factor. Van der Zee demonstrated that otters in his study area showed a strong preference for rock crabs and a marked reluctance to catch kelp fish. In Britain the pattern is reversed, Eurasian otters preying on fish rather than crabs but there is no evidence to show whether this is due to selection by the otter or to differences in availability.

Sea Otters

Estes *et al.* (1981) carried out a wide-ranging study of sea otter diets in six populations across much of the species' range. The most westerly sites were at the extreme end of the Aleutian chain on Amchitka and Attu Islands and the most southerly in central California at Piedras Blancas and Point Buchon. The other two sites were at Prince William Sound in Alaska where they studied populations at Green Island and Sheep Bay. In each of these areas, one population (the first named) had been long established and was thought to have reached an equilibrium while at the other otters had only recently established themselves, were at a lower density and likely to continue increasing in numbers. In addition to recording the items in the diet, Estes *et al.* noted success rates, length of dives, time spent eating prey on the surface and the sex and age (adult or juvenile) of animals being watched.

Figure 3.12 illustrates their findings on diet — low density areas on the top row and the corresponding high density areas below. Three important points emerged from these results. First, that the sea otter's diet varied through its range, presumably in relation to the availability of prey. In other words it is an adaptable predator. Bivalve molluscs dominated the diet in Prince William Sound, urchins in the Aleutians and urchins and crabs in California. Second, fish were not usually taken very frequently by sea otters; they are invertebrate specialists. Third, the diet in the longer established populations differed from that in the areas which had been more recently colonised.

In each case the type of prey eaten most frequently in the 'recent' areas was taken less often by the corresponding long-term colony. In California the urchins at Point Buchon were replaced by crabs and turban snails at Piedras Blancas. At Prince William Sound mussels replaced clams as the most frequent items in the denser population. In the Aleutian Islands the difference was less marked than elsewhere but there was significantly lower predation on urchins and a corresponding higher frequency of fish

Figure 3.12   The diets of sea otters in: (A, D) the Aleutian Islands; (B, E) at Prince William Sound; (C, F) in California. The areas in the upper row were colonised more recently

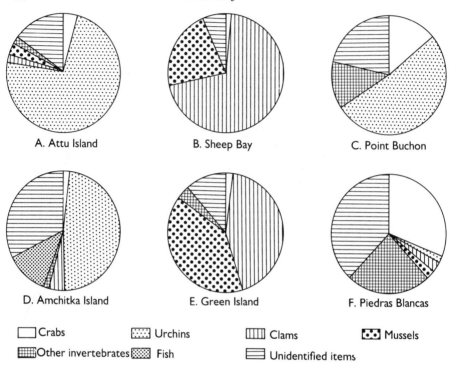

A. Attu Island   B. Sheep Bay   C. Point Buchon

D. Amchitka Island   E. Green Island   F. Piedras Blancas

☐ Crabs   ▦ Urchins   ▥ Clams   ◌ Mussels

▦ Other invertebrates ▦ Fish   ☰ Unidentified items

Source: Estes, Jameson and Johnson (1981).

in the dense population. Many of the unidentified items at Amchitka were thought to be small urchins. As fish tend to be larger than sea urchins, their importance was undoubtedly underestimated by this frequency estimate and analyses of sea otter stomachs at Amchitka indicated that fish formed 50 per cent to 60 per cent of the bulk of the diet (Kenyon, 1969).

There was considerable variation in the number of species preyed on by otters, ranging from three at Sheep Bay to 17 at Piedras Blancas but the variation between the three main areas was greater than that between pairs of neighbouring colonies. There was, however, a marked tendency for the evenness of the diet to be greater in the long-established populations, predation in these colonies was spread more evenly across the range of prey types rather than being concentrated on one or a few.

All this suggests that as sea otter populations increase, their selective predation on preferred species tends to reduce the numbers of that type of prey and they have to turn to alternative food. This cannot be proved by comparative studies of this sort but there is also evidence from areas at different stages of colonisation which shows that this is so. This is considered in more detail in Chapter 4 where the effects of sea otters on their prey populations are discussed.

Figure 3.13   Abalone shell

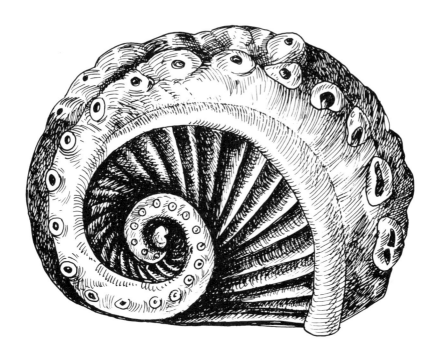

Fish are evidently an important component of the sea otter diet at Amchitka and Estes and his colleagues pointed out that as well as turning to fish because they had reduced populations of sea urchins, sea otters may have also indirectly increased the availability of the fish. This is because the reduction in numbers of herbivorous urchins allowed the kelp beds to increase in extent (see Chapter 4) which increased the abundance of fish which live in the kelp.

Estes *et al.* found that abalones (*Haliotis* spp. — Figure 3.13) were a minor item in the diet of sea otters in California and were not taken at all elsewhere. However, they pointed out that at Point Buchon, abalones formed nearly a quarter of the items caught by otters two years prior to their own study and other studies on the foraging of sea otters (see below) have shown that they show a strong preference for feeding on these large meaty molluscs when they can.

Apart from the prey referred to above, sea otters eat various other types of food including limpets, sea cucumbers, scallops, chitons, anemones and annelid worms. Perhaps the most bizarre habits are those of otters in Monterey Bay which eat tinned octopus. This depends on an unlikely association between sea otters and beer and cola drinkers. When empty cans are thrown into the sea small octopuses creep in and use them as refuges. The sea otters have evidently learned this and collect the cans which they tear open with their teeth to extract the succulent contents.

Summary. Like other otters, sea otters are adaptable opportunists but retain a specialist interest in invertebrates. This may reflect a close affinity with the clawless otters. Fish are taken but only when other food is relatively hard to find. As much of their prey consists of sedentary species they do not normally have to chase their prey and this may enable them to select prey in ways which are not possible for river otters (see Foraging Tactics below).

PREDATORY BEHAVIOUR

If you look down into the clear water of a hill or moorland stream it seems that hunting fish must be an easy task for otters but seen from within the underwater world is very different. Philip Wayre (1979) remembered his first dive into a river as being like a dull November afternoon with visibility as little as a metre. If the water is like that on a clear day, imagine the problems for an otter on a dark night, in the rapid water of a stream in spate or in a muddy lowland river. Yet otters can fish in these conditions, so how do they do it?

Although it is possible to watch wild otters fishing if you go to remote places, normally all that can be seen is activity on the surface when the otter comes up to breathe or to eat the prey that it has caught. What happens below can only be guessed at. Exceptionally the otter can be watched swimming under water in the sea but the actual hunting takes place in thick beds of kelp (*Laminaria*) so that the otter has to be followed by watching the rising chain of bubbles (Watson, 1978).

Most of our knowledge of hunting behaviour comes from studies of captive animals, either in pools or tanks, or from tame otters which can be temporarily released. From these sources, it is possible to build up an outline of the way in which the otter hunts, although the natural pattern of hunting may differ.

Sea otters are unlike other otters, partly because they feed mainly on immobile invertebrates in relatively deep water which require different techniques for catching but also because divers have been able to follow them under water and watch them foraging. On account of this sea otter foraging behaviour is dealt with separately. The following sections concentrate on otters hunting in fresh water, mainly for fish. The hunting process is divided into three stages: seeking, chasing and catching.

Searching for Prey

Otters vary their searching methods according to conditions, particularly the depth of the water. In very shallow water where it cannot conveniently swim the Eurasian otter will walk along the bottom with its head under water looking out for fish and turning over stones with its nose to search for crayfish, bullheads, and so on. The African clawless otter does the same but uses its front paws for turning stones and grasping prey.

When the water is a little deeper the otter swims on the surface with its head submerged and, if the water is more than 30 to 40 cm deep, submerges completely, enabling it to swim more swiftly as it uses its whole body rather than just its limbs. In an artificial pool 40 cm deep the otters swam along the bottom but in deeper pools (150 cm) they stayed at depths of 30 to 60 cm while searching for fish (Erlinge, 1968b).

Otters have a characteristic method of diving in which the back is arched and the otter dives vertically downwards, the hind limbs and tail following the line of the body in a graceful curve. This propels the otter towards the bottom more rapidly than the shallow dives used when the otter swims near the surface. This deep diving technique minimises the time taken to reach the bottom which, in water more than a metre or two deep, is very important since the time taken travelling to and fro takes a substantial proportion of time during each dive.

In a study of coastal otters in Scotland, only 19 per cent of 120 dives were successful but these successful dives were, on average 36 per cent shorter than unsuccessful dives (Kruuk and Hewson, 1978). It was calculated that on average it took these otters 7 seconds per dive travelling to and from the bottom, a distance of 2–3 m. In view of this, it is unlikely that otters normally hunt at depths much greater than this. Although there have been reports of river otters caught in crab or lobster pots at depths as great as 18.5 m (Scheffer, 1953), this is probably exceptional. Of 22 casualties recorded in South Uist, one otter was caught in a trap in water 15 m deep but all the rest were in water less than 6 m deep and most were caught at depths of 2–4 m.

Detecting Prey. Under favourable conditions, that is in clear, well-lit water, otters seem to depend mainly on sight for detecting prey. Even on dark nights there is usually some light from the sky and scales are very reflective so an otter may see the occasional gleam of light from the side of a fish. In murky water or on very dark nights other senses have to be used and experiments have shown that Eurasian otters can use their facial whiskers to find prey (see Chapter 2). The vibrissae are sensitive to vibration so an otter could not detect a fish if it was motionless. In still water, therefore, the otter would have to get close enough to the fish to disturb it and make it move before detection was possible. This, together with the fact that the whiskers are probably only sensitive at close range, explains why the experimental otter took four times longer to catch fish in darkened water than in clear. In running water, fish need to swim in order to stay in the same place, so by hunting upstream, the otter should find detection easier.

Chasing Prey

Captive otters often pursued fish from below, at a distance of 0.5 m to 1 m, probably because this gave the otter the best view of the fish and also made it difficult for the fish to see the otter (Erlinge, 1968b). Sometimes the fish was caught from below without a chase because the otter's approach was not detected.

In shallow water and with bottom-living fish the otter has to adopt a different strategy. Clawless otters have more difficulty in catching fish in shallow water than deep, presumably because they cannot swim properly but have to run and leap after the fish. Crabs and frogs on the other hand move less rapidly and are caught as easily in shallow water as deep (Rowe-Rowe, 1977a). It has been suggested that other species of otters sometimes drive fish into the shallows to catch them but the success of this may depend on the size of the fish. A large fish in shallow water would certainly be more vulnerable than a small one.

It is very important for the otter to keep close to a fish it is chasing and if the fish manages to get more than 2−3 m ahead of the otter, even in clear water, contact is lost and the otter begins searching again. In murky water, the critical distance is probably rather less. Dunstone (1976) observed similar behaviour in the mink, although this species seems to prefer to do its searching from a vantage point on the bank or side of the pool. The mink's visual powers under water are much poorer than the otter's, however, and it loses track of fish if they manage to get more than about 30 cm in front of it.

While chasing fish, the otter swims at its maximum speed using the hind end of the body for propulsion and the fore limbs for steering, pushing off rocks, the bottom or, in a tank, the sides. Although the otter needs to take a breath every 20−30 seconds or so, in water that is not too deep, this need not necessarily interrupt the chase. If the fish swims anywhere near the surface, the otter can break through, take a breath and continue the chase without pausing or losing contact. Otters sometimes pursue fish for 2−3 minutes in this way. If the fish is not caught immediately, the otter tries to tire it, as few fish are capable of swimming at high speed except in short bursts. A trout, for example, can reach a speed of nearly ten body lengths per second, but this is only sustained for about one second. The highest speed that can be kept up for five seconds is 4−5 lengths/second, which is equivalent to 1 m/sec. for a 200 mm fish and not beyond the powers of an otter.

Clearly, continuous pursuit is not possible when hunting bottom-living fish in deep water and this may be one of the reasons for the low capture rates of coastal otters. These otters cannot chase the same fish continually as they must return to the surface to breathe and searching and pursuit have to begin again after each breath so there is little opportunity to tire a fish out.

A strategy employed by many carnivores to improve hunting efficiency is co-operation, most highly developed in social animals such as lions and African hunting dogs. As Eurasian otters are largely solitary, opportunities for co-operative hunting are limited to family groups and there is no evidence that a co-operative strategy is normally employed. However, Sheldon and Toll (1964) watched a female American river otter hunting co-operatively with her cub:

> They swam on the surface until about ten feet apart, dived and swam rapidly toward a shallow cove, apparently herding fish before them . . . There seemed to be a high degree of success in this type of fishing as usually, both animals came up with fish.

Some species of otter are more gregarious than river otters and Harris (1968) claimed that:

> some races of Indian otters form groups to make co-operative hunting expeditions, the members forming a large semi-circle and gradually driving the fish before them towards the shallows.

It has also been suggested that giant otters co-operate to drive fish into shallow backwaters although Duplaix (1980) saw no evidence of this in over 100 hours of observation, despite seeing parties of up to eight otters feeding together. She concluded that the general disturbance created by several otters hunting in close proximity may have confused fish and made escape more difficult but each otter appeared to hunt independently even if close to its neighbours.

As pointed out earlier, the behaviour patterns of fish vary and this may affect the success of otters in catching them. Of particular importance is the response to attack by a predator. In the wild, observations of fish chased by tame otters show that some species, particularly the slower-moving ones, tend to take cover in weed and among rocks when chased by otters. This is apparently not an effective stratagem, at least during daylight, as the fish were easily caught by the otters (Wayre, 1979).

In a study of the predatory behaviour of captive mink, Poole and Dunstone (1976) found that the behaviour of the fish tended to be unpredictable and that they used such tactics as sharp turns and swimming in a zig-zag pattern to try and evade the pursuing mink. Mink also took longer to catch minnows if the number in the tank was increased but when goldfish were increased in number there was no change in the time taken to catch one. Minnows form shoals but goldfish do not which suggests that shoaling decreased the predator's efficiency, probably because the mink had to make a choice between a number of fleeing fish scattering in all directions. On the other hand, a shoal is more conspicuous than a single fish particularly in the complex environments in which otters normally hunt and shoaling is not an appropriate strategy for all species of fish.

Catching, Killing and Consuming

Eurasian otters usually catch fish with their jaws, but sometimes an otter will grasp a fish in its paws and then pass it to the mouth to be bitten (Figure 3.14). Fish are normally caught by the belly, probably reflecting the otter's preference for attack from below, but may sometimes be taken by the tail, back or head. Small fish are eaten at the surface but larger ones are taken to the side to be consumed. Although fish are not eaten in any set pattern, live fish are normally eaten from the head, possibly to ensure that they are rapidly killed.

Otters do not eat the heads of large fish and in some cases the vertebral column is also left. Normally, however, the otter leaves few or no remains except of extremely large fish. I have only twice seen fish half-eaten by otters, once on the bank of a Devon stream where I found a 30 cm length of eel and on another occasion beside a remote lake in Sweden. In the second case the fish was freshly killed and we may have disturbed the otter before it finished its meal.

These observations do not coincide with a popular theory of fishermen and water bailiffs that otters will often kill a salmon or sea trout and then leave it after taking 'a bite out of the shoulder'. Water bailiffs spend a good deal of their time patrolling long stretches of river and are likely to notice such fish when they are left by otters but the frequency of the event can easily become exaggerated. Also the bite is in reality more than just a mouthful, half a kilogram or more might be eaten, a substantial meal for an otter (Figure 3.15). Bailiffs have described to me

Figure 3.14   River otter catching a fish in its forepaws

how they would collect the partly-eaten fish for their own consumption but perhaps if they did not do so, the otter might return later to finish to task itself.

There are a small number of observations which suggest that otters do return to kills, for example Pring (1958) includes a report that:

> an otter returned the next night and finished eating all but the jaw bone and scrap of head of a 1.25 to 1.5 lb (570−680 g) Rainbow Trout which it had taken from the mill leat and half eaten the previous night.

Figure 3.15   Partly-eaten salmon

Rowe-Rowe (1977a) compared the feeding behaviour of clawless otters and spotted-necked otters. Spotted-necked otters usually caught prey in their mouths. Perhaps because of this, they were very wary of large crabs (over 50 mm in width) which were likely to nip their faces while clawless otters which used their nimble fingers to manipulate crabs, ignored the occasional tweak. Clawless otters also caught fish in their hands, passing them to the mouth and biting their heads.

The manual dexterity of the clawless otters enabled them to handle prey sufficiently well to eat in the water but, unless it was very small, spotted-necked otters took their prey to the bank to consume so that they could hold it down with their forepaws. There was a tendency for each species to start eating from opposite ends especially if the fish were over 60 mm in length. Clawless otters started at the head and spotted-necked at the tail. This reflects the differences in their dentitions, the powerful molars of the clawless otters enabling them to crush the heads of all but the largest fish while the sharp teeth of the spotted-necked otter mean that they find it easier to eat the flesh and leave the head of most fish.

Like sea otters, clawless otters occasionally use tools to help them deal with their prey. During a year of low rainfall in Zimbabwe, water levels dropped to expose large areas of mudflats behind several dams in a National Park. At two of these, numerous middens were found consisting of the broken remains of mussel shells (*Aspartharia wahlbergia*) scattered around hard objects such as rocks, bottles and pipes. Otter trails led to these from the water's edge some 5 m away. As the waterline receded the middens were abandoned and new ones started. The mussels were 60 to 120 mm in length and the shells required considerable force to break. The otters achieved this by hurling them at the anvils. Scats taken at that time included fragments of shell but a subsequent collection of 100 scats taken over a longer period included none, suggesting that the otters only attempted to eat the mussels during times of drought (Donnelly and Grobler, 1976).

The Foraging Behaviour of Sea Otters

Although sea otters have good underwater vision, they find their prey mainly by feeling for it. Shimek (1977) watched a sea otter while he was diving and described how in 15 seconds it managed to feel its way around three granite boulders, the holdfast of a giant kelp plant and into a crevice, collecting two snails as it went. It did not seem to be looking for prey and held its head back while reaching into the crevice and patting the boulders with its paws. Kenyon (1969) observed similar behaviour in a captive female which was offered a bucket of turbid water containing 200 small crabs, four mussels and some pebbles. The otter rested its chin on the bucket's edge while feeling in the muddy water with its paws and within a few seconds had pulled out the four mussels, leaving the other contents behind.

On another occasion Shimek watched an otter foraging with its head down in a cloud of silt and only its flippers visible. Closer inspection, after the otter had surfaced, revealed a series of holes 30 to 40 cm in diameter and about 20 cm deep on the bottom. On at least two consecutive dives the otter returned to the same hole and enlarged it, kicking with its flippers to hold the body down while the forepaws and head were used to excavate the silt and cobbles on the bottom. Simultaneous observations at the surface showed that the otter was feeding on specimens of the fat innkeeper worm (*Urechis caupo*) but it did not apparently take any tube worms or purple olive shells (*Olivela biplicata*) which were also to be found in the substrate. The sea otter is obviously capable of being selective in what it picks up. Shimek's observations indicate that while the tactile sense is probably most important in finding prey, the otter probably uses vision to find the area in which it is going to search, for example to enable it to return to a previously started excavation.

Much of the prey of the sea otter is effectively immobile (urchins and molluscs) or fairly slow-moving so the otters, once they have found their prey, do not need to chase it, merely pick it up and carry it to the surface to be eaten. Some food may offer a little resistance. Limpets and chitons cling firmly to rocks but even if they cannot be simply picked up in the paws they can probably be fairly easily prised off with the teeth. Abalones which are effectively giant limpets are quite another matter. The whole of the underside of the abalone consists of a massive muscular foot which is used to grip the rock by suction. Since the average size of abalones may be over 200 mm they must sometimes take a considerable amount of work to dislodge. This is confirmed by observations which showed that while most items of prey can be collected in a single dive, it sometimes takes six or seven dives to bring up one abalone (Ostfeld, 1982).

For some time it was not clear just how the sea otters managed to pry loose these tenacious animals. Hildebrand (1954) suggested that the teeth were used and pointed out that the incisor teeth of sea otters were often worn on the outside as if they had been abraded while the canines were being used to lever up the outside of the shell. He also noted that when brought to the surface abalones often had pieces missing from the shell as if bitten by the otter. Other people suggested that the otters might take the abalones by surprise and tug them off before they had a chance to grip tightly. In fact the otters use a weapon, usually a rock, with which to bludgeon the unfortunate molluscs. Several dives are needed to pound the abalone into submission but finally it lets go and is brought to the surface by the sea otter. This has been observed from below the surface by Houk and Geibel (1974) who watched a sea otter take three dives to dislodge a 120 mm-long abalone. The same rock was used on each dive but it was discarded after the abalone had been collected. The otter alternately lay on its front with its head bent up hammering with the rock held in front of it and then turned over onto its back, head to one side, and pounded over its shoulder.

One type of food which has to be chased by sea otters is fish. No one has observed sea otters hunting fish from under water, presumably because this happens very rarely in California, fish being mainly eaten by otters in the Aleutians. Not surprisingly sea otters take mainly sluggish bottom-dwelling fish although these are probably less abundant than more active species. Kenyon pointed out that marine mammals that eat fish normally have many sharp pointed teeth to catch their prey and then swallow it whole while sea otters are not adapted for this. He believed that they normally caught fish in the forepaws, brought them to the surface and then killed them with a crushing bite at or near the head.

The fish were held in the forepaws, chunks torn off and then swallowed after a moderate amount of chewing. Some lumps of fish flesh in the stomach were as much as 50 mm across indicating that the food was not much broken up in the mouth.

The ways in which sea otters deal with other types of prey depend on size and the presence or absence of a hard shell. Octopuses are treated like fish although otters are unable to kill them as rapidly. However, the writhing arms and suckers which grip the face, limbs, body or even inside the mouth do not seem to disconcert the otters at all and they are capable of dealing with specimens up to 2 kg in weight.

Small urchins and small or soft-shelled molluscs are crushed and eaten in their entirety but larger urchins, mussels and clams are broken up first. The tests of large urchins are fractured and broken with the teeth or paws and the contents scooped out by the incisors (this may cause the wear described above). Crabs are torn apart and although legs and pincers have been found in sea otters' stomachs, thoroughly crushed, the carapaces have not, presumably because the contents have been scooped out and the shell discarded.

One of the best known aspects of sea otter behaviour is the habit of using a stone anvil to break open the shells of clams or mussels (Figure 3.16). The otters lie on their backs holding the mollusc between their paws with the anvil on their chests. After a few tentative taps, possibly to line up the shell, they proceed to batter the mussel against the stone until the shell is broken and the contents can be consumed. Hall and Schaller (1964) observed otters feeding on mussels at Point Lobos, Monterey, California and found that although the mussels were not very large (averaging some 50 mm in length) it took an average of 35.5 blows to break them open. The stones appeared to average about 125 mm across

Figure 3.16 Sea otter using a rock to break a clam shell

weighing perhaps 500–600 g but were not very constant in shape and it seemed that otters would collect any stone of about the right size. One otter watched by Hall and Schaller caught 44 mussels but only used six different stones during a single feeding session. While diving and searching for more mussels, the stones were tucked into the flap of skin under the otter's forelimb. Otters also seem to concentrate their foraging on mussels for long periods. One otter in particular spent 86 minutes feeding on a single mussel bed and collected 54 mussels during that time.

Foraging Tactics. The fact that otters might concentrate their foraging on particular species of prey during a foraging session suggests that they choose what type of prey to feed on. A study of the factors governing that choice was made by Ostfeld (1982) near Santa Cruz in California where the otter population had only recently been re-established. He found that the main items in the diet were kelp crabs (*Pugettia producta*), red abalones (*Haliotis rufescens*), *Cancer* crabs, urchins (*Strongylocentrotus franciscanus*) and clams (*Gari californica*).

Having determined that these species were being taken by otters, he attempted to estimate their 'profitability' by calculating the average energy value of each item and dividing this by the average time taken to collect one. He then determined the otters preferences and found that the order was: (1) *Cancer* crabs and abalones — strongly preferred; (2) sea urchins — preferred; (3) kelp crabs — taken less frequently than predicted by their abundance. Since the rank order of preference was the same as the order of profitability, Ostfeld concluded that the otters were trying to maximise their intake of energy for the minimum effort expended.

He also demonstrated that during one feeding session otters tended to concentrate on one type of prey and did not often switch from one species to another. When switching did occur, it was more likely to happen after a series of unsuccessful dives. In some cases otters were foraging in areas where only one type of prey was likely to be found but at other times it was clear that the otters tended to ignore a type of prey which was present. Switching was less likely to occur with the more abundant species such as clams, urchins and kelp crabs than with *Cancer* crabs and abalones which, though widespread, were at lower densities than the other species. For example, 27 per cent of sea urchin captures were followed by switching to a different species but switching occurred after 42 per cent of abalone captures. Most consistent of all was predation on clams (10 per cent switching) probably because they were found in soft substrates where the other species were rare. In order to switch, the otter would have had to move to another area.

Food Consumption

Satiation probably inhibits otters from searching for more food (see below), but at what stage is satiation reached? Erlinge found that captive otters were moderately replete after 400–500 g and satiated after 900–1,000 g of fish and he estimated the daily consumption to be 1–1.5 kg for an adult otter. The intake of two adult male otters weighing slightly above the average (12.25 kg and 10.9 kg) were recorded for one week in winter when the mean temperature was close to freezing. They consumed 1.5 kg and 1.4 kg per day respectively (Wayre, 1979) and since otters eat less food in warmer weather this must be near the maximum for captive otters.

Wild otters, which have to expend more energy in obtaining their food, might be expected to eat rather more than the captive ones and males rather more than females. On these grounds it seems reasonable to suggest that daily consumption is of the order of 15–20 per cent of body weight.

Kenyon (1969) made observations on a captive female sea otter which averaged 4 kg of food per day, equivalent to 23 per cent of her body weight. Although one normally expects larger animals to eat relatively less than smaller ones because of their lower metabolic rates, this discrepancy in otters is not surprising since sea otters have a metabolic rate higher than other species because of their fully aquatic habits (see Chapter 2).

Surplus Killing and Predation on Domestic and Enclosed Prey

A facet of carnivore behaviour that man often bitterly regrets is surplus killing. The most familiar example of this is the carnage which may be caused by the fox in the hen-house but Kruuk (1972) recorded several examples from the wild including a polar bear killing narwhals, spotted hyenas killing and maiming Thomson's gazelle, foxes killing black-headed gulls and a leopard killing goats. In each case considerable numbers of prey were killed on a single night and there was a great deal of waste involved. Usually one or a few predators killed large numbers of prey, many times more than they could possibly eat and little or nothing was eaten from each carcass.

Other observations, particularly on social carnivores such as lions and wild dogs, show that individual animals often kill more than they need in order to provide food for other members of the social group. At its simplest a mother may kill more than she can consume in order to provide for her dependent offspring.

Another potential benefit from small-scale surplus kills is that prey might be cached and then consumed at a later date and a number of carnivores including foxes, polecats and leopards do this. However, Kruuk pointed out that large-scale surplus killing could be positively detrimental to the predator in that it might reduce the potential food supply in the future. He concluded that foxes could have wiped out a black-headed gull colony he was studying had predation continued at the high levels he observed. In addition, any subsequent benefits of surplus killing would be limited by decay of the carcasses or their removal by scavengers.

Kruuk emphasised the fact that predators appeared to make surplus kills when they were not hungry but had already eaten enough to be satiated. He suggested that hunting behaviour could be divided into four phases: searching, hunting, catching and killing. Once an animal was replete, searching and perhaps hunting behaviour might be inhibited, but if catching and, particularly, killing behaviour was not, the replete animal would then be in a position to take advantage of any opportunities which presented themselves. If the predator trips over potential prey it kills it.

Normally the anti-predator behaviour of the prey, fleeing or hiding for example, would prevent this happening on more than a small scale but, under certain conditions, the anti-predator responses to the prey do not operate. The black-headed gulls, Thomson's gazelle and goats were all killed on very dark nights when, if they had tried to escape, they might have injured themselves or run into the jaws of the predator. The narwhals were trapped in a small pool of ice and were scooped out by the bear when they came up to breathe.

Interestingly, although verbal accounts of surplus kills of poultry often imply a frenzied attack by the predator this does not seem to have been the case in the few instances which could easily be followed. Kruuk found that the foxes and the hyenas walked quietly among the prey rather than rushing bloodthirstily from one tender throat to the next.

It is clear that surplus killing occurs rarely in the wild. I know of no cases where otters have been involved in surplus killing of unenclosed animals but there are a small number of occasions on which otters have caused problems to enclosed stocks.

Otter predation on livestock is rare but attacks by predators on any animal kept by man tend to cause annoyance, often in inverse proportion to the trouble taken to prevent it. Information on such attacks tends to be anecdotal and difficult to quantify and since the culprit is not usually seen at work blame is attributed on the basis of circumstantial evidence.

In the past, the otter has been regarded as a pest principally on account of its fish-eating habits and man's conviction that every fish eaten by a predator is one less for him to catch. The truth of this idea is examined in the next chapter, but here it has to be accepted that if otters do get into fish stews or hatcheries, they can cause considerable damage. King *et al.* (1976) suggested that medieval monasteries relied heavily on fish stews to supplement their diet and might have been seriously inconvenienced by the attentions of otters. Contemporary accounts are rare but Harris mentioned two instances, in one of which three otters were reputed to have killed 2,000 yearling trout in one night — a formidable task!

An anonymous writer quoted by Laws (1978) claimed that:

> When compelled by hunger, the otter is known to quit the stream, and to travel to a distance overland, and to commit ravages among the farmer's stock, devouring rabbits and barn door fowls, and even young pigs and lambs.

However, Harris was able to find only one confirmed instance of poultry killing and this was carried out by an otter with a steel trap on its leg. In another incident, in Shropshire, a duck farm was set up with an otter proof fence around it. However, the fence also enclosed an otter which is reported to have killed £600 worth of ducks (Shepheard and Townshend, 1937).

More recently, complaints were made by the residents of Colonsay and Oronsay, islands off the west coast of Scotland, that otters were killing poultry and waterfowl. Birds were found to form a small proportion of the diet of otters and at one site 5 per cent of the spraints contained feathers.

It was clear that this was having no effect on the population of eider ducks, as had been feared, but reports of otters taking poultry were substantiated by the finding of hen feathers in spraints from two sites. There were no terrestrial predators on the islands and few precautions were taken. Some fowl were not shut in at night and roamed along the shoreline where they were easy prey for the otters.

Incidents such as these are unusual and, on the whole, the likelihood of otters taking ducks or poultry is low and would be even lower if all owners took the trouble to pen their flocks securely at night.

Occasionally otters are accused of taking even larger prey such as sheep though the evidence is usually circumstantial. In one case in the 1970s a total of 82 sheep were reputedly killed by otters on the west coast of Scotland over a seven year period. This included yearling and adult sheep several times bigger than an otter as well as lambs. Incriminating evidence included the fact that otters were seen near kills and that the methods of killing were supposedly characteristic of otters. None of this stood up to critical examination.

4 Relations with other animals

The relationships between otters and man are examined in Chapter 7, and in this chapter the interactions between otters and three other groups of animals are considered: those that eat them, those that they eat and those that compete with them, in other words, predators, prey and competitors.

PREDATORS OF OTTERS

Otters are sometimes referred to as 'top carnivores' which means that they are usually at the end of food chains and do not form a normal part of the diet of larger predators. Large carnivores may feed on smaller carnivores but generally do so very rarely, simply because they are always much scarcer than other prey such as rodents and ungulates or other herbivorous animals. There is even some evidence that carnivores can be distasteful to eat. MacDonald (1977) offered tame foxes lumps of badger, weasel and fox flesh and on each occasion the carnivore meat was rejected although small pieces of rabbit meat, offered at the same time, were eaten or cached. Whole corpses were treated in the same way although sometimes the corpses of the carnivores were urinated or defaecated upon.

It seems likely then that a large carnivore would only kill and eat an otter if it encountered one by chance, was big enough to overpower it and, probably, was fairly hungry. Field observations of such an event are extremely unlikely and none have been recorded although it has been suggested that in Russia, wolverines eat Eurasian otters (Novikov, 1962) and that in South America, jaguars kill giant otters (Duplaix, 1980). However, neither these, nor any other authors, offer any evidence to confirm these suggestions.

Otters in tropical regions might occasionally be eaten by large reptiles although here too evidence is lacking. For example, Procter (1963) concluded that spotted-necked otter dens around Lake Victoria were probably safe from most predators except pythons but he did not make it clear whether or not the snakes actually ate otters.

Sea otters, on the other hand, by congregating together, lay themselves open to systematic predation because the groups are easily found. Their size and habit of staying offshore considerably reduce the range of predators that are able to attack them and only a large marine animal would have much chance of taking an adult. The cubs are easier prey, however, and on Amchitka Island are taken by bald eagles (*Haliaeetus leucocephalus*), at least during the nesting season (see Chapter 6). It has been suggested that killer whales (*Orcinus orca*) may prey on sea otters (Kenyon, 1969) but there are no observations of this occurring even though killer whales have been seen near groups of sea otters. Sea otter fur has been found in the scats of arctic foxes (*Alopex lagopus*) (Harris,

1968) although this small species commonly scavenges along the shoreline and may have been feeding on carrion. When in 1971 winter weather conditions led to the deaths of substantial numbers of sea otters mainly from malnutrition some carcasses were scavenged by red foxes (*Vulpes vulpes*) and wolverines. At least one otter had probably been killed by one of the predators when it was already in poor condition (Schneider and Faro, 1975).

The only undisputed evidence of predation upon adult sea otters comes from California where Ames and Morejohn (1980) found that between 9 per cent and 15 per cent of dead sea otters they examined had been attacked and killed by white sharks (*Carcharodon carcharias*). Since the remains of sea otters have never been found in shark guts it is unlikely that otters form a significant item in the normal diet of the sharks and it is even possible that the sharks kill the otters but do not eat them.

Overall, the only predation on otters that has been adequately documented is that on sea otters by bald eagles and white sharks. Other species of otter undoubtedly do fall victim to larger predators from time to time but it is quite likely that it only happens sporadically and that other forms of mortality are much more important.

OTTER PREY

The interactions between predators and their prey are usually complex and it is often difficult to separate causes and effects. In Chapter 5 it is suggested that the abundance and distribution of prey may affect the behaviour of otters; the following section shows how otters could, and in some cases do, affect the abundance of their prey.

The impact of otter predation on prey populations has only been adequately assessed in two areas. In Sweden, Erlinge collected data which suggested that the effect of Eurasian otter predation on fish and crayfish populations was negligible, while in Alaska and California it has been shown that sea otter predation on sea urchins and abalones can be so intense that the whole community of underwater life is altered.

River Otters

Much has been said about the otter's supposed effect on populations of fish, particularly of game fish, but during the twentieth century the view that otters are simply noxious vermin has changed considerably. This is partly due to a change in attitudes to predators generally brought about by a better understanding of the ecology of predation, but otters have also benefited from the favourable image of them portrayed by authors such as Henry Williamson and Gavin Maxwell. In addition, in Britain and many parts of Europe there is now a new *bête noire* for the fishermen to anguish over, the feral mink.

As long ago as 1880, correspondence was generated in *The Field* by an article emphasising not only the pleasure of otter hunting, but also the damage that otters do. In reply it was pointed out that the otter feeds mainly on 'eels and coarse fish, thereby rather benefitting a trout stream'. Fitter (1964) believed that the decline of otters in Poland resulted in a decrease in fish populations because the otters had been taking mostly sick fish and, once they had gone, disease spread rapidly among the fish population. Unfortunately, these beneficial effects are speculative and the potential benefits of otters have, until recently, been dismissed in favour of the more obvious fact that otters eat salmon and trout.

In captivity it is not difficult to demonstrate that otters selectively prey upon slower-moving and damaged fish, so it seems quite feasible to extrapolate this to the wild and suggest that diseased and debilitated fish could be taken disproportionately frequently. No one has demonstrated this for otters, but in the Netherlands, it has been shown that 30 per cent of the roach taken by cormorants in one area were parasitised by the tapeworm *Ligula intestinalis* although only 6.5 per cent of the fish population were infected by the worm (van Dobben, 1952). Clearly the diseased fish were being removed selectively, which could help to slow the spread of the disease. Sometimes, however, the opposite occurs since many species of parasite make use of predators as alternate hosts, infecting the carnivorous species when it eats an infected primary host. The carnivore then disperses the parasite, often in its faeces and usually at a different stage of the life cycle. As predators are usually more mobile than their prey this is an effective means for the parasite to ensure its wide dissemination.

Tapeworm segments (proglottids) have been found in otter sprints from time to time, some probably ingested with prey and passing straight through the gut, others having been shed by worms parasitising the otter. I have only seen these in four sprints, two beside a lake in Sweden and two in Devon. In Montana, Greer (1955) found that 5 per cent of the river otter scats he collected contained *Ligula* proglottids but since birds are normally the alternate host of this species, one may conclude that they were parasitising the prey rather than the otter. On the other hand, Erlinge found proglottids of an unidentified tapeworm regularly in the sprints of one otter over a period of two years indicating that these had been shed by a tapeworm in the otter's gut.

The selective removal of diseased individuals and also very young and very old prey has been demonstrated in other predators where prey is actively pursued rather than being ambushed. With some types of prey this may have a beneficial effect in that predation is concentrated on the non-breeding part of the population. However, as yet there is little evidence that this 'sanitation effect' actually limits the spread of disease in a population or that otters are significant carriers of fish parasites.

Normally, the number of fish in an area is determined by the amount of space or food available rather than by the level of predation. Salmonid fish are territorial, each fish claiming an area large enough to feed itself and then defending it vigorously. Those fish unable to establish a territory near their hatching site drift downstream until they find a suitable vacant site. If they fail to do so they will die of starvation, disease or predation. As a result, of the average brood of trout eggs, fewer than 5 per cent survive the first year of life. As the fish grow, their territories expand and the weaker fish are displaced so that after the first year about half the fish in a particular age group die annually. Under normal circumstances, many of these surplus fish are taken by predators such as otters, herons, kingfishers and bigger fish. If, on the other hand, the predator takes a territory-holding fish, there will always be other fish available to take over the territory.

Below the size of fish taken by man, therefore, the predators merely remove a proportion of the doomed individuals. Once the fish reach a size of 20 cm or so, another predator comes on the scene, namely man. Theoretically, it would be possible for man to catch all the fish which might be expected to die each year, without affecting the fishing for future years. To do this he would also need to take fish which would normally have been eaten by other fish predators including otters. In practice, fishing in inland waters is not usually that intense and in addition, the otter takes mainly the smaller fish, below catchable size.

Turning to coarse fisheries, the problem of otter predation is different because in Britain, at least, anglers return their catch to the water and are not, therefore, proper predators themselves. They too have argued that predation reduces the number of fish available for them to catch. Population regulation in coarse fish differs from that in salmonids because they are not territorial but there is still a high mortality of fish each year in a stable population. People have argued that returning the catch to the water is a bad policy since a dense population of fish leads to a reduction in growth rate and in maximum size (Owen, 1974). Similarly, it has been shown that a reduction in population density can sometimes lead to an increase in the average size of the fish. For example, studies of the fish in a Swedish lake showed that by substantially reducing the population and reducing the spawning rate the average size of fish was increased by 50 per cent in eight years (Alm, 1946). Following up this line of argument, some people have even recommended the encouragement of predators on certain waters to improve the catch.

Although one can argue strongly for the beneficial effects of otters as against the harm they might do, it is important to realise that neither side has proved its case. On balance I suspect that predation on fish by river otters is usually neutral and that neither encouraging nor controlling otters has any significant effects on fishing.

Erlinge (1967b) attempted to quantify otter predation on fish at Lake Sövdesjön and to compare it with the level of fishing by man. He knew that there were four otters on the lake and assumed that they took between 1.0 kg and 1.5 kg fish per day while information on the extent of human depredations came from fishing returns. Table 4.1 shows the

Table 4.1   Estimates of the quantities of fish caught by otters and by fishermen on Lake Sövdesjön (Sweden) in one year

	Eaten by otters (kg)	Caught by fishermen (kg)
Cyprinids	975	1,500 – 1,750
Perch and ruffe[a]	450	unknown
Pike	120	1,000 – 1,200
Eel	50	365 – 400

Note: a. *Gymnocephalus cernua*.
Source: Erlinge (1967b).

figures he calculated for otter predation and the catches by fishermen indicating that man takes about twice as many cyprinids (bleak, bream, rudd, tench) as the otter and nearly ten times as many pike and eels. In addition to man and otters, the fish populations are also preyed upon by herons, mergansers, grebes and, particularly, other fish such as pike. Erlinge calculated that the thousand or so pike taken by fishermen each year would themselves have consumed about 5,000 kg of smaller fish in that time, had they survived. This in itself is more than three times the total weight of fish consumed by the otters each year. It is clear, therefore, that the otter consumes a very small proportion of the total biomass of fish taken by predators during a year. Despite losses to these various predators, Erlinge considered that fish populations in the lake were limited by food and not by predation.

The River Klingavälsån flows out of Lake Sövdesjön and it was here that Erlinge investigated the otter's effect on the crayfish population. By marking and recapturing crayfish he was able to estimate the number present and compare it with the numbers taken by otters and man, the two main predators. Between them, they removed nearly half the population each year, man taking about 50 per cent more than the otter. As the crayfish population was able to withstand this level of exploitation from year to year, it would seem that man and otter were not competing. Whether increasing the length of the fishing season or the intensity of fishing would have led to competition could not be determined.

Erlinge also found that when the crayfish population was devastated by disease, it recovered quickly despite continuous predation by the otters. In areas where crayfish were sparse, this scarcity could be attributed to unsuitable habitat or to fish predation and Erlinge concluded that otters do not depress crayfish populations whether they are dense or sparse.

As one might expect, it is not possible to draw any firm conclusions about the effects of otters on fish populations. Le Cren (1962) stated that:

> fish have remarkable powers of self-regulation in their abundance, including the ability to compensate for extra mortality they may suffer.

By the same token, one should be wary of arguing a beneficial effect when otters catch fish which fishermen consider to be pests such as eels. Having argued that trout, roach and bream populations are not depleted by otter predation, one can hardly suggest that eel populations are. Similarly, although otters may well selectively prey upon damaged fish, there is no evidence that this has any effects on the population as a whole.

Sea Otters

By contrast, the effects of sea otters on populations of their prey are not only more easily measured but also dramatic. A number of surveys carried out in Alaska and California have shown that within a few years of the arrival of sea otters in a new area the populations of their favoured prey begin to decline. The abalones and sea urchins, which they prefer to eat, feed on seaweeds and the pressure of their grazing normally prevents the growth of these plants. Once the grazers have been reduced in

Figure 4.1   Sea otter foraging in kelp

numbers, the plants, particularly kelp (*Macrocystis* spp.), begin to grow luxuriantly (Figure 4.1). Similarly, comparisons of areas where otters are well established with those in which they are absent or only recently arrived show marked differences in the subtidal flora and fauna as well as in the otters' diet (see Chapter 3). Indeed the elimination of sea otters from much of their ancestral habitat combined with their slow spreading and recolonisation has resulted in a fascinating natural experiment in predator – prey interactions.

Fishermen were the first to remark on the effects of sea otters, claiming that the otters had reduced abalone populations off the Californian coast. There is little doubt that fishermen were themselves overexploiting the stocks of abalones (Duplaix, 1978) but there is also evidence that the otters had played a part in reducing the numbers in the areas where they foraged. Surveys of abalones and sea urchins carried out at Pacific Grove in California showed that in the 1970s, abalones and sea urchins were small, scarce and confined mainly to crevices (Lowry and Pearse, 1973; Cooper *et al.*, 1977). Only one abalone out of more than 200 sampled was larger than the minimum catchable size for fishermen. Bigger ones would not fit into the crevices and were, therefore, more vulnerable to the otters.

No one had made a detailed survey of the shellfish before the sea otters re-established themselves in the area but one report claimed that densities of sea urchins of six per square metre had been typical. In 1962 when sea otters were still few in number in this area, the subtidal rocks were '. . . covered with urchins and abalones spaced only a few feet apart . . . the general appearance of these rocks is bare' (McClean, 1962). By 1972 the sea otter population had reached a density of 20 per km^2, the density of sea urchins and abalones was down to 0.2 per m^2 and the subtidal rocks supported a forest of kelp 50 to 150 m wide some 50 m offshore.

RELATIONS WITH OTHER ANIMALS

In the Aleutian Island chain Estes and Palmisano (1974) compared the communities in the littoral (intertidal) and sublittoral regions of two islands, Amchitka and Shemya. The population of sea otters on Amchitka had built up to between 20 and 30 per km^2 of suitable habitat and they estimated that the otters' food intake was about 35 tonnes per km^2 per year. Semya, 400 km away in the Near Island group, was separated by deep oceanic channels and sea otters had not re-established themselves there after extermination in the previous century.

At Amchitka, the sea floor was carpeted by brown seaweeds, mainly kelp, and sea urchins were scarce and confined to crevices in shallow water. Below 10 m in depth the number of urchins increased but all were very small. Estes and Palmisano suggested that the otters might not find it energetically worthwhile to dive so deep for small urchins and therefore only took the larger specimens. By contrast, at Shemya where there were no otters, urchins were abundant and in shallow water they carpeted the bottom. The average density at a depth of 3 m was over 400 urchins per square metre and many were large, some reaching 80 mm across. Below the littoral zone there was a distinct lack of plant life due to urchin grazing although brown seaweeds could be found on the shore in the intertidal region. Even these had been grazed and all the plants growing round pools and channels, which harboured urchins when the tide was out, had been partly eaten. Similarly, barnacles and mussels were 200 times more abundant at Shemya than at Amchitka because they were not swamped by the growth of kelp.

The kelp is an important component of many food chains and its abundance at Amchitka probably results in a much higher productivity in the nearshore region. Estes and Palmisano concluded that this was why bald eagles and harbor seals (known in Britain as common seals — *Phoca vitulina*) and some species of fish were abundant at Amchitka but not at Shemya.

Paradoxically, in making the habitat more productive and able to support populations of eagles and seals, the otters had made it less suitable for themselves. As the populations of their preferred prey decreased, the otters turned to other sources of food which were more difficult to find or catch. When otters were first establishing themselves at Amchitka, sea urchins and abalones dominated the diet and fish and crabs formed less than 10 per cent of their prey but by the 1970s fish constituted over half the bulk of the diet and crabs were also being taken much more frequently (see Chapter 3).

Estes and Palmisano suggested that the sea otter is a 'keystone' species — one which has a profound effect on other members of the ecological community. Thus, changes in the numbers of sea otters, either reductions caused by over-exploitation or increases because of protection, have resulted in dramatic changes in the structure of the nearshore community.

More recent studies in California north of Santa Cruz where sea otters are absent have shown that the community can also be drastically altered by water movements. Cowen *et al.* (1982) found that urchins were dispersed and algal cover reduced after severe storms. They concluded that while sea otter predation modified intertidal communities in some areas, elsewhere storm-induced water movements were at least as important.

Nevertheless, comparing the role of the sea otter as a predator in the nearshore community with that of the piscivorous river otters reveals a marked difference. The sea otter can have a major impact on community structure and river otters, apparently, little or none.

COMPETITION

Before considering the relationships between otters and their potential competitors, it is important to define clearly what is meant by the word competition. There is a tendency for people to assume that two species which eat the same food are competing with one another, but this is not necessarily so. Strictly speaking, competition occurs when two species share a resource which is actually or potentially limited. In other words, there is not enough to go round, at least at certain times. This is a very important point because, as we have seen with salmonid populations, there may be a considerable surplus of a prey species available which, if not eaten by the predator, would die anyway. It is only when the whole of this surplus is insufficient to feed the predators and they have to start feeding on the 'capital' that competition will occur. Notice also that the definition uses the word 'resource' not food. Sometimes competition is for dens or resting places or other essential resources. In this discussion, however, I shall be considering mainly the possibility of competing for food.

It is also important to remember that when competition occurs, one species is excluded or ousted by another. The exclusion may be temporary, perhaps in winter when food is scarce, or permanent such that one species cannot live in the same area as its competitor. Unfortunately, it can be very difficult to determine whether or not competition takes place in the wild.

What then are the potential competitors of the otter? In theory at least, any medium-sized aquatic predator could compete with one species or another of otter, ranging from cormorants to crocodiles or from ospreys to pike. In practice most attention has been paid to the possibility of competition between otters and other mammals, particularly those which are closely related. This is not to say that the otter does not compete with grebes, kingfishers or piranha fish but the non-mammalian species have very different methods of hunting and this in itself tends to reduce the likelihood of competition for food. Since competition is most likely in animals of similar size and habit, it is not surprising that there has been some interest in the relationships between different species of otters which are sympatric (live in the same areas).

In South Africa, for example, Rowe-Rowe (1977c) studied the diets of clawless and spotted-necked otters and compared these with the diet of the water mongoose (*Atilax paludinosus*) which lives in the same area. This is another semi-aquatic carnivore, although it belongs to a different family — the *Viverridae* which includes genets and civet cats as well as the mongooses.

In Europe attention has been focused on interactions between feral American mink another semi-aquatic mustelid and the Eurasian otter.

Studies of mink have also been undertaken in its native North American habitat where it is sympatric with the American river otter.

I shall deal first, and in most detail, with the mink/otter relationship, partly because I have a personal interest in the problem, having long been a defender of mink, and partly because, as an introduced alien species, the mink has generated considerable interest and controversy in those parts of Europe which it has colonised.

The American Mink

Mink, like otters, are members of the family *Mustelidae*, but belong to the stoat/weasel/polecat branch of the family, the *Mustelinae*. There are two species of mink, almost identical in size and appearance, one native to America called *Mustela vison* and the other native to Europe, though not Britain, known as *Mustela lutreola*.

The American mink has long been prized for its luxurious fur. In 1867 the first captive breeding colony was established, forming the basis of an enormous industry which now produces millions of pelts each year. In the 1920s and 1930s, live mink were exported to establish fur farms in European countries and it was not long before the first animals escaped. Mink were recorded wild in Sweden in 1928, in Norway in 1930 and in Britain in 1938. In Russia mink were deliberately released so that they could be trapped for their fur.

The first records of mink breeding in the wild in Britain occurred during the mid-1950s and by the early 1960s, there was concern over their possible effects on native wildlife and their all too obvious effects on free range poultry. As a result of this, in 1962, the Government invoked the Destructive Imported Animals Act, 1932, which controlled the keeping of mink and officially designated them as pests. Since then, like otters in previous centuries, mink have had numerous accusations made against them, and have acquired a reputation which they scarcely deserve. The accusation to be considered here is that mink compete with otters for food or reduce the numbers of otters by driving them away from otherwise suitable habitat.

Relations Between Feral Mink and Otter

Although mink live mainly by water and are accomplished swimmers, they take a smaller proportion of fish in their diet than otters, usually between 20 per cent and 60 per cent of the total. Thus while there is a considerable overlap in the diets of the two species, mink take substantial numbers of some prey such as birds and mammals which are only of secondary importance or less to otters. A study of the diets of mink and otter on a productive lake and a moorland stream in Devon showed that in both cases, fish were three times as important to otters as they were to mink (Figure 4.2). Overall the diets overlapped by about 40 per cent but there was some seasonal variation (Wise, 1978). As fish are most difficult to catch in the summer, their lower availability is more likely to result in competition at this time than during the autumn and winter when they are easier to catch. In fact the overlap in diets during the summer was less than in the colder months, mink taking advantage of an abundant supply of young rabbits while the otters continued to specialise in fish. Contrary to the popular view, therefore, if there is

Figure 4.2   The diets of mink and otters in Devon

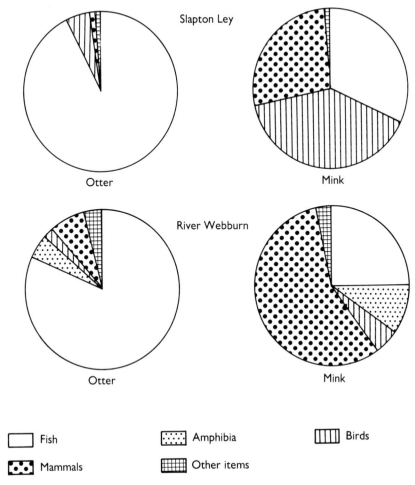

Source: Wise, Linn and Kennedy (1981).

competition, the otter is superior to the mink at exploiting the shared resource. More likely though is that the mink does not compete as there is another source of more easily caught prey.

Of the most important shared items on the river, otters took 2½ times as many salmonids as mink while the mink took eight times as many rabbits. Similarly at Slapton ducks, coots and moorhens dominated the diet of the mink while otters took a much higher proportion of roach, eel and pike.

Erlinge (1969, 1972b) compared the diets of mink and otter living in the same areas in Sweden and his conclusions were similar. He found that the diets overlapped by 55 per cent to 75 per cent depending on the area and the time of year and that overlap was greatest in winter when food was hard to find. Although few items were taken exclusively by one species or the other, mink tended to take a higher proportion of mammals, birds and crayfish while otters took fish and frogs more frequently. Significantly, Erlinge also found that the diet of otters on one lake did not change after the mink arrived.

The fact that a substantial proportion of the mink's diet consisted of items of minor importance to the otter tends to minimise the possibility of competition and, in addition, there is evidence in some areas of differences in the size of fish taken by the two species. Thus Erlinge found that all trout taken by mink on one of his study areas were less than 15 cm in length whereas a quarter of those eaten by otters were larger than this. The same effect was found with cyprinids (Table 4.2) where mink were concentrating on fish under 15 cm in length. Overall, Erlinge found that about 30 per cent of the fish taken by otters exceeded the largest taken by mink. However, there were no differences in the sizes of fish taken by mink and otters in the study areas in Devon.

Habitat Use. It is not easy to obtain an accurate assessment of the density of otters and mink but both Erlinge (1972b) and Wise (1978) used the density of scats as an approximate indication of the intensity of use of different parts of their study areas by the two species. In each case they found that otter spraints formed a higher proportion of the total on main rivers and lakes than on tributaries and peripheral lakes. In Devon this may have partly reflected differences in the availability of prey favoured by mink, such as rabbits, but in both areas fish were more abundant in the main rivers and lakes.

More convincing evidence of the competitive exclusion of mink was obtained by Erlinge on the Nobyån stream and its surrounding marsh. This was a good habitat for mink in the summer and densely populated, while otters visited it infrequently, hunting mainly in the lakes. During the winter, when the lakes were frozen over, otters moved to the stream and at that time the mink numbers decreased considerably. Erlinge considered that this was due to interference from the otters and that the mink then moved to the suboptimal, peripheral lakes and streams.

Table 4.2 A comparison of the size of fish eaten by mink and otters on the River Svartån in Småland (Sweden)

		No. eaten by mink	No. eaten by otter
Pike	large	2	41
	small	16	34
Trout	large	0	7
	small	7	22
Cyprinid	large	0	36
	small	11	84

Notes: a. Large pike are more than 200 mm long.

   b. Large trout and cyprinids are over 150 mm in length.

Source: Erlinge (1969).

Interference. On some of the more productive lakes in Erlinge's study area the otter population was high but mink numbers were low. Two lakes in particular had suitable den sites, an abundance of food and appeared to be optimal habitat for mink, yet although mink were common on nearby streams, they failed to colonise the lakes.

Erlinge believed that the otters prevented the mink from successfully exploiting these areas by interference and suggested that this might take the form of physical attacks. As evidence for this he cited two Russian ecologists who, in another paper (Grigor'ev and Egorov, 1969) reported that:

> In the opinion of some hunters and state fur purveyors, the otter is a serious enemy of the mink, rapidly ousts it, wipes it out and . . . checks the growth of its numbers.

Clearly the Russian view of the mink/otter relationship is diametrically opposed to that of many people in Britain. Grigor'ev and Egorov found remains of six mink in a total of 880 otter spraints suggesting that the otters in this area were occasional predators of mink.

Following his work on otters, Erlinge turned his attention to smaller mustelids, particularly stoats (*Mustela erminea*) and weasels (*M. nivalis*). He made some observations of the relationships between these two species and between stoats and polecats (*M. putorius*) which also shed light on the relationship between mink and otter. Observations of stoats and polecats in captivity showed that when the two species were put in the same enclosure, the stoat was always very vigilant and carefully observed the movements of the polecat, keeping as far away from the larger animal as possible. If the polecat noticed the stoat, it would hunt it as if it were prey. This may be because larger predators look upon smaller ones as potential food but as carnivore meat seems to be unpalatable (at least to foxes, see above) they may only do so when hungry. Alternatively they may recognise the smaller predator as a potential competitor and hunt it in order to exclude it from their foraging area.

Whichever is correct, Eurasian otters do sometimes hunt mink and where mink are likely to encounter otters frequently, they should devote at least some attention to the activities of otters and avoid them as much as possible. Where otter populations are very dense, the likelihood of a meeting is particularly high and if mink are to avoid the risk of being attacked, this must be at the expense of constant vigilance.

One way to avoid otters is to leave the area entirely, which mink seemed to do on the Nobyån stream in winter, another is for mink to adjust their activity pattern so that they rest when otters are active and vice versa. Mink are often mainly nocturnal but they can be active at any time of day and can adjust their pattern of activity according to the degree of human disturbance, the habits of their prey and whether or not they are feeding young. So far no one has found clear evidence of temporal separation in the activities of mink and otter but the option may be available to the mink.

In competing with the otter, the mink has two disadvantages. First, it is a much smaller animal, an adult female otter weighing three to four times more than a large male mink. This makes the mink vulnerable to attacks or threats of attacks from the otter. Second, mink are less specialised in their feeding habits than otters and are less well adapted to catch fish.

On the other hand the mink has two important advantages. The fact that it is a generalist means that the mink is able to supplement the fish in its diet with birds and mammals much more easily than the otter. This enables it successfully to exploit habitats which are unsuitable for otters because of the inadequate food supply. In addition, the mink appears to be much more tolerant of man than the otter. Mink do not need so much bankside cover for their dens as otters and frequently live in close proximity to man. I have caught mink in the middle of a small market town and have had records of mink living and rearing young in or under farm buildings. Otters do travel through towns and may occasionally have dens close to human habitation but are usually much more wary of human presence than the mink and, being larger, need more cover and bigger dens.

It is undoubtedly factors such as these which have enabled the mink to survive and successfully spread in Britain at a time when the otter has been in decline. Indeed the otter's decline may itself have made it easier for the mink to spread since a potential competitor had been much reduced in numbers and range.

Finally, there is the often repeated story of mink attacking and eating otter cubs. It is extremely unlikely that a mink would take the risk of seeking out and entering the den of a potential predator. Were it not for the fact that so many people claim to know someone who has seen it happen, the idea could be dismissed as ludicrous. Some of my attempts to substantiate these claims have ended with inconclusive evidence, a mink seen carrying a small brown animal for example, others have failed because the original observer cannot be traced. I have come to the conclusion that if mink have ever killed otter cubs it is such a rare event as to pale into insignificance alongside the damage that man has done to the otter population in Britain over the last 30 years.

Otters and Mink in North America

In North America the mink is sympatric with the river otter throughout its range and the fact that the two species have lived in the same habitat for a considerable period of time indicates that they have evolved compromises in their ecology and behaviour to avoid competing. If they had not, they could not co-exist. A study of the diet and activities of mink and otter in Idaho illustrates some of the ways in which they do this (Melquist *et al.*, 1981).

A total of 26 mink and 37 otters were radio-tracked during the period 1976 to 1979; the activities of mink were monitored for 889 hours and otters for 3,437 hours. From this a picture of the activity patterns, habitat use, den use, foraging tactics and interactions between the two species was built up. A total of 657 mink scats and 1,902 otter scats were collected to determine the diet.

Predictably, fish were found in over 90 per cent of the otter scats and 59 per cent of the mink scats. Mammals, birds and invertebrates were only taken occasionally by the otters but frequently by mink. In other words, both species were feeding in similar ways to their European counterparts. Again, competition was likely to be for fish and the otter took a greater number and wider range of species than the mink.

In this area, otters caught larger fish than the mink and this enabled them to exploit species such as large-scale suckers (*Catostomus macrocheilus*) and northern squawfish (*Ptychocheilus oregonensis*), which ranged from 35−45 cm in length. Neither of these species was taken by mink nor were mottled sculpins, a bottom-dwelling species. This may have been because the mink, searching for prey from boulders and logs above water, did not see these often immobile and well camouflaged fish. Both species preyed on small cyprinids, 7−12 cm in length, which were found in 29 per cent of mink scats and 24 per cent of otter scats.

Fish of the salmonid family were the most frequently taken group in the otter's diet (63 per cent of scats) but were generally of less significance to mink (10 per cent of scats). However in one stream, from August to November, salmonids and particularly kokanee were important to both species, being found in 39 per cent of mink and 76 per cent of otter scats. The stream was mostly 10−15 m wide and consisted of deep pools, interspersed with shallow riffles but was also characterised by the fact that the downstream third consisted of an enormous log-jam caused by trees and logs piling up after the spring floods. This area was intensively studied in order to examine the interactions between mink and otters. Seven mink and eight otters were radio-tracked along a two kilometre stretch of the stream between August and November in the years 1976 to 1979.

At this time of year up to twelve otters lived in the area. The cause of the aggregation of otters was the spawning run of the kokanee which left the lake and travelled upstream to spawn in August. During this period otter predation on the fish increased rapidly (Figure 4.3) till kokanee were found in 69 per cent of scats in August and 90 per cent in September. Then the proportion fell as the spawning run tapered off. Mink on the other hand took very few kokanee as they travelled upstream in August and September but concentrated their predation in October and November when dead fish were washed up on the shore after spawning.

Observations of mink hunting in the wild confirm those made on captive mink. The mink hunted from the shoreline or from floating logs, diving in after their prey while the otters hunted in the water. Mink were more nocturnal than otters probably because this enabled them to hunt mammalian prey more effectively, but there were no times of day when either species was always inactive. Both species spent a considerable amount of time foraging around the log-jam but apart from this they concentrated their activity in different areas. Patterns of habitat use varied from month to month but mink spent between 35 per cent and 80 per cent of their time on the stream bank or in riparian vegetation and none in the open water while otters spent up to 70 per cent of their time in open water but little or none on the bank.

Direct interactions between the two species were not seen, probably because neither was observed for very long, but active mink and otter were known to pass within as little as 5 m of one another. Mink also passed close to dens in which otters were resting and vice versa and the

Figure 4.3   Changes in the level of predation on kokanee by mink and otters during the spawning season

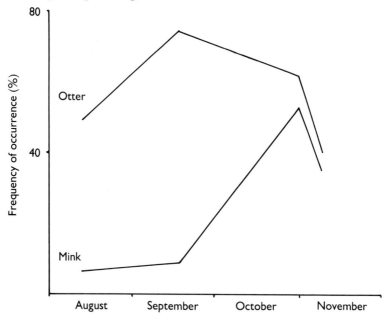

Source: Melquist, Whitman and Hornocker (1981).

most frequently used dens of each species were only 3 m apart.

This suggests that the relationships between mink and American river otters are not the same as those between mink and Eurasian otters, in some places at least. In this small intensively used area although the different foraging methods of the two species reduced the likelihood of direct encounters, they showed no signs of actual avoidance. There was also little overlap in the sources of food exploited because of the different hunting techniques. Although surprisingly large numbers of otters congregated in the area in addition to the mink they did so because food was plentiful and easily caught so competition was unlikely. Why Russian otters should wish to eat mink while American otters are happy to live next door to them is less clear.

African Otters

Rowe-Rowe (1977c) investigated the dietary differences between African clawless otters and spotted-necked otters which live sympatrically in Natal and, because the water mongoose lived in the same area, he collected scats from all three species to compare their diets (Figure 4.4).

In all three species frogs formed a substantial secondary item in the diet but it is evident that water mongooses concentrated on birds and mammalian prey while spotted-necked otters monopolised fish predation. Crabs were a frequent item in the diets of all three species but for the clawless otter they were the mainstay. This means that although spotted-necked otters and mongooses each had effective 'feeding refuges' the more

5 Social organisation and communication

As well as interacting with other animals, otters interact with members of their own species and much of the following chapter is concerned with this. It also deals with the movements of individuals and the areas in which they live.

Otters exploit a wide range of aquatic habitats. The Eurasian otter, for example, can live on the coast or in estuaries as well as in fresh water. It may feed in small streams, mighty rivers, lakes, ponds or marshes. Some rivers and streams used by otters are rich and productive, others have a poorer supply of fish. Factors such as these have a profound effect on the movements of otters, particularly the distances over which they travel, and may also, together with other factors, influence their social behaviour. Suppose, for example, that an otter fed exclusively on a species of fish which was uniformly distributed throughout a lake and a river that flowed from it. If the lake was 1,000 m long and 500 m wide while the river averaged 10 m in width, there would be as many fish in the lake as in 50 km of river as both would have an area of half a square kilometre. If the number of fish in the lake was sufficient to support one otter then it would be possible for another to live on the river but, while the lake otter would have to travel 3 km round the perimeter of its home range, the otter on the river would have to walk or swim 50 km to get from one end to the other.

In real life things are more complicated but this example does illustrate how the 'shape' of water can effect the otter's way of life. There is in fact an even more extreme case if one looks at coastal otters where an otter could conceivably find all the food it needed within a few hundred metres of shoreline. If you add to this the fact that lakes, streams and coasts all vary in topography as well as the type, abundance and availability of prey it is hardly surprising to find that otters show a range of life styles in order to cope with these conditions.

The first part of this chapter deals mainly with two aspects of an otter's way of life, the area in which it lives and its relationships with other otters. Most otters live on their own or in small groups and direct contact between otters other than within the groups is infrequent. It is evident, however, that otters have an efficient method of indirect communication using scent and the second part of the chapter deals with this.

HOME RANGES, TERRITORIES AND SOCIETIES

The terms 'Home Range' and 'Territory' have similar meanings and are often, mistakenly, used interchangeably but the meanings are quite different and it is important to understand how before looking closely at the way they may be applied to the otter.

Home range is used to describe the area of land or water in which a particular animal normally lives. The area includes all the places visited by the animal in its usual day-to-day travels and includes such essentials as feeding and drinking places, resting sites, refuges and breeding sites together with all the areas passed through in between. Home ranges may be used by individual animals, pairs, families or larger social groups and they may be isolated from, adjacent to or overlapping with the home ranges of other members of the same species. Sometimes it is convenient to consider the range of an animal over a particular time span such as a season or a year and these seasonal or annual ranges can be distinguished from the 'life-time range' of an animal which is the area enclosing all its movements from birth to death.

The word territory is normally used in a much more restricted sense and, strictly speaking, refers only to an area which is actively defended by an animal or group against other members of the same species. Often it is much more difficult to determine the boundaries of a territory since you need to observe or at least infer that they are defended. In addition, defence is not necessarily carried out by fighting. Territorial behaviour includes threats, displays and marking or signalling behaviour of various kinds as well as actual physical conflict. In fact sightings or even signs of actual fights are not very common.

A problem for mammals, particularly carnivores, is that their home ranges are often rather large compared to the size of the animal so that it may take hours or even days to patrol completely the whole border. If another animal intrudes it may take some time for the owner to reach the spot and in some cases it may not know that the incursion has occurred until after the invader has left. The consequences of this are that exclusion of other members of the species by fighting or display cannot always be complete. Defence of a territory is, therefore, often carried out indirectly by the use of signs. These include scraping, marking and the depositing of faeces, urine and/or scent, and may be reinforced by aggressive behaviour if the intruder is actually encountered in the territory.

As knowledge of the habits of animals increases, it becomes more and more difficult to fit them into neat categories. Home range is a convenient term for describing the area in which an animal lives but, as implied above, it is more difficult to be sure whether or not you are dealing with an animal that is territorial. Some animals only defend part of their home range so that there are degrees of territoriality. At one end of the spectrum are animals that normally only avoid intruding on one another's 'personal space', which may extend for a few metres or tens of metres around them. Others may defend a proportion of their home range, perhaps a central 'core area' which is much used or a breeding den or only defend a territory for part of the year. At the other extreme are animals which exclude other members of the same species from the whole of their home range.

In the same way, one cannot draw a sharp distinction between solitary mammals and social species. There are degrees of sociality. Any mammal that remained completely solitary throughout its life would not leave many offspring! The smallest social unit in otter societies consists of a female with her most recent litter, and this may be extended by the presence of the male parent or young of previous litters. Many small and medium sized groups of animals are now known to consist of related individuals, usually on the mother's side.

Recent ideas in behavioural ecology have centred around the advantages and disadvantages to individuals of the behaviour they exhibit. Territorial behaviour is seen as an attempt by an individual or group to monopolise resources within the home range. If the animals are well adapted to their environment one would expect the benefits of such exclusivity to outweigh the costs in terms of time and energy spent in defence, the risk of damage during physical conflict, and so on. Similar considerations apply to social groups. The benefits of living in a group may include co-operation in hunting and defence against predators; the drawbacks may include sharing the food one has caught with other group members or interference with one's own hunting.

A major aim of behavioural ecologists has been to make quantitative predictions about animal behaviour and to test these on animals. The problem with otters is that, except for the sea otter, it is extremely difficult to obtain the data that are needed on a sufficient scale.

RIVER OTTERS

In this section, no distinction is drawn between Eurasian and American river otters. This is partly a matter of convenience but more importantly because they are very alike in habits and I believe that in a similar habitat they would behave in a similar way.

In Britain it was once generally believed that otters led a solitary existence, travelling gypsy-like from river to river and only settling down while the female reared her young. This idea is conveyed very clearly in Henry Williamson's book *Tarka the Otter* written in the 1920s in which Tarka's experiences are based on ideas of otter habits developed from Williamson's own observations and those of the otter hunters he knew at that time.

In a few days, for example, Tarka travelled from Braunton Burrows at the mouth of the Rivers Taw and Torridge to Great Kneeset and Cranmere Pool on Dartmoor where the rivers rise. A journey of some 50 km as the crow flies and many more as the river flows. Later Tarka followed the Taw back down to the estuary and traced one of its tributaries up onto Exmoor, returning via the River Heddon and the North Devon coast, a round trip of over 100 km. During his life Tarka ranged over an area of some 2,000 km^2.

It is impossible to know just how accurate a picture this is of a typical Eurasian otter, and until recently I would have said that the distances travelled by Tarka and other otters mentioned in the book were much exaggerated. Now I am not so sure, recent research suggests that otters may have extremely large home ranges, while at the other extreme, some have very small ones.

Studies of Otter Movements

The recent increase in knowledge of otter movements can be attributed to the development of suitable methods of catching and radio-tracking otters. Previously the only information which could be considered reliable came from studies in Sweden where Erlinge (1967a, 1968a) followed otters by tracking them, mainly in snow.

Swedish winters can be relied upon to produce reasonable quantities of snow each year and Erlinge was able to follow the otters on skis. During the day time he would follow the journeys made by otters the previous night and every so often more snow would fall, effectively wiping the slate clean. Although he could not reliably identify individual otters from their footprints, he could distinguish between large otters (adult males), family groups (medium sized plus small footprints) and medium sized otters. By tracking on consecutive days, he was able to build up a picture of the movements of individual otters or family groups. At other times of the year he was able to obtain some information from tracks in mud or sand or when an otter deposited a series of characteristic spraints, containing an unusual food item or tapeworm segments.

Erlinge used two study areas. One, in southern Sweden (Scania), included four lakes together with the River Klingavälsån which connected them and was approximately 50 km by 20 km in extent. A second area, 300 km further north in Småland, was 50 km by 40 km and consisted of over a dozen lakes, the streams running between them and the main river, the Svartån. Most of these lakes exceeded 2 km in length and the largest were about 5 km long. In both areas many species of fish were present but trout were absent in the southern study area. Waterfowl were abundant in both areas and crayfish were present in Scania.

In North America, Melquist and Hornocker (1983) followed the movements of American river otters by radio-tracking. They used small transmitters encased in capsules which were implanted into the body cavity through a small incision. Altogether they tracked a total of 39 otters between 1976 and 1981.

Their study area measured 64 km by 32 km and lay on the North Fork Payette river system between the Salmon River Mountains and the West Mountains in west-central Idaho. The waterways consisted mainly of streams feeding the North Fork Payette River and the Cascade reservoir, some of which were only a few metres across. Eleven species of fish were recorded by electric fishing including five species of salmonids.

Two recent studies of otter movements have been carried out in Scotland. Jim and Rosemary Green worked on a tributary of the River Tay in Perthshire and Jane Twelves studied coastal otters on South Uist, an island in the Outer Hebrides. Don Jefferies and Tony Mitchell-Jones of the Nature Conservancy Council took part in both projects and developed the radio-tracking system.

Beaver traps were used to catch the otters but owing to the legal position in Britain it is not possible to implant transmitters. Instead they were attached to harnesses which were designed to pass round the neck and forelimbs of the otters. These were fixed with rivets designed to rust through and release the otter after a period of three months or so. In fact, although one adult male was tracked for 98 days, other otters managed to wriggle out of their harnesses within a month. Some otters were injected with a solution of zinc chloride. This contained doses of radio-active zinc which were too small to harm the animal but enabled their spraints to be identified with the aid of a sensitive scintillation counter. In this way, information on these otters' movements was obtained for four or five months after the harnesses came off. The methods are described in detail in a paper by Mitchell-Jones et al. (1984) and the results obtained from

Perthshire have also been written up (Green *et al.*, 1984). The data obtained in South Uist are still being analysed (Twelves, pers. comm.).

The Perthshire study area included 84 km of waterway ranging from small fast-flowing streams to slower more productive lowland reaches. The largest lake on the system, some 10 km long and a kilometre wide, was in the upper part of the system at about 100 m above sea level. All the other lakes were much smaller and formed a relatively small (but not unimportant) proportion of the total waterway. Salmonids dominated the fish fauna throughout the system but perch and eels were common in the lower-lying parts of the area, particularly the lowland lakes. Three otters were tracked, an adult male and two adult females.

In South Uist, Twelves tracked otters on the sheltered eastern coast of the island. This consists of a low-lying area of treeless land covered in peat. It is intersected with long sea lochs, some of which stretch several kilometres inland. There are numerous small islands and reefs offshore and, inland, many freshwater lakes which support populations of eels. The length of coastline in the areas is extremely high because of its convoluted nature.

Home Range Size

Table 5.1 shows the sizes of home ranges of otters in three of the areas and there is obviously a great deal of variation. One female otter tracked by Twelves had a home range of only a quarter of a square kilometre so there is a range of values extending from a few hundred metres across for this coastal otter to home ranges between 50 and 80 km in extent for some otters in Idaho. Mainland Scottish and Swedish otters come second and third respectively on the scale, and coastal otters in Shetland with home ranges a few kilometres in length (Watson, 1978) fourth. However, this neat arrangement does mask a considerable amount of variation within categories in each area. For example, the home ranges of adult male otters followed by Erlinge varied by a factor of two (10 to 21 km

Table 5.1 Home range length (in kilometres) of river otters

Type of otter	Idaho		Perthshire		Sweden	
Solitary juvenile	31.8	(4)				
Solitary yearling	49.0	(4)	20.0	(1)		
Adult male	50.0	(1)	39.1	(1)	15.3	(8)
Adult female	44.3	(3)	16.0	(1)		
Family group	34.0	(5)	22.4	(1)	4−6	(6)[a]
					10−12	(1)[b]

Notes: a. Family groups at lakes.
b. Family groups on rivers.
c. Figures in parentheses indicate the number of otters, or groups, tracked.

Sources: Idaho, Melquist and Hornocker (1983); Perthshire, Green *et al.* (1984); Sweden, Erlinge (1967a).

across) and there was even greater variation amongst the population in Idaho. The smallest range included 8 km of waterway and was used by a solitary juvenile female in autumn while a male during its second summer had a range of only 10 km across. By contrast, another male of the same age had the longest range of all — 78 km of river.

One would expect juvenile otters to increase their home ranges as they get older and in Idaho the average range size for solitary juveniles increased from 15 km in the autumn to 27 km in winter and 38 km by the spring. Thereafter it changed little. Family groups which stayed together during the winter had larger home ranges but also increased them, from autumn (average — 26 km) to winter (30.5 km). The home range length of a family group that lived along a stream in Sweden was nearly twice that of family groups which included lakes within their ranges emphasising the importance of the area available for fishing in determining range size.

Melquist and Hornocker obtained very little information on the movements of adult male otters. One was tracked as a juvenile and a yearling but they only obtained three fixes for it as an adult, in the spring of its third year and its estimated range of 50 km is probably conservative. The home ranges of adult male mustelids are often considerably bigger than those of females and this was true in both Sweden and Perthshire. In both areas the ranges of male otters were more than twice the size of females. Part of this might be explained by differences in body size. Bigger animals need more food and therefore a larger range. However, the difference in range size is more than would be predicted by differences in body size alone.

The lakes and streams studied in Sweden were more productive than those in Scotland and had a higher fish population which might partly explain the differences in range sizes between the areas. However, the structure of the habitats is also very different and in particular the lakes in Sweden formed a much higher proportion of the total area. Conventionally the home ranges of river otters have been measured in lengths of river, lake shore or coast. Totalling up the areas of aquatic habitat available to the otters in Scotland and Sweden shows that Swedish otters had a much greater area of water within their home ranges than their Scottish counterparts. Indeed the Scottish male seemed to have a smaller area of water in its range than the family groups in Sweden. In other words, otters living in the more productive area had more water available to fish in. Two factors may explain this. First, that otters may feed mainly close to the shore, either because there are more fish there or because it is easier to catch them, perhaps because the water is shallower. The lakes in Scotland were small and otters may have used much of the total area whereas in Sweden they were much larger, up to 1 km across and otters may have confined their fishing to a fairly small proportion of the area of water. Second, in Sweden the area available for fishing in winter is much less than at other times because the lakes freeze over.

The lengths of home ranges in Perthshire and Idaho were much greater than in Sweden so one would expect that if otter density were measured in terms of the number of otters in a given length of waterway it would be greater in Sweden. In fact this is not the case. Erlinge estimated the

Plate 1 Sea otter eating a crab (Photo: Pat Morris)

Plate 2 Eurasian otter (Photo: Mary Pearson)

Plate 3 Giant otter (Photo: Pat Morris)

Plate 4 Spotted-necked otter (Photo: Ernest Neal)

Plate 5 A partly eaten bream in Sweden. The otter was probably disturbed during its meal.

Plate 6 Asian small-clawed otter (Photo: Pat Morris)

Plate 7 Otter tracks on a beach in the Outer Hebrides (Photo: Will Lewis)

Plate 8 Typical 'spraint station'. Bright green grass shows where the spraint piles are (Photo: Will Lewis)

Plate 9 Sign heap made of sand

Plate 10 Otter spraint on a rock in a Devon stream

Plate 11 Eurasian otter eating an eel (Photo: Ernest Neal)

Plate 12 Contents of spraint. This shows the scales of roach, perch, pike and salmon and the bones from perch, eel, roach and trout

Plate 13 Otter holt under a rock on the west coast of Scotland

Plate 14 Otter holt in peat on South Uist (Photo: Ernest Neal)

Plate 15 Slapton Ley. Productive and fringed with dense reedbeds, it is much used by otters

Plate 16 Sympathetic management by a Water Authority. Only the trees leaning over the water have been removed. The stumps have been left to regrow

Plate 17 Otter being fitted with a radio-transmitter (Photo: Don Jefferies)

density of otters to range from 3.6 to 5.6 otters per 10 km of lake shore and 1.7 to 2.8 per 10 km of stream, while Melquist and Hornocker estimated the density of otters in Idaho to vary between 1.7 and 3.7 per 10 km of stream. The overall density of otters in Perthshire could not be determined but it was found that there were seven or eight family groups in 98 km of river. This is equivalent to 0.75 breeding females per 10 km which compares favourably with an estimate of 0.5 breeding females per 10 km of waterway in Idaho.

So, although the length of otter home ranges varies considerably, the density of otters is more constant. Before trying to explain this apparent contradiction, it is necessary to describe the spatial distribution of home ranges and the relationships between otters in them.

Spatial Distribution

Figure 5.1 illustrates the arrangements of home ranges which Erlinge found amongst adult otters and family groups. The main features are:

(i)   Male otter home ranges were contiguous and although there was sometimes a degree of overlap, it was small in relation to the total size. The main part of each adult male's home range was not used by other adult male otters.

(ii) Family group home ranges tended to be centred on inflows or outlets of lakes and were not usually contiguous. Overlap between ranges was unusual and was very small when it did occur.

(iii) The home ranges of males overlapped with those of family groups and one male sometimes had part or all of the ranges of two family groups within his own. The range of one family group might be overlapped by more than one male.

The question arises as to whether the home ranges of adult males in Sweden were territories in the strict sense of the word because of the overlap that occurred. In addition, other otters intruded on the home ranges of adult males in Erlinge's study area. These transient and temporarily resident otters were thought to consist of sub-adult otters and, possibly, non-breeding adult females. Erlinge concluded that otters were territorial since if they were not he would have found much more overlap between the ranges of males and of family groups.

In Idaho, American river otters behaved quite differently and overlap of ranges was extensive. In each of four different parts of their study area Melquist and Hornocker found two adult females sharing the same general range and although only one adult male was tracked, trapping results indicated that male ranges also overlapped considerably. The overlap was most marked during the spawning run of the kokanee (see Chapter 4) when up to twelve otters congregated at the spawning beds in one area.

As only three otters were tracked in Perthshire, it is not possible to give precise details of the pattern of home ranges in the area. The two females were in different parts of the study area and not contiguous, although one of them did overlap with another adult female. By studying footprints it was shown that the range of the male overlapped with two

Figure 5.1 *The distribution of home ranges of male otters and family groups in Småland (after Erlinge, 1968a)*

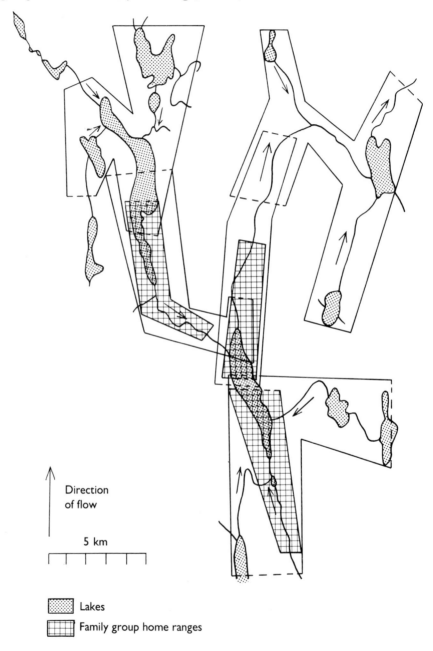

Direction
of flow

5 km

Lakes
Family group home ranges

other adult males but the extent was not easily determined. In one case it may have been nearly 5 km, a considerable distance but no more than an eighth of his total range. He also overlapped with the ranges of three breeding females, one of which he mated with.

In subsequent tracking of a sub-adult male they found that although its movements overlapped those of the adult male in space they tended not to do so in time. Concentrating its activity in the upland parts of the study area it only ventured into the area of overlap when the adult was absent.

Twelves found that although each otter in her study area had one main holt (resting site), plus a few subsidiaries, all the holts were visited by other otters, of both sexes, indicating that some overlap occurred. However, she did find that two females whose ranges were both overlapped by the same male did not use the same areas, one keeping to the north half of his range and the other to the south.

Other observations of coastal otters suggest that a considerable amount of overlap in home ranges occurs in this habitat but the precise relationships are not clear. Watson reliably determined the home range of one family group which extended along 2.5 km of shore and he recognised at least five otters living along a 7 km stretch of the coast. Kruuk and Hewson (1978) who watched otters fishing but could not recognise individuals, concluded that the otters hunted in communal foraging areas.

It is evident that river otters living on the coast and in Idaho do not defend exclusive territories but the behaviour of those in Sweden and Perthshire is less clear cut. Certainly no one has found distinct territorial boundaries in these areas but although one cannot draw the boundaries of territories on a map, or measure their length, territorial behaviour still occurs and prevents the home ranges of otters of the same sex from overlapping except at the edges.

Patterns of Movement

Otters, particularly males, can cover considerable distances in quite a short time. The greatest overnight distance recorded by Erlinge was 16 km and males in his study area regularly travelled as much as 10 km in one night. Family groups were less mobile, especially when the cubs were young.

Melquist and Hornocker did not follow otters throughout their travels but estimated them from consecutive daily fixes. They found that the maximum distance travelled by an otter in 24 hours was 42 km by a dispersing yearling male. The average distances travelled were low, however, probably because no account could be taken of otters deviating from the direct routes between resting sites. Averages ranged from 1 km to 5 km per night depending on season and type of otter. Otters seem to travel least in winter and most in summer and the greatest distances were covered by yearling males which averaged about 5 km per night but there were no data for adult males.

In Perthshire the male otter was tracked through the whole of some activity periods and several records of the total distance covered were obtained. These averaged 5.4 km with a maximum of 16 km while females moved shorter distances averaging 3.6 km for one female and 1.0 km for the other. Maximum distances for females were also less at 8.9 km and 3.9 km respectively.

The movements of female otters could be separated into two types, travel movements, when the otter moved consistently in one direction and foraging movements, when the otter systematically covered a small part of its range, often in a zig-zag pattern. The male otter on the other hand tended to combine foraging and travelling and even moved through productive areas without stopping to explore them. It was assumed that he fed as he travelled. Rates of travel could be very fast. The female otters averaged 1.4 km/hr in travelling across their ranges with a maximum of 3.0 km/hr. The male averaged 1.7 km/hr travelling upstream and 2.4 km/hr with the current but his highest downstream speed, during a spate, was 4.4 km/hr. On one occasion he travelled over 12 km downstream at a rate of 3.8 km/hr.

The females regularly travelled through the whole of their ranges but showed no consistent pattern of movement from day to day. Most travelling consisted of rapid journeys between feeding areas. The male on the other hand showed a somewhat regular pattern of activity whereby he travelled away from his activity centres to the boundaries of his range at intervals and spent a couple of days on the periphery before returning. Visits to the various boundaries did not take place on a predictable pattern but there was an underlying rhythm of activity over four days showing first an increase and then a decrease in the distances travelled. Similar cycles were detected by Erlinge (Figure 5.2) and he concluded that the male otters were patrolling the boundaries of their ranges, keeping a check on potential intruders and reinforcing the scent marks which signalled their continued occupancy of the range.

In Sweden, Perthshire and Idaho 'centres of activity' were recognised. The authors did not all define these exactly but it is evident that in each

Figure 5.2   Diagrammatic representation of the movements of two otters in adjacent home ranges over a period of 24 days. The ranges overlapped at B

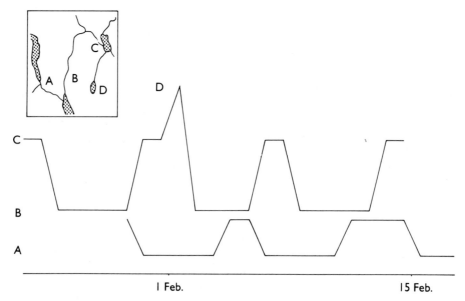

Source: Erlinge (1968a).

case they refer to parts of the range in which the otters spent a relatively high proportion of their time. In Sweden, centres of activity were fairly large ranging from 1 to 5 km across. Family groups had activity centres in the mid-part of their ranges, usually at the outflows of lakes. These were areas which were mainly used during the summer when the cubs were small, probably because they were good sites for rearing young. The centres of activity of male otters tended to be larger and in some cases were near the borders of their ranges, even in areas of overlap.

Melquist and Hornocker defined centres of activity as areas in which otters spent more than 10 per cent of their time and, perhaps because of this more precise definition, recorded more than one centre per home range, with a maximum of five. In Perthshire, two centres of activity were identified in the range of one female. Both of these centres were at lakes and during tracking 73 per cent of her time was spent at one of these. The secondary centre was at the other end of her home range and consisted of two more lakes. The otter foraged in both of these areas but the intervening waterways were used only as a thoroughfare. The male also used two centres of activity both of which were well within the boundaries of his home range. The second female used her range more evenly and no distinct centres could be found.

Melquist and Hornocker found distinct seasonal changes in the movements of otters whose home ranges encompassed the spawning grounds of the kokanee. During the spawning season the otters tended to congregate on the beds and not move away from them until the season was over. In Sweden seasonal changes also occurred, particularly in the winter. At this time activities were confined to the streams and other areas of open water, mainly at the outlets of the lakes. Sometimes this led to aggregations of otters and at one time Erlinge counted seven or eight otters along a four or five kilometre stretch of stream. This suggests an increase in tolerance of the presence of other otters during severe conditions. Following break-up of the ice, there was a considerable increase in activity as otters re-occupied areas that had been abandoned in the winter with much marking being recorded at this time.

Dispersal of Young. In Sweden, during the autumn cubs were small and the family groups only travelled short distances, averaging 2.7 km per night but as the cubs got older the distances increased to 3.8 km in winter and 6.9 km in spring. Eventually the cubs reached a size when they were able to live independently of the mother and this happened in the spring following birth, when they were about one year old. Some groups kept together, albeit somewhat loosely, into the summer and Erlinge concluded that in these cases the female did not have another litter to care for.

A young male otter which had been injected with radio-active zinc chloride by Jenkins (1980) expanded its home range from the lake on which it had been reared out into the nearby river between the ages of eight and eleven months. Its range increased during this period until radio-active spraint had been collected from 68 km of the river but it is not known when it parted from its mother.

In Idaho young otters became independent of the mother at varying ages between November and March but often stayed within their mother's range after that time. Dispersal seemed to occur in April or May when the young otters were 12 or 13 months of age. Two young otters that were radio-tracked during dispersal covered great distances before settling in their own home ranges. One young male travelled 104 km in 30 days, ending up some 32 km from its natal area. A young female travelled even further, covering 192 km in 50 days only to find the ideal situation in a home range adjacent to and slightly overlapping with the one she had been brought up in. Two young male otters on the other hand had not shown any signs of dispersing when contact with them was lost at 16 and 25 months old. Melquist and Hornocker concluded that young otters were under no pressure from adults to disperse and whether or when they did so depended on their own inherent urges.

Relationships Between Otters

Although there was variation both in the size and spatial distribution of home ranges, one factor which was common to all these studies was that adult otters of both sexes tended not to associate with other adults except for reproductive purposes.

Erlinge found that adult males were solitary apart from during the breeding season although they would sometimes travel with a family group for part of a night. Similarly, in Idaho, practically all observations of adult males with other otters took place during the mating period. Adult females and family groups on the other hand were more sociable and occasionally travelled in company with unrelated juvenile or yearling otters. One particular adult female with no cubs of her own spent a considerable amount of time with a family group.

Clearly the family group is the most important unit of otter society. Other associations are less common and shorter lived although the mutual tolerance of otters in Idaho permitted a certain amount of sociability. This was particularly evident in autumn when otters congregated in the spawning areas and one year a group of seven otters consisting of an adult female plus two family groups was observed together several times. In another study carried out in America one group of otters was observed during the winter, when many of the waterways were iced up. This group, of six otters, was regularly seen along a stretch of the Tomahawk River in Wisconsin and was believed to consist of at least one adult male, an adult female plus sub-adult and juvenile otters (Beckel-Kratz, 1977). However, as none of the otters was caught or marked it is difficult to know how accurate the identifications were. The group was larger than a single family group and was very cohesive, using the same den as well as travelling and feeding together.

Despite some tolerance of one another's presence otters in Idaho did not form any long-term groups larger than the family. Interactions between individual otters were rare, only 3 per cent of behavioural observations involved mutual grooming or other social behaviour. It seems that the otters were tolerant rather than sociable. There was no aggression but otters did sometimes seem to avoid one another. For example, an otter arriving at an activity centre that was already being used would pass through rather than stop to forage.

Erlinge did not witness aggression between wild otters or find signs of it but he concluded that territories were maintained by 'threatening signals' mainly the deposition of scent. On the other hand Stephens (1957) spoke to a number of people who claimed to have seen otters fighting, some of whom said that each otter tried to bite the penis of its rival. Some of the dead male otters examined by Stephens and by Fairley (1972) had fractured bacula so there may be some truth in this although there is no conclusive evidence that the territories of wild otters are defended so vigorously. On the contrary, most authors emphasise the importance of avoidance in the social behaviour of otters.

One factor which may help to promote the avoidance of fights is that resident otters know their place in the social hierarchy. Some are subordinate to others and their behaviour reflects this. In an area of overlap or when a boundary transgression occurs the subordinate animal may go to great lengths to avoid the dominant which appears to ignore the presence of its inferior. Erlinge described how on a lake that was used by two male otters one would always boldly cross the centre of the lake to deposit spraint at the far inlet. When the other otter was also at the lake it kept to the shores, often lurking in the vegetation until the dominant animal had gone. If it was away from the lake, it did not re-enter via the inlet when fresh spraint from the other animal was there. The male otter tracked in Perthshire was dominant to a younger male otter but was itself dominated by its downstream neighbour. The factors determining dominance are unknown but age, experience and prior possession could all play a part.

Although dominance relationships described here have been between members of the same sex they also occur between males and females. Normally, males are tolerant of females and vice versa but after giving birth female otters may temporarily become dominant to males. One captive female otter repeatedly attacked a male in her enclosure when cubs had been born although a second female in an adjacent pen continued to be tolerant of a male under the same conditions. The wild male which was tracked in Perthshire also appeared to adopt a submissive role towards a female with young in his range.

Resource Distribution and Social Organisation

At the beginning of this chapter it was pointed out that territorial behaviour can be seen as an attempt by an animal to monopolise a resource or to restrict the access of other animals to it. The abundance and distribution of resources also affects other aspects of otter social organisation such as home range size as well as density and patterns of movement. Three resources which are likely to be particularly important to otters are food, resting sites and mates.

Food. It is obvious that the abundance of food for otters varies from one area to another but it is important to realise that it will also vary considerably from place to place within one otter's home range. Also, some parts of the home range may be easier for foraging than others. On an upland stream the deeper pools are likely to be easier for an otter to hunt in than rapid rocky stretches. There may also be change with time as fish gather for spawning, and good feeding areas may be inaccessible owing to spates or ice at certain times of year. Food does not occur in discrete, separate clumps, but from the otter's point of view richer easier areas can be looked upon as more profitable food 'patches' separated by areas where it is not worth spending too much time and energy in hunting. Centres of activity in otter home ranges may correspond to such food patches or groups of patches.

In some home ranges they might be large, a lake for example, in others rather small, a deep pool in a rapid river, or temporary such as a spawning ground. In the latter cases an otter would need more than one patch, perhaps several in order to provide feeding throughout the year. Larger home ranges would be necessary where patches were spread out, smaller ones would be possible when they were close together. Predictability is also important. If you can rely on known feeding areas there is little need to spend time looking for others. If there is a risk of their disappearing or being temporarily depleted, it would pay to travel further afield in the hope that others might be found.

We know little of the distribution of food within the areas in which otters have been studied and it is impossible to prove that it determines home range size or spacing but it seems reasonable to suggest that it is at least an important factor.

Resting Sites. In undisturbed areas, otters are not particularly fussy about where they sleep and on the coasts of Shetland they often sleep in the open (Miles, 1984). Even in areas with moderate disturbance otters sometimes choose sites which are above ground, albeit in cover. Green *et al.* (1984) differentiated between holts, which were holes in the ground and couches, above it. They identified 24 couches, most of which were in thick vegetation such as sallow scrub or rhododendrons although a few were under piles of sticks and branches and one was in a depression amongst bankside vegetation only 30 cm high. They also found 24 holts which were usually tunnels into the river bank among roots and boulders.

The average distance between sites was 1.5 km overall and varied from 135 m to 3,650 m but the dens were not regularly distributed, tending to be clumped near centres of activity. They concluded that even after radio-tracking an otter for many days, there were still some resting sites they had not discovered and it seemed that there was no lack of suitable sites on their study area. In another part of Scotland, on the west coast, Trowbridge found an average density of twelve den sites per kilometre.

Otters were opportunistic in their use of dens in Idaho as well. Old beaver dens were most frequent but the otters used a variety of sites, enlarging existing tunnels or dens, using stick piles, riparian vegetation, heaps of rocks, and so on. One otter used 88 separate resting sites over a period of 16 months.

If sleeping sites are not limiting, breeding dens might be. Breeding females might be expected to be more particular in their requirements and to need secure and undisturbed places in which to bring up their cubs, preferably close to a productive food supply. In remote areas this might not pose a problem although it could strongly influence the distribution of female home ranges.

Mates. A male otter could increase the number of offspring he sired in a year by increasing the number of females he mated with. From the males' point of view, therefore, females are a resource worth competing for and, within limits, the more females he has access to the better. Females do not have this option and would gain nothing, in terms of numbers of young, from mating with more than one male. The best strategy for females is to try to mate with a male that is likely to sire successful offspring.

The simplest way for a male to obtain exclusive access to females is to stake out a large territory which includes sufficient good habitat for the ranges of several females and to ensure that other males are kept out. Obviously there are limits to this, the larger the territory the more difficult it will be to defend and the more females within it, the more attractive it becomes to rivals.

These factors may explain the relatively large ranges of male otters in Sweden and Scotland and why the edges of male otters' home ranges are not necessarily determined by good feeding areas. The adult male tracked in Perthshire had at least three breeding females within or on the periphery of his home range. His activities were concentrated on the main river while the females also used the tributaries. During his regular patrols he would travel at least part of the way into the range of each female and this was presumably sufficient to determine whether or not they were receptive. Erlinge says that male otters:

> frequent above all the main passages of otters in the area and may show great interest in a particular part due to, for instance, the presence of a female otter in heat.

The question arises as to what happens with a female whose range is overlapped by more than one male. Perhaps this is a time when dominance is important. If the subordinate were to encounter the female first he could attempt to court her but if challenged by the dominant he might have to give way. Female choice could also play an important role if she knew which male was dominant. It would normally be best for her to mate with the dominant male since this is likely to be 'fitter' than the subordinate.

Dominance, Territoriality and Resources. Trowbridge stated that:

> ... in most situations otters are not territorial. Rather they have large home ranges, probably too large to be economically defendable, and between males at least, there exists an absolute dominance hierarchy.

My own view is that this is only partly correct. It seems clear that male otters can be territorial, if they were not, the ranges of males in Sweden and Scotland would overlap much more, as they do in Idaho. This is not invalidated by a certain amount of overlap at the extremities or by the fact that immature animals may intrude into the ranges. There is no reason why defence of a territory should not be selective, only against other adult males for example, or that exclusion should be complete, especially where territories are large.

The regular trips made by male otters to the borders of their ranges seem to be a form of territorial behaviour and in this respect they differ from the females. However, female otters with their families may also be territorial, at least at certain times. The fact that Erlinge never found more than one family group in one area suggests that territorial behaviour occurred. In Perthshire, there were marked changes in activity on a lake after cubs were born to a female living there. From the time of birth until the cubs were two or three months old the number of spraints in a zone 400 m round the breeding den dropped dramatically. Previously another female otter had been radio-tracked in that area but it was evident that after the birth of her cubs other otters avoided the area close to the den.

Otters are not always territorial of course, Melquist and Hornocker saw no overt signs of territoriality and the reasons for this are difficult to discern. It may simply be because the American otter is a different species but I am inclined to doubt this, particularly as coastal Eurasian otters also seem not to be territorial. It is also difficult to see how the balance between the costs and benefits of holding territories could be so very different for the two species. The main difference between them is in their reproductive biology, American river otters having a much longer gestation period (see Chapter 6). It seems improbable that this causes the differences in territoriality and a more likely cause is the distribution of food.

The absence of territories in Idaho may be a response to a food supply in which patches are widely dispersed, unpredictable or not very productive. Otters might, therefore, require extremely large home ranges which are uneconomic to defend. If this is so, one would expect American otters in more productive regions to have a social system more similar to those in Europe. Interestingly, even in Sweden the home ranges of resident otters were found on the central more productive lakes and rivers. Otters living in the peripheral lakes and streams did not seem to establish territories.

What of coastal otters? These seem also to be aterritorial, despite a very rich food supply in the littoral region. Here the problem of defendability lies not in the distances that need to be travelled (home ranges are small) but in marking out and defending boundaries at sea. Scent cannot be used and short of carrying out continual sentry duty, it is impractical for an otter to mark or defend its feeding areas. In addition as the feeding areas are apparently extremely rich and can support a number of otters the benefits of defending the food supply are low.

The same does not apply to females and the small home ranges should make it more feasible for males to defend an area containing more than one female without travelling the huge distances needed in other areas. However, the constraints imposed by having the sea as part of the boundary still apply. Would rivals be more likely to intrude when they can come in from the sea rather than overland? Perhaps under these circumstances dominance is a better strategy. Although the evidence for dominance hierarchies comes from areas where otters hold territories, there is no reason why one should not develop in areas where they do not. Dominant otters would still have the first opportunity to mate with females and the females would also have the option of choosing a preferred, dominant male.

The advantages of territoriality to subordinate otters are less obvious but they may have opportunities to mate when more than one female comes into oestrus at the same time. They are also in a strategic position to take over a neighbouring home range or to move up the hierarchy when a dominant male dies.

SEA OTTERS

As in river otters the male sea otter contributes nothing to the rearing of the young and the most important unit of sea otter society is the family group, the female with her latest young. Unlike all other species of otters, however, sea otters are usually found in groups, known as rafts or pods ranging in size from a few tens to several hundred animals. The largest group recorded consisted of around 2,000 sea otters in Bristol Bay, Alaska. Even so, the otters do not seem to be all that sociable. They do not form sub-groups of closely related animals, for example. Of 3,621 behavioural observations made by Shimek and Monk (1977) only 5 per cent were in the category 'interacting'. Since this also included aggressive and courtship behaviour, it does not suggest that very much time is spent in social intercourse. The most frequent interactions other than these were play-fights, mainly between young male otters. The reason for this lack of social behaviour is that there is no advantage to sea otters in being sociable, they do not need the help of other otters for foraging or grooming and they have no predators against which group defence would be appropriate. There is little to be gained from spending time building up social contacts and sea otters aggregate in groups only because certain areas are suitable for resting and foraging. As the areas for resting are large and the food supply very difficult to defend most otters would gain little from trying to establish a territory.

The sexes tend to remain in separate groups and to some extent in separate areas also. Females with their young have larger home ranges than the males and use separate resting or hauling out places. Most adult males were found in all-male rafts which in some areas at least were found in the more exposed regions of the coast, near headlands. Predictably, the home ranges of otters from the same raft overlap much more than those from different rafts but there is no evidence of avoidance or territorial behaviour. Otters feed and rest in different parts of their home ranges and foraging areas are generally closer inshore. The size of home ranges varies considerably (Table 5.2) and those at Monterey were much smaller than those at San Simeon. The differences between the two areas may be due to differences in resource distribution although information on this is lacking. Ribic suggested that the smaller home ranges in Monterey were due to greater disturbance but it is hard to see why this should be so.

Some males established separate home ranges from the rafts and these were the smallest of all. Unlike other sea otters these males were territorial and other males were only tolerated in the territories as they passed through but not if they tried to remain in them. Females were subjected to investigation by the territory holder, presumably to determine whether or not they were receptive but were permitted to rest within the territory, at the risk of attempted matings by the resident. Otters of either sex which foraged in the territory were likely to have their food stolen.

Table 5.2   Home range size of sea otters

Monterey:

Females	80 ha	(8)
Territorial males	35 ha	(4)
Non-territorial males	44 ha	(7)

San Simeon:

Females	540 ha	(12)
Males	325 ha	(8)

Note: a. Data for San Simeon include only resident otters.
b. Figures in parentheses indicate number of otters studied.

Sources: Monterey, Loughlin (1980); San Simeon, Ribic (1982).

Fighting occasionally occurred when a neighbouring territory holder transgressed the territorial boundary (Loughlin, 1980; Calkins and Lent, 1975). Fights were usually bloodless and consisted of chasing or rearing vertically out of the water and lunging at the head and neck. On one occasion an intruding otter was attacked after it had tried to pull a female into its own territory while the resident was under water, foraging. Elsewhere, a territorial male made several attacks on the male member of a mated pair (Vandervere, 1970).

Although territorial males enclose their own feeding areas in their territories, sex seems to be the main benefit of territory holding. Non-territorial males are able to intercept and court females by searching for them within the female rafts but the major advantage of territory holding may be that the activities of other males in the territories are controlled. Territorial males are, therefore, able to court and mate with a female with less risk of harassment from potential rivals. If this is so, one would expect territorial males to have a higher rate of mating success than other males. Again, female choice may also be important. Only the strongest and most fit males are likely to be able to defend territories and females would benefit their offspring by mating with the territorial males.

Within home ranges, movements of females and non-territorial males were mainly between feeding and resting areas but adult males also patrolled the borders of their range sometimes swimming vigorously with much splashing. This may act as a visual and audible signal which together with occasional clashes with neighbours enables the otters to delineate the boundaries of their territories.

Sea otters are capable of travelling considerable distances beyond the normal home range although the frequency with which this occurs is not known. Three male otters which were radio-tracked by Ribic (1982) travelled distances of 80 km south of her study area within a few days of release. Whether this was due to the disturbance of being captured, because they were dispersing young or to seasonal migration could not be determined. A female otter also moved away from the vicinity of capture but returned and travelled between two areas 43 km apart on a roughly monthly cycle. Daily distances were as much as 25 km for the female and 35 km for one of the males. Other long distance movements have been recorded when sea otters were translocated in order to establish new colonies. Most of these movements took place over longer periods, between a month and a year although similar distances were involved. The fastest rate of movement recorded was an otter which travelled 48 km in less than 22 hours.

Determination of the density of sea otters is made difficult not by the problem of finding and counting otters but in deciding what boundaries to use for measuring the sea area. Kenyon used the thirty fathom (55 m) contour which is very deep water for otters to feed in although otters do sometimes travel beyond this limit. This is undoubtedly why Kenyon's estimates of density, which fell mainly in the region of 12 to 16 animals/km^2, were rather lower than the estimates made by Estes and Smith (1973) who used a more conservative outer limit. They concluded that the density of otters at Amchitka was in the range 20–30 otters/km^2 of available habitat.

OTHER OTTERS

Most of the information on the social systems of other species of otters is anecdotal and difficult to evaluate. Two studies of giant otters, by Duplaix (1980) and Laidler and Laidler (1983), together with one of African clawless otters by van der Zee (1982), provide reliable preliminary data on these two species.

It has often been suggested that otters are sociable creatures, apart from river otters which are rather solitary. The evidence for this is not very strong although large groups of otters of some species have been recorded. Procter (1963) recorded one observation of 20 spotted-necked otters in Lake Victoria, Tanzania and of 39 sightings he reported, 15 contained more than six otters and must, therefore, have been larger than a family group. However, he also said that most of the otters that were seen regularly were in groups of 'about five animals', a more likely size for a family group.

Twenty also seems to be about the largest group of giant otters recorded although groups in the range three to eight are normal. Duplaix herself saw one group of 16 otters while working in Surinam and she estimated that it consisted of five adult males, five adult females and six sub-adults. However, her records show that the accuracy of age assessment may have been poor and most of the groups she saw consisted of one or two adults of each sex and varying numbers of young. The six groups which she studied in detail consisted of one adult of each sex but in four of them there were young of two sizes, sub-adult and cub. This suggests that a second litter may be born before the first disperses. A typical 'extended family group' included seven otters, an adult of each sex and five young, two sub-adults and three cubs. In Guyana the Laidlers observed two family groups which joined together for a short period and this undoubtedly explains many of the larger groups that have been recorded. There was some evidence of territorial behaviour but in

Duplaix' area it only happened in some seasons and in Guyana it was confined to a small core area at the heart of the home range.

Although Rowe-Rowe (1978) claimed that family groups of the African clawless otter consist of two adults plus two or three young, observations by van der Zee suggest that in coastal populations this is not always so. In the Tsitsikama Coastal National Park he recorded 142 sightings of otters of which 78 per cent were of single individuals. Forty per cent of the remainder were reliably identified as including only a female with cubs and there was only one observation which definitely included a male 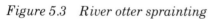 and female otter together with (two) cubs. This suggests that in this area at least, clawless otters are no more sociable than river otters.

The ranges of the clawless otters overlapped although van der Zee believed that there was temporal separation in use of the habitat. Minimum home ranges were between 4 km and 6.5 km of coast and the density of otters was between four and ten per 10 km of coastline.

Overall the impression gained is that family groups are fundamental units of society in otters. In some species they may include the male and, in giant otters at least, young from two consecutive litters. Other groupings include single otters which attach themselves temporarily to family groups and the short-term linking of separate family groups. These do not last for more than a very short time.

Although the large rafts of sea otters may seem to be an exception, they can be viewed in a similar light. There is little or no social bond between individuals other than mother and cub and the attachment seems to be more to place rather than to other otters.

SCENT COMMUNICATION

Otters spend a great deal of time sniffing both at their own spraint and that of other otters. Usually after a detailed investigation the otter turns round and deposits a fresh contribution close to that already present (Figure 5.3). Spraint is dispersed widely along the routes travelled by otters and instead of the one or two defaecations per night which might

Figure 5.3   River otter sprainting

be needed for elimination, several spraints are produced, often quite small and sometimes consisting of only a few bones and a quantity of mucus.

Fresh spraint has a characteristic smell, not unpleasant, which is recognisable as 'otter' to humans and is quite distinct from that of other carnivores. The smell is quite persistent and can be detected by the rather feeble human nose on spraint which is evidently weathered and a few weeks rather than days old. Indeed, it is still quite strong on spraint I collected twelve years ago and keep in small glass phials for demon-stration purposes.

It has been recognised for many years that otter spraint is important in the social behaviour of otters. People used to say that it was simply for 'territory marking' but in the last 15 years or so the biology of scent marking has been more closely investigated. A study by Trowbridge (1983) at Aberdeen University has recently unravelled some of the complexities of scent communication in Eurasian otters.

Production of Scent

Members of the mustelid family are noted for their scent glands most of which are to be found in the anal region. Particularly renowned are the scent glands of the skunk, powerful organs which can project an awe-inspiring smell an impressive distance. Otters are fortunately less well endowed but possess two pairs of glands in this region, the anal glands and the proctodeal glands which discharge respectively just outside and inside the anus.

The significance of the two sets of glands is unknown but the anal glands have been described in some detail by Gorman et al. (1978). They consist of two types of secretory tissue, a storage sac surrounded by muscle and a duct for discharging the contents. The bulk of the material in the sac consists of proteins and mucopolysaccharides, secreted by sudorific tissue, in which is dispersed droplets of fatty material produced by sebaceous tissue.

Trowbridge investigated the chemical characteristics of the scent by extracting it from spraints with ether and subjecting the extract to analysis by gas chromatography. This enabled her to show that there was a complex series of compounds in the scent of which she could recognise nearly a hundred separate components. One of these was found to form a high proportion of all the samples and might simply have spelled otter. It was less volatile than most which means that it would have lasted a long time. Other components varied in proportion between otters but remained constant for one individual over at least 25 days. This suggests that each otter has a characteristic chemical fingerprint in its scent by which it might be identified.

Why is the scent deposited on spraint and not just smeared or sprayed onto the ground or a tree or rock? This may be connected with the individuality of the scent. Many other species of mammal produce scent marks which are invisible to the eye although all too obvious to the nose. The smell of male cats is familiar to many and in the country one often catches the distinctive smell of fox. These strong scents are unmistakable indicators of the presence of fox or cat but if several foxes or cats were to scent mark in the same place it might only add to the overall power of the smell. Such a cocktail of smells would not necessarily convey much information because they would interfere with each other and mask the individuality of the scent. A resident fox might learn no more than that other foxes were present. Otter scent is much less strong at least to the human nose and the behaviour of otters shows that they are not concerned with the general smell in the region of the spraints, their attention is directed specifically at the faecal material. The spraint appears to be a visual indicator of where to sniff. Since different otters use the same sprainting sites this may be a mechanism to ensure that they can determine which particular otters have been in the area.

Distribution of Spraint

If spraint is used to attract the otter's nose to a particular place, how is the otter attracted to the spot where the spraint is deposited? Obviously, familiarity would be sufficient in the case of a resident otter but if, as is generally assumed, the information is meant to be passed on to any otter passing by, it is important that it should be easily found.

One factor that promotes this is that otters tend to deposit spraint in conspicuous places, at least from otter eye level. Large boulders and tree roots, the trunks of fallen or leaning trees, the bases of bridges, concrete work around weirs, spillways and sluices are all typical otter sprainting sites. In addition spraints are often found in the vicinity of major topographical features such as the confluence of two rivers or where a small stream joins a river. The inlets and outflows of lakes and islands whether in lakes or rivers are also favoured by otters. Finally otter spraint is found along otter trails, sometimes at 'conspicuous places' but occasionally simply deposited in the middle of the path.

Trees and rocks may occur at frequent intervals along a lake shore or river while inflows, confluences and so on tend to be much scarcer. Otters could use every possible tree root or boulder or they could save up their spraints for places where there are major features. In fact, of course, they do neither, and research by Jenkins and Burrows (1980) mainly on the River Dee in north-east Scotland and by Trowbridge, at two sites on the west coast of Scotland, help to show what factors determine the distribution of otter spraint.

Jenkins and Burrows regularly recorded the distribution of spraints along a 26 km stretch of the Dee in 1977 and 1978. They analysed their results by dividing the river into 2 km sections and counting the number of spraints and spraint sites they found in each. They then tested to see whether the spraints were distributed at random or not. They found that in some months they were but that in others there was a tendency for the sites to be somewhat clumped. Areas where sites were clumped were likely to be those places where there was woodland beside the river and they concluded that otters preferred to use areas where there was good bankside cover.

This research shows that otters do not distribute their spraints uniformly, but the fact that the sample units were 2 km of river obscures much of the detailed information on spraint distribution that Trowbridge was able to pick up in her study area. She measured the distances between individual piles of spraint and used these in her analysis of randomness.

She found that the distances between piles of spraint were not random and that spraint piles were clumped into groups which were usually 40 m or more apart. She called the groups 'spraint stations' and noted that they usually included all the following features:

(i)   trails leading from the sea to some feature of interest to otters such as a den or freshwater pool; 81 per cent of the stations had a freshwater pool and 41 per cent a den or resting site;
(ii)   spraint piles along the trails, particularly at the beginning and end and at the edges of pools;
(iii) no land trails from one spraint station to the next, otters evidently travelled between spraint stations by sea.

Figure 5.4 illustrates a typical spraint station.

Spraint stations were not dispersed at random either and tended to be evenly spaced along the coast mainly at distances between 40 and 70 m apart. The distance between stations was not determined by the distribution of pools or dens although otters preferred pools that were larger than average. The significance of the pools was not clear but they may have been used for drinking, washing and grooming or playing. Van der Zee (1982) found that African clawless otters living on the coast frequently visited freshwater pools or streams after leaving the sea and before going into their dens.

Trowbridge also discovered well-worn trails which ran across the peninsula, and were up to 3 km in length. These tended to follow small

Figure 5.4   A typical spraint station

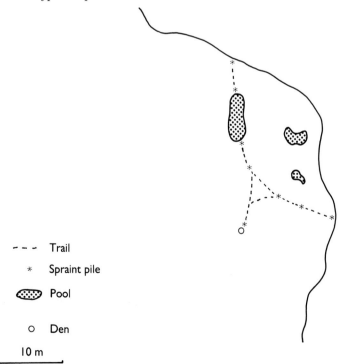

- - -   Trail

*   Spraint pile

▨ Pool

o   Den

10 m

streams and spraint piles were distributed at random along them, probably determined at least partly by the distribution of tussocks on which they were deposited. The average density of spraint piles on these trails was 20/km, much lower than the density on the coast itself where the average was 266/km.

She explained the distribution of spraint as being the most effective way of dispersing signs so that an otter entering an area would very soon encounter a spraint site. She pointed out that in coastal areas otters have fixed trails on land but not at sea. An otter could come onto land from the sea virtually anywhere along the coast but wherever it did so it was likely to be only a few tens of metres from the nearest spraint station and would, therefore, soon become aware of the presence of other otters in the area. On tracks and beside rivers where movement is channelled along particular routes it is not necessary to have spraint piles so close together and on rivers, where ranges are so much larger, it would be very difficult to sustain such a high density of marking.

It has often been suggested that otters might use spraint to mark the boundaries of their home ranges but Trowbridge pointed out that this seems to arise from a misinterpretation of one of Erlinge's papers. He said that intensity of marking by otters was highest in the areas of overlap but this does not necessarily mean that individual otters mark more in these areas, merely that there are more otters doing the marking. The reverse was proposed by Kruuk and Hewson (1978) who believed that otters on the coast marked more frequently near to their dens than away from them. This did not coincide with Trowbridge's findings at a site further north but she also revisited the area in which Kruuk and Hewson had worked and found that the spraint distribution there was similar to her main study area. She concluded that Kruuk and Hewson had underestimated the numbers of den sites and also failed to find a high proportion of the spraints. This does not mean that otters do not spraint near their dens. On the contrary there are often several spraint piles near a den but they do not do so significantly more often than in areas between dens.

The conclusion that must be drawn from her work is that otters tend to distribute spraint throughout their home ranges in such a way as to maximise the likelihood that other otters will find it.

The Message

The importance of scent marking to otters is illustrated by the elaborate and time-consuming behaviour associated with it (see below). Otters produce numerous faecal pellets, coat them with scent, carefully disperse them as they move around and spend some time in investigating the scent marks of otters. What information is carried by this scent and how do the otters use it?

The scent could provide otters with some or all of the following information: individual identity of the animal which produced the spraint, its age, sex, breeding condition and status. In addition, the time since deposition could also be gauged as the more volatile components of the scent would evaporate more quickly and its character would change.

In a series of carefully designed experiments, Trowbridge was able to show that a tame otter could distinguish the scent of several different otters, some of which were familiar to him, while others were not. The sex of the otters made no difference although it was not possible to show whether or not he could tell the sex of the donor from its scent. Different spraints from the same animal were treated as if they were the same, confirming the results of the chemical analysis which showed that the scent profile of an otter was stable over a period of time.

Even if otters are unable to determine sex, age or status from scent, they may still be able to extract some of this information when they encounter the spraint of animals with which they are familiar. Otters could recognise each other from their scent in the same way that we recognise people from their voices. By this means males, for example, could keep track of the animals to which they were subordinate or dominant, or follow the movements of known females.

Although not all Eurasian otters maintain exclusive territories, those that do may use spraints as a first line of defence. The frequently encountered scent of a territory-holding animal would be a powerful reminder to an intruder that it risked being attacked. In Sweden, otters were more likely to intrude on a neighbouring home range when fresh spraint was not present. For example, when a male otter was killed its range was taken over by a neighbouring and previously subordinate otter within a week (Erlinge, 1968a).

In the ranges of territorial otters, spraints may help to promote avoidance of the dominant by the subordinate otter in areas of overlap but spraint may also have an important function in the home ranges of otters that are not territorial. Melquist and Hornocker suggested that in the large home ranges used by otters in Idaho, individual animals might settle at one activity centre for a period of time and by profuse marking deter other otters from staying in the same area. This would maintain a degree of 'personal space' for the animal, which in effect becomes a territory holder, albeit for a limited period, and reduce the risk of conflict or interference with foraging. However, this system is flexible and when rich food supplies are available during the spawning season several otters share the same activity centre.

Observations on the differences between the sprainting behaviour of male and female otters were made by Hillegaart et al. (1981) who studied two pairs of otters in enclosures. They found that males sprainted more than twice as frequently as females (seven times per hour when active) and deposited most spraints near the edges of their enclosures. Females spent more time and deposited more spraints close to the dens than near the boundaries but after cubs were born both females sprainted mainly in the water. This suggests that spraints are concealed to prevent detection by potential predators. The behaviour of the females towards the males also changed at birth, both became dominant to their mates and one repeatedly attacked the male as it left its den.

The observations by Green et al. (1984) of a reduction in sprainting activity but an increase in dominance by a wild female with very young cubs closely parallels these observations. It is particularly interesting to find that when the female becomes dominant she produces fewer spraints or at least deposits them inconspicuously. Evidently copious and conspicuous production of spraint is not necessary for advertising dominance.

The territorial behaviour of females seems to be mainly concerned with a relatively small part of the range near the natal den. When good breeding sites are far apart the home ranges of females with family groups are separate. Where they are closer together, overlap is more likely to occur. Males on the other hand devote more time to the boundaries of their ranges and less to particular areas within them.

OTHER FORMS OF MARKING

Several people have noticed that otters produce a substance which is variously known as tarry spraint, white jelly or anal gland secretion. This was studied by Gorman et al. (1978) who believed that it originated from the anal sacs and noticed that production seemed to vary in correspondence with the apparent oestrous cycle of the female. A more detailed study by Trowbridge showed that this was not so. She could detect no rhythm in jelly deposition and found in fact that it was mucus from the gut, normally only produced when all solid waste had been eliminated. Since the jelly often smelled of otter it may simply have been used as a vehicle for the carrying of scent when an otter wished to make a mark but had no solid faecal material to deposit it on.

Other methods of marking used by otters consist mainly of variations on the theme of scraping. At its simplest this may consist of a few scratch marks in mud or gravel, only recognisable as otter from the adjacent footprints or the presence of a spraint. Sometimes the substrate may be scraped together and the spraint deposited on it but simple scraping of this sort can be elaborated in one of two ways.

The term 'sign heap' is often used to describe small mounds of sand, gravel or mud scraped up by otters and also for little tufts of grass or other vegetation which is scraped or twisted together and crowned with spraint. Sometimes there is no spraint visible but the unmistakable odour of otters can be distinguished by the experienced nose. The largest sign heap I have seen was made in sand on the edge of a freshwater loch on South Uist and was 10 cm high and 15 to 20 cm in length. For sheer effort, however, the prize must go to an otter (or otters) which produced a total of 48 sign heaps at Slapton Ley during a few days in January 1976. All these were found along the shore of a small pool, connected to the Lower Ley and about 50 m in diameter. The sign heaps, consisting mainly of dried rush and reed were scattered along the margin and quite a high proportion had spraint on or beside them. I have no idea what caused the activity although the otters must have had a busy few days.

The second way in which scraping develops is into earth moving and clearing. When I went otter watching I occasionally heard the otters scratching away in loose shale below the willow trees. The result of their efforts was a sizeable trench around which spraints were scattered. The excavation never exceeded a metre or so in length and perhaps 10 to 15 cm in depth, probably because they filled it in as fast as they dug it out. Erlinge found similar excavations in areas of intense marking activity. Elsewhere, I once found an oval area about one metre long which had been scraped bare of vegetation to reveal the peat below. Half a dozen spraints were scattered in and around this area but it disappeared after a few weeks as the vegetation grew back.

This type of activity is taken to extremes by giant otters which make large 'camp sites' in the bankside vegetation. These are used for resting, grooming and feeding as well as defaecation (Duplaix, 1980). They are separate from den sites, which also have latrines near them, and seem to have much in common with the sprainting stations described by Trowbridge. A notable feature of all camp sites is the clearing of vegetation, often over a large area. Plants are torn down and trampled into the ground so that sites are usually very conspicuous when viewed from the water, the bare bank at the camp site contrasting strongly with the dense vegetation elsewhere. Camp sites may be as much as 28 m in length but usually average 8 to 12 m along the water's edge and 6 m or so away from it. There are usually a number of separate latrine sites at each, mainly around the periphery and, after defaecating, the otters trample their faeces into these areas.

All these activities seem to have one end in view, to make the sprainting site more conspicuous. Where vegetation is thick, as in the South American forest, clearing of the vegetation makes a very obvious gap along the river bank. On level ground, sand spits or gravelly shores, where there are no natural eminences, the otters scrape up the substrate to form one.

Another form of marking which is important to many species involves the use of urine. The interactions between dogs and lamp posts are very familiar although less well known is the fact that many members of the cat family also urine-mark by directing a jet of urine backwards to spray bushes or trees. In these species the urine acts as a carrier for scent but in other species, particularly amongst ungulates, sex hormones, or their breakdown products in the urine, are used to determine the stage of the female's oestrous cycle.

Unlike dogs, foxes, and so on which eke out their urine in order to mark as many times as possible, otters produce copious quantities and there is no evidence that urine is used for marking like spraint. Trowbridge pointed out that otters live in damp places and are often wet themselves so urine might be washed away quite quickly and would not be a satisfactory long-term marker. On the other hand, it could be useful in the short term, possibly as a signal that a female was ready to mate. By collecting urine samples daily from a captive female otter she was able to show that the concentration of one compound, oestradiol, varied through the oestrous cycle in a similar way to other mammals. However, it was not a reliable indicator of receptivity because the peak concentrations in some cycles were lower than the troughs in others. It is still possible that urine is used to signal receptivity in otters but if so other compounds must be used.

CONCLUSIONS

The studies of otter movements and social systems that have been carried out recently represent many years of hard work by several people but the main conclusion that has to be drawn is that more information is needed. The results clearly illustrate the adaptability of otters but, because of this adaptability, it is very difficult to explain differences in otter behaviour in different circumstances. Trying to find underlying principles is like trying to complete a crossword when you only have a quarter of the clues. At the moment one can explain away some of the variations in otter behaviour by reference to supposed variation in resources. Until more information is available on the distribution and abundance of these resources such 'explanations' have to suffice but we are still far from fully understanding the social organisation of otters.

6 Life history

The life history of otters is another area in which there is much scope for further research. Our knowledge of when otters breed and how often, how long they live, what causes their deaths and a host of other fascinating questions is patchy to say the least. This is not altogether surprising but it is unfortunate that much valuable information has been wasted. Of the hundreds of thousands of otters that have been killed for the fur trade, no more than a few hundred have been systematically studied.

The information on which this chapter is based is very fragmentary. I have had to rely more on casual observations than elsewhere and would not be at all surprised to find that further research contradicts some currently held views. In addition, although some information is available from wild populations, many observations reported in this chapter have been made on captive animals and these should certainly be interpreted with caution. One would expect well-fed captive animals to live longer and die from different causes to wild animals. Captivity can modify various aspects of breeding biology such as birth intervals and the number and survival of young. There is also the distinct possibility of misinterpretation where people have made brief or casual observations on wild or captive animals and made incorrect assumptions about the behaviour they have seen. I am quite sure that observations of play, aggressive and sexual behaviour have, on occasions, been confused and since written records are inevitably coloured by such interpretations it can be very difficult to separate fact from fancy.

REPRODUCTION

Breeding Seasons

Although humans and most domestic animals do not breed seasonally, or at least not obviously so, we tend to assume that most wild animals have a well-defined breeding season. This is not always the case and although some species have short, well-defined breeding seasons, others can breed at any time of the year. There are even variations within species. Eurasian otters have a distinct breeding season in some parts of their range but not in others. Sea otters can have their young at any time of the year but there is a peak of births in both the Alaskan and Californian populations and they are at different times of the year.

Needless to say, establishing the dates of births of wild otter cubs is fraught with difficulty, not least because the cubs are very rarely seen until they are several weeks old when their age has to be estimated from their size. Although some naturalists and huntsmen are remarkably confident in their ability to do this, the growth rate of litters can be very variable (see below) so estimates of the age of single litters should be treated with caution. With a large sample the errors should be spread

Figure 6.1   Distribution of birth dates for Eurasian otters in Britain

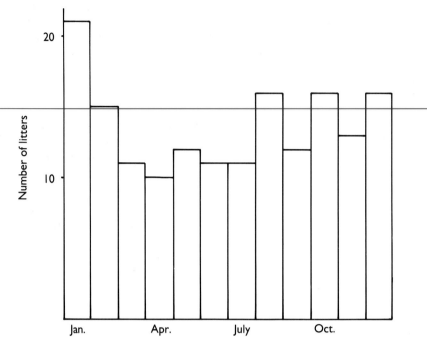

Source: Harris (1968).

through the year so that if otters did have a distinct breeding season it should still be detectable even though some estimates might be a month or so out.

Figure 6.1 illustrates the estimated birth dates of 164 litters of Eurasian otters and shows that there is no significant variation in numbers of births between months or seasons. In Scotland, on the other hand, although there is no evidence of seasonality in births, survival of litters is probably lower in severe winters (Jenkins, 1980). Further north, breeding in Sweden is seasonal and young are born in the spring (Erlinge, 1967a) although it is interesting to find that two captive female otters kept near Stockholm in semi-wild conditions had their young in late June and early July (Hillegaart *et al.*, 1981). These otters were penned with two males in early April and mating must have taken place within a few weeks of this time indicating that females can breed later in the year if they are not mated at the normal time.

While there seems to be no particular benefit to otters in southern Europe to breed seasonally, further north it is advantageous for otters to ensure that their young are well grown before the waterways freeze over in winter. One might expect a similar system to prevail in North America but the evidence available suggests that birth in American river otters is not correlated with latitude, even as far south as Florida and cubs are normally born between February and April (Harris, 1968). In Oregon, for example, otters give birth during April (Tabor and Wight, 1977) and in Idaho, at a similar latitude, the young are born in late March or early

April (Melquist and Hornocker, 1983). There are, unfortunately, no data on the breeding season from the tropical and southern parts of its range.

Sea otters in the Aleutian Islands can give birth at any time of the year although most births occur between April and June with a peak in mid-May (Estes *et al.*, 1978) but in California, births are concentrated in the period December to February (Sandegren *et al.*, 1973). The authors offer no explanations for these differences but interactions between food availability and the timing of severe weather seem likely to be the most important factors.

Little is known of other species although evidence from zoos suggests that breeding in Asian small-clawed otters is not seasonal. Procter (1963) concluded that spotted-necked otters had their young in September in Tanzania, but on the basis of only one year of observation. Duplaix (1980) believed that giant otters normally have their young at the beginning of the dry season in Surinam.

Evidently otters of at least some species can adjust their breeding season to suit local conditions or even not have one at all. When the climate and availability of food is very variable they may give birth at the most favourable time of year or immediately after the harshest time so that the young are well grown before they have to face the most rigorous conditions.

Breeding Cycles

As one would expect, in seasonally breeding mammals the reproductive system undergoes profound changes through the year. Apart from changes associated with pregnancy there are differences between females in oestrus (ready to mate) and those in anoestrus (quiescent), particularly in the amounts of hormones secreted by the ovaries and other glands. These hormones ensure that at the right time of year the ova are ready to be released, the uterus is ready for pregnancy, and so on. They also affect the behaviour of the female to ensure that she is receptive to the male at the appropriate time. Changes in the male may also occur and can be quite conspicuous. After the breeding season the testes become much smaller and may even retreat into the abdomen so that adults are similar to immature males in their external appearance. As the breeding season approaches the testes begin to enlarge again and sperm production restarts. In male American river otters the testes begin to enlarge in November reaching maximum size in the spring (Liers, 1951).

Even in species which breed throughout the year behavioural and physiological changes occur, at least in the female. If a female does not conceive when she first comes into oestrus after a pregnancy or on reaching maturity she will go through a period of a few weeks during which she is not receptive and will then come back into breeding condition. In seasonally breeding mammals there may be a series of short cycles during the breeding season within which the female varies in her willingness to mate and ability to conceive.

The main reason for these cycles is the considerable importance of synchronising copulation and ovulation sufficiently closely to ensure that fertilisation takes place. The hormones controlling the cycle modify the female's behaviour so that she is most receptive when she is most likely to conceive. This may be aided by the process of induced ovulation whereby a female that is ready to ovulate does not do so until stimulated by copulation. Many carnivores are thought to be induced ovulators (including American river otters) and the fact that mating is often prolonged and vigorous in carnivores may be related to this.

The only information on oestrous cycles in otters which is based on more than casual observation was obtained by collecting daily urine samples from a female Eurasian otter (Trowbridge, 1983). The concentration of oestradiol was measured as this is secreted at different levels through the cycle. In otters the concentration was very variable and no regular cycle was distinguished but it seemed that the otter ovulated at intervals ranging from 17 to 51 days with an average of 36 days.

Behavioural observations of captive American river otters suggest that shorter cycles occur in this seasonally breeding species. Females come into oestrus about three weeks after giving birth and remain on heat for a period of 42 to 46 days unless mating takes place. During this time they vary in their willingness to mate and after a female has been highly receptive there is a period of six days when a male is more likely to be rejected (Liers, 1951).

Courtship and Mating

Kenyon (1968) described how male sea otters in Alaska searched for females in oestrus by cruising in a characteristic manner round the areas in which females congregated. They adopted a face down swimming posture, moving more rapidly than usual and when they encountered a female they would approach and attempt to embrace her with their forelegs or rub and sniff at her body. If she was receptive a period of rolling and frolicking ensued but otherwise the male was rejected by a snap or a push from the forepaws or flippers. Males seemed to approach all females indiscriminately, pairing off when they eventually found one that did not reject their advances. Similar behaviour was observed by Vandevere (1970) in California except that although the males sniffed at the genital regions of all the females that they encountered they did not attempt to court them all, presumably concentrating on those that were in or approaching oestrus. Pairing lasted for a few days only, presumably while the female remained on heat and was terminated when the female abandoned the male, swimming away while he was under water foraging.

Neither of these authors distinguished territorial from non-territorial males, so it is unclear whether there is a difference in behaviour between them. Descriptions of the behaviour of territorial males suggests that they only make advances to females within their own territory (Loughlin, 1980) which might reduce their opportunities to do so. On the other hand a well placed territory on a route regularly travelled by females would enhance the opportunities and once a receptive female is in the territory the risk of harassment by other males would be much reduced. Fisher (1939) found that competition for females, presumably by non-territorial males, was keen and on some occasions a male was pounced on by one or even two others when attempting to mate.

Female sea otters live in large groups and scent can only be used as an indicator of reproductive status at close quarters. Under these circumstances, territory holding and cruising strategies seem to be an economical way for males to discover females in oestrus. One might also expect females to have a strategy for choosing males but as yet there are no observations to confirm that they do. When females rejected the advances of cruising males it was assumed that this was because they were not receptive but it is also possible that they were exercising choice. They may 'prefer' to mate with other males, possibly those with territories.

The more solitary species such as river otters rarely get a chance to sample large numbers of females in this way and must rely on other cues to determine when and where a receptive female is likely to be found. In the seasonally breeding American river otter the problem is reduced to finding where the female is but in the Eurasian otter, at least in areas where breeding is not seasonal, both problems have to be tackled. The potential value of scent in breeding was discussed in Chapter 5 and it is generally believed that a male otter detects the presence of an oestrous female from scent and then endeavours to find and court her. The reliability of the system may be judged by the behaviour of a male otter that was radio-tracked in Scotland (Green *et al.*, 1984). On two successive nights he travelled through a part of his range which was occupied by a female and showed no undue interest in the area but each of the following two nights were spent with this female and a great deal of calling and chasing took place. Although mating was not observed, there is strong evidence that it took place and cubs were present there the following year. After two nights of intense courtship the male spent a further five days in the vicinity of the female instead of pursuing his normal pattern of travelling but was not seen in company with her again.

In the more sociable species of otters, males and females are in daily contact so the need for establishing a temporary bond is obviated and no special behaviour is required for the male to determine when the female is on heat. It is a pity that there are very few detailed accounts of the mating behaviour of these otters since one might expect differences from the more solitary species. Zeller (1960) said that a female giant otter showed no desire for play when in oestrus although it is difficult to decide whether he means play with her keepers or with other otters. By contrast, accounts of courtship and mating of sea otters and river otters all stress the fact that courting otters engage in play and chase one another before mating (Figure 6.2). For these species, where males and females are normally separate, courtship may be important in overcoming a natural wariness between individuals. Wayre (1979) described a typical mating sequence in the Eurasian otter as follows:

> Copulation was preceded by vigorous 'play', the dog chasing the bitch in and out of their pool and all over their large enclosure. At times both otters swam and dived together, twisting and corkscrewing through the water. There was also much mock fighting, the pair facing each other, submerged except for their heads and lunging at each others faces and necks.

Mating took place shortly after this.

Most observations suggest that otters usually mate in water but it seems that in some species they do not always do so. A particular problem

Figure 6.2   Courtship swimming

for otters is that the broad base to the tail makes intromission rather difficult during normal dorsal mounting and most species seem to get round this problem by the male twisting his body round the female's although still clasping or gripping her from behind. Male sea otters use their forelegs to hold the female round the thorax and their teeth to grasp her upper jaw or nose, while in other species the female is usually gripped by the scruff of the neck. Wayre noticed that in the mating of the two otters described above the male used his forelimbs to hold the female around the abdomen. It would seem simpler for male otters to adopt a ventral (face to face) approach and Yadav (1967) has observed this in captive spotted-necked otters but Kenyon was adamant that it is not normal in sea otters and Harper and Jenkins (1981) found that an inexperienced male otter was less successful in achieving intromission when he tried this approach.

In mustelids mating can be very vigorous and the female is often gripped at the back of the neck by the male's teeth. Female mink often lose one or two square centimetres of skin from their necks during copulation. Otters would appear not to go to these lengths, perhaps relying on a longer courtship to win the female's co-operation. Even so females may occasionally suffer some injury and bloodied and scarred noses seem to be an occupational hazard for female sea otters which are held by the face during mating (Foott, 1970).

Mating is a risky business when the pair are less vigilant than normal and hampered in their ability to flee. They may also be made more conspicuous by their activity. This is less of a problem for carnivores, especially large ones, and while in some herbivorous species copulation may only last for several seconds, some carnivores, particularly in the weasel and dog families, may copulate for many minutes or even an hour or two. Otters seem to be in the middle of the range with successful copulations apparently lasting between ten minutes and half an hour. Like many other carnivores, however, they do mate several times during the female's period of receptivity, presumably to maximise the chances of conception occurring.

Gestation and Birth

Determining the length of gestation for species which breed seasonally is quite easy, particularly if they have a conspicuous rutting period like red deer or grey seals. In other species post mortem examination of reproductive organs can be very informative and some of the details of the breeding cycles of American river otters and sea otters were worked out in this way. With aseasonally breeding animals the only reasonably sure method is to observe them in captivity and this is the sole source of information for other species of otters.

Recent successes at breeding Eurasian and other otters in captivity have confirmed the observations made by Cocks in the nineteenth century that Eurasian otters have a gestation period of about nine weeks (Wayre, 1979). Most otters produced litters within a few days either side of 63 days after they were observed mating. Gestation periods of similar length have also been recorded in the giant otter, the smooth-coated, spotted-necked and Asian small-clawed otters and these are much as expected for carnivores in this size range.

American river otters and the sea otter are exceptional in having gestation periods much longer than other species of otters. The maximum gestation period recorded for the river otter was 12.5 months and the minimum 9.5 months (Liers, 1951), while in sea otters estimates range from 4 to 12 months. Although this may appear very odd, such extended pregnancies are known in a number of other animals, particularly amongst the weasel family but including roe deer, grey seals and some kangaroos. It is easy to explain how it takes 12 months for an American river otter embryo to develop and only two for a Eurasian otter but more difficult to understand why it should do so.

After fertilisation has taken place, the egg undergoes a number of changes. As it moves down the fallopian tube from the ovary to the uterus, it divides repeatedly until it reaches a stage known as the blastocyst, consisting of a ball of cells about 1 mm across surrounded by fluid and a thin membrane. Normally it would then embed in the uterine wall in preparation for the next phase of growth but in some species of mammal this implantation is delayed and development suspended for anything from several days to several months. This is known as delayed implantation. In the American river otter the blastocyst remains in the uterus until the following January or February when it implants in the uterine wall and continues to develop normally until about eight weeks later when the young are born. In sea otters implantation dates are more variable and the exact length of the two phases of pregnancy are unknown. Kenyon suggested that like fur seals, sea otter embryos probably took four or five months to develop after implantation but although sea otter cubs are much larger than other species they are virtually always single and there is no reason to suppose that gestation after implantation should take so very much longer than in other species of otters.

Interestingly, the most recent observations on sea otters in California indicate that total gestation may be only four months and the author suggests that there may be no delay in implantation at all (Vandervere, 1983). A more likely explanation is that in this area the period of delay was short, perhaps two months, followed by two months of normal gestation. If this is so, then it may be that, like the European badger, sea otters can vary the delay in implantation from a few to several months.

The reasons for delaying implantation are sometimes quite obvious; in grey seals which only come ashore to give birth and to mate, one can see the benefits of combining the two activities into one season. If stoats (*Mustela erminea*) had no delay they would need to mate in winter in order to ensure that births occurred in the spring. By delaying implantation, stoats avoid having to undergo the stresses of the mating season at a time when, in northern temperate regions at least, food is more difficult to find. A similar reason may underlie the delay in implantation in sea otters if it enables them to avoid mating when sea conditions are particularly rough. On the other hand it is difficult to see how the same arguments could apply to river otters in North America, particularly as the Eurasian otter seems quite capable of mating in winter in Sweden.

The factors which lead to implantation are unknown although it is obvious that hormonal changes in the female must be involved. Shortly before implantation, glands in the wall of the uterus undergo changes which enable the blastocyst to become embedded. The factor controlling this in some members of the weasel family is day length. For example, by artificially increasing the length of the day it is possible to shorten the gestation period of the marten (*Martes americana*) by making the blastocyst implant prematurely. In the river otter such an increase in day length occurring naturally after mid-winter could trigger implantation, at least in the northern parts of its range. Most Alaskan sea otters seem to implant in spring and Californian ones in the autumn so if day length is responsible in this species, implantation must be triggered by increasing day length in the north and decreasing day length in the south, although other factors could also be involved.

No one knows for certain what happens when wild otters are ready to give birth but it is thought that they usually try to find a quiet undisturbed part of their range for the natal den. Some people believe that otters often have their cubs away from water although it is difficult to understand why they should do so unless there are no suitable dens at the waterside. In addition to a secure den it is obviously important to have a good food supply nearby, particularly when the cubs are small to minimise the time they are left while the female goes hunting. Stephens (1957) in describing otter breeding sites summarised the prevailing views on where otters are likely to have their young:

The bitch generally chooses her nest up a small sidestream and away from the main river and floods, and rarely are two families found nearer than five miles apart. Alternatively the nest may be out in woodland or in a pile of sticks or brushwood, or high up in a hill tarn or reservoir. In parts of Scotland otters are often said to travel miles overland to a remote highland loch to breed. One occasionally hears tales of such lochs being ruined by a family of otters learning to fish there. In Norfolk the nests may be situated out on the reed-beds and in parts of Cornwall, besides Scotland, it is quite common for cubs to be born in caves around the coast or on islands in the salt marshes. In every case there is sure to be an abundant food supply near at hand, so that the bitch can feed and rear her cubs without exposing herself to too much danger.

Shortly before birth, captive Eurasian otters add considerable quantities of bedding to the nest to form a bulky structure with a hollow in the centre in which the female lies (Wayre, 1979). By this stage the male otter will have been removed from the enclosure. In the wild it is often assumed that the female Eurasian otter will be alone but a male otter in Scotland concentrated his activity in the vicinity of a female he had mated with at the time the cubs were born (Green *et al.*, 1984). He not only reduced the length of his travels and stayed in the same area for several nights but also became much more cautious and his emergence time was delayed.

Sea otters give birth to a solitary cub in the water, or occasionally on the beach. No one has reported seeing the birth of a sea otter cub although Sandegren *et al.* (1973) observed a female shortly after giving birth and watched her with the cub for the first few hours of its life.

During that time the predominant activity of the female was grooming the cub which rested on her chest. She spent 2.5 hours doing this continuously before stopping for fifteen minutes to attend to her own coat. By this time the cub was dry and fluffy and it floated beside her until she finished cleaning herself and placed it back on her chest. The cub, dependent on dry, air-filled fur for insulation and buoyancy could not survive long unless given this meticulous attention.

The variation in weight of newborn otters is remarkable, from the tiny Asian small-clawed otter cub weighing only 40 g or 50 g to sea otter pups which can exceed 2 kg in weight. This range can be explained almost entirely in terms of the sizes of adult otters and the number of young they bear. Kenyon found that the average weight of sea otter cubs was 1.85 kg which is between 8 per cent and 9 per cent of the weight of an average female. The best estimate of birth weight for American river otters comes from Hamilton and Eadie (1964) who found a foetus weighing 132 g which was close to birth. Taking the weight of an adult female as 6 kg this is equivalent to 2.7 per cent, so a litter of three would weigh about 7 per cent and a litter of four about 9 per cent of the female's body weight. There are only two estimates of the body weight of newborn Asian small-clawed otters, one was born dead at Chester Zoo and weighed 52 g (Timmis, 1971) and the other was reared by Philip Wayre's wife after being rescued from its parents weighing 35 g. The larger of these is about 1.4 per cent of the average body weight of an adult female so a litter of five would weigh 7 per cent of the female's weight. A litter of five giant otter cubs averaged 200 g in weight two days after birth weighing altogether between 4 and 5 per cent of the weight of an adult female. Bearing in mind that only the sea otter weights were based on a large sample it would seem that the normal litter weight in otters is probably in the range 5 per cent to 10 per cent of the female's body weight. This is unexceptional in carnivores of this size, for example in red foxes the mean litter weight is in the region of 10 per cent of the female's body weight (data from Lloyd, 1980) and in European badgers it approximates to 3 per cent (data from Neal, 1977).

Litter Size

Although female sea otters have occasionally been found with two embryos, only one survives to birth and females have never been seen with two cubs. Other species are more variable in their litters, ranging between one and six young although the latter is unusual except in the Asian small-clawed otter. Table 6.1 indicates the average litter sizes in populations of various species and Figure 6.3 shows the range of sizes in some of these. In each case, as far as possible, all the litters were recorded so there is no bias towards the extremes. Larger litters than these have been reported for each species except the Asian small-clawed otter. In this species litters smaller than those shown have been recorded.

Harris (1968) reported four cases in which Eurasian otters had litters of five or six but these are evidently not typical. Interestingly, American river otters kept by Liers seem regularly to have produced litters of four and he recorded none of two cubs, the most common size for Eurasian otters.

Table 6.1 Average litter sizes of otters

Source	Mean litter size	N	Comments
Eurasian otter			
Stubbe (1977)	2.3	70	Wild; data from questionnaire
Wayre[a]	2.4	26	Captive; counted at birth
Erlinge (1967a)	1.9[b]	11	Wild; tracked in snow
Wayre (1981)	1.8	17	Captive; reared to independence
Jenkins (1980)	1.1	16	Wild; tracked and seen
American river otter			
Tabor and Wight (1977)	2.8	39	Wild; counts of embryos
Liers (1951)	3.4	7	Captive; counted at birth
Hamilton and Eadie (1964)	2.0	15	Wild; counts of embryos
Asian small-clawed otter			
Wayre[a]	4.4	10	Captive; counted at birth
Wayre (1981)	0.8	16	Captive; reared to independence
Giant otter			
Duplaix (1980)	2.1[b]	7	Wild; seen with adults

Notes: a. Data from *Otters: Journal of the Otter Trust*, 1976–82.
 b. Excludes families which reared no cubs.
 c. N = number of litters counted.

The data in Table 6.1 suggest that wild American river otters may have a tendency to produce larger litters than Eurasian otters. This may be partly because the figures for American otters were counts at or before birth while all but one of those for Eurasian otters were based on counts at a later stage. Tabor and Wight (1977) and Melquist and Hornocker (1983) calculated that by the beginning of winter the average number of young per adult was 2.3 and 2.4 respectively but in neither case were individual litters counted. Non-breeding females and mortality of adult females as well as cubs between birth and winter makes these figures unreliable as indicators of cub survival.

Asian small-clawed otters also have large litters, four or five seems to be normal in captivity, but although these otters breed readily they are not so successful at rearing their young. The cubs are sometimes abandoned or ill-treated by one or both parents though this may be connected with the differences in behaviour of captive animals rather than with any natural deficiencies in their abilities as parents. Even Wayre, otherwise extremely successful at breeding otters, has suffered mortalities in the region of 80 per cent in this species while only 22

Figure 6.3   Litter size in river otters and Asian small-clawed otters

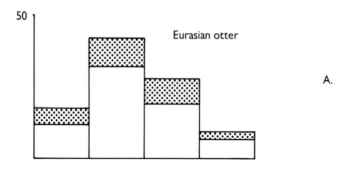

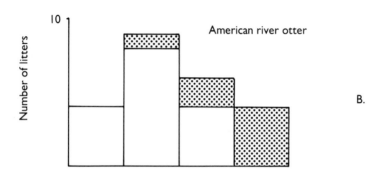

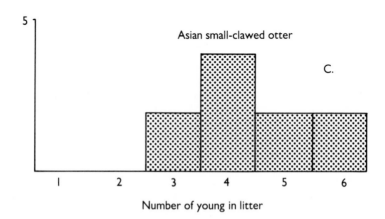

Number of young in litter

Sources: A — Wayre (Journals of the Otter Trust from 1977–82) (shaded),
Stubbe (1977); B — Liers (1951) (shaded), Hamilton and Eadie (1964);
C — Wayre (as above).

per cent of Eurasian otters born in his collections failed to reach independence.

A certain amount of mortality between birth and independence is inevitable in wild as well as captive populations and for many species of mammal the first year of life is a time of particularly high losses. Jenkins (1980) concluded that in four of the 17 family groups he watched no cubs were reared to independence while of those that did rear cubs successfully the average number was 1.4 per family. Further north, in Sweden, Erlinge followed eleven family groups and in all but one of these there were two cubs. Erlinge did not record any losses of young between the time they first travelled with their mother and becoming independent but the difficulties of tracking otters when there was no snow may have concealed some losses. On the other hand the fact that Swedish otters have adjusted their reproductive cycle to ensure that their young are born at the most favourable time of year will have increased their success in rearing young.

It is possible that in Sweden the predictability of severe weather makes a seasonal strategy appropriate so that a higher proportion of cubs in each litter is reared to independence. In Scotland where winters can be less severe, the fact that fewer cubs survive each litter on average may be offset by the possibility of a shorter average interval between births. A Swedish otter losing a litter would have to wait a full year before starting afresh while a Scottish otter could do so more quickly.

Duplaix' observations on giant otters (Table 6.1) also only included 'successful' families but it is notable that in this species the number of young observed per family group was quite high. So far, no one has managed to follow families of wild otters from the moment of birth to independence so it is impossible to determine the mortalities at each stage. However, it seems likely that about a third of the otters born will die during the first year of life (see below).

Growth and Development of the Young

Except in the case of the sea otter whose young are, of necessity, somewhat precocious, the newborn otter is a remarkably helpless creature — blind and scarcely mobile it spends most of its time either suckling or sleeping. Wayre (1979) has built special breeding dens in which he can observe and film the development of young otters and his book contains some remarkable photographs illustrating this. Most other people breeding otters have had to content themselves with occasional peeps into the breeding chamber up to the time when cubs begin to wander outside and so their accounts are much less detailed.

Wayre found that at first the cubs suckled every three or four hours for periods of ten to fifteen minutes (Figure 6.4). He wrote:

When hungry they struggle upwards through the fur of the bitch's belly searching for her teats, twittering softly until they find them. They suckle vigorously, wagging their little tails from side to side and kneading the bitch's stomach with their front paws.

Otter milk is extremely rich and it is hardly surprising that otters do not thrive on cow's milk which has only one-sixth of the fat content. This

Figure 6.4   Female otter suckling two cubs

is probably because the female hunts in water so that when she returns to her cubs after foraging she is damp. In order to avoid chilling, the young have a high metabolic rate and therefore require a concentrated source of energy (Ben Shaul, 1962).

Despite this nutritious diet, the development of young otters is slow. A young mink is independent and fending for itself after three months but Eurasian otters of that age have not usually learned to swim. The cubs' eyes are fully open by four or five weeks and although they can crawl at this stage they are still unable to hold their heads up. At seven weeks they first take solid food and they begin to run, albeit somewhat unsteadily (Figure 6.5). They also leave the nest in order to defaecate a short distance away but do not begin to play outside the den until they are ten weeks old. Although by this time they are taking considerable quantities of solid food brought by the mother they are not fully weaned until fourteen weeks of age (Wayre, 1979).

The first swimming attempts take place at about three months and the exact procedure seems to vary between families. In some cases the bitch appears to take an active role by carrying or dragging the cubs into the water but in other families she merely leads them to the water's edge leaving the cubs to take the final steps into the water to follow her. It is apparently not unusual for some cubs to be more adventurous and the more reluctant individuals seem to follow their mother and siblings in order to avoid being left behind.

At first the cubs' fluffy coats give them a great deal of buoyancy so although they float quite well, diving is rather difficult. Within a few weeks, however, they are as capable of swimming below the water as at the surface and by four months they are sufficiently competent to catch their own food for the first time. By this time they are following the female on her nightly travels, which increase in extent as the cubs get

Figure 6.5   Otter cub

older (see Chapter 5). Even so, the young otters have a long apprentice-ship before they leave the family group and fend for themselves.

There are a small number of observations on the growth rate of otter cubs in captivity but for some of these it is difficult to be sure of the exact ages of the cubs when they were first weighed. Otter hunters in Britain believed that otter cubs reach about 3 lb (1.4 kg) at three months of age and then increase in weight by about 1 lb (450 g) per month. These are convenient and memorable figures but they do not of course take any account of natural variations between litters or the sexes. In two litters of American river otters, one with two cubs and the other with five, the otters in the smaller litter each weighed nearly twice as much as those in the larger by the time they were four months old (Harris, 1968). There are also differences in the growth weights of male and female otters within the same litter. Figure 6.6 is based on records of two otter cubs, estimated to be two months old when they were received. The male was consistently a third heavier than the female and although she increased in weight at almost exactly 1 lb a month, his monthly weight gain was always higher. Thus, the male reached a weight of 5 kg some twelve weeks earlier than his sister.

African clawless otters are somewhat heavier than Eurasian otters and at two weeks of age the cubs in one litter weighed between 700 g and 1,400 g. A fortnight later, when their eyes opened they were 1,800 g, about twice the weight of Eurasian otters of comparable age. Needless to say, the growth rate was correspondingly greater. Between eight and sixteen weeks of age the African otters gained weight at about 300 g per week while Stephens' otters increased at 200 g (male) and 100 g (female) per week.

Bearing in mind that there are differences in growth rate between litters and within them, as well as between captive and wild otters, it is clear that it is very difficult to judge the age of a young otter from its size.

Figure 6.6   Increase in weight of captive Eurasian otter cubs

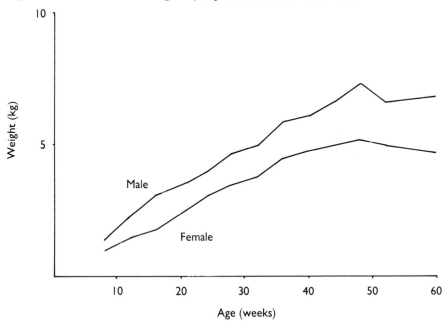

Source: Stephens (1957).

Age at First Breeding and Frequency of Litters

River Otters. American river otters normally reach maturity at two years of age but in captivity young males may not be very successful at breeding (Liers, 1951). Liers concluded that a male could not be relied upon as a breeder until it reached five to seven years of age and claimed that of 70 male otters he kept, 46 did not succeed in breeding. A similar experience is reported by Jenkins and Harper (1982) who reared a male Eurasian otter. They measured the size of his testes twice a week and showed that they reached maximum size by the time he was 20–22 months old. Although he shared a pen with a female from this age and they copulated frequently when she was receptive, she did not produce any cubs. Elsewhere, on the other hand, a captive male Eurasian otter of only 17 months successfully mated with a female five months older and a single cub was born (Wayre, 1980).

One female river otter kept by Liers first mated at 16 months of age and gave birth to a litter of four cubs nine months later although most female otters in his collection did not mate until they were two years old. Anatomical evidence indicates that female American river otters normally first mate at two years of age and that young males first produce mature sperm at about the same time (Hamilton and Eadie, 1964; Tabor and Wight, 1977). It seems probable, therefore, that both sexes in both species normally reach maturity by the time that they are two years old. In American river otters the females will have their first litter around their third birthday but Eurasian otters, by virtue of their shorter gestation, may do so somewhat earlier. In the wild, young males may have to wait rather longer to become fathers because of competition with older males.

In species with delayed implantation or a short annual season of births, there is little chance of producing more than one litter in a year and although it was once believed that Eurasian otters could breed twice yearly, the long period when the cubs are dependent on the mother precludes this in most species. Indeed there is even some doubt as to whether female otters normally breed every year or not. In captivity, where frequency of litters is usually governed by management techniques rather than nature, otters can certainly do so and female Eurasian otters have on several occasions given birth to two litters within fifteen months.

American river otters come into oestrus shortly after giving birth in the wild (Hamilton and Eadie, 1964) as well as in captivity (Best, 1962) so they too must be capable of breeding each year. However, Erlinge (1968a) suggested that otters in Sweden may not breed every twelve months and since otters seemed to be seasonal in his study areas this implies that females only have a litter in alternate years. His evidence for this was simply that during the rutting season the family groups remained together and since he never observed a dog otter accompanying a family group, the females must fail to come into oestrus while they are accompanied by young.

What happens where Eurasian otters do not breed seasonally is unknown but it is evident that they could easily have a birth interval longer than twelve months but shorter than two years. Perhaps a significant advantage of aseasonal breeding is that it gives ample time to allow the young to reach independence without restricting the females to a full two year cycle.

Sea Otters. There are hardly any concrete data on maturity in sea otters and Kenyon (1969) had to base his assessment solely on one female otter which was tagged at approximately one year of age and then shot and recovered one year later. By that time her teeth were those of a young adult but her reproductive system was immature and Kenyon concluded that female otters do not breed before they are two years old. By extrapolating her weight gain in her second year, he concluded that she would probably reach adult weight by three years but, less plausibly, he suggested that the age of maturity in sea otters might be similar to northern fur seals. In this species only 3 per cent of the females are pregnant at four years and 40 per cent at five and Kenyon suggested that perhaps most female sea otters did not become pregnant until their fifth year. Unfortunately, this assumption has been repeated rather un-critically since then and although one might expect the larger sea otter to take a little longer to reach maturity than the river otters, there is no obvious reason why it should take more than three years to do so.

As for males, Schneider (1978) believed that they do not mature until five or six years and that they do not become active breeders until some years later. This also seems a very slow rate of development but it may be connected with the establishment of territories. It is obvious that more information is needed before any confident statements can be made about maturity in sea otters.

Kenyon concluded that sea otters bred in alternate years but this was partly based on his assumption that gestation lasted for a year. More recent research suggests that the gestation period is shorter and that females can breed each year (Woodward, 1980).

LENGTH OF LIFE

The two problems in determining how long otters live are that first, unless an animal is born in captivity or at least caught when immature, it is difficult or impossible to determine how old it is when it dies. Second, animals kept in captivity under ideal conditions may well live much longer than they would in the wild whilst those kept in poor conditions will probably have a much shorter life than normal.

There are a number of records of otter longevity in captivity which indicate how long an otter can live, less information is available on the longevity of otters in the wild. Most information on captive otters has been collected by Harris (1968) supplemented with data from Liers (1951). Many of the records seem to refer to the length of time an animal was kept captive rather than its actual age at death although in a few cases the full length of life is known.

There are nine records of American river otters exceeding ten years of life and of these, four lived beyond their fifteenth year and one exceeded 20 years to die at the ripe old age of 23. There are fewer records for Eurasian otters and Harris reported five instances in which otters lived between 8.5 and 12.5 years. He also noted two long-lived smooth-coated otters of which one died at eleven years and four months and the other at 15.5 years. It is unlikely that there are great differences between species of otters although large animals tend to live longer than small ones, so sea otters may have slightly greater life expectancy than river otters and small-clawed otters slightly less. Overall, one may conclude that otters in captivity can reach an age of ten to 15 years but only rarely exceed 20 years.

Looking at these figures, it is interesting to note Wayre's comments on the death of his otter Kate at 8.5 years. Her death was caused by pneumonia and 'other associated conditions of old age' which emphasises the point that the figures in the above paragraph are selected to show the maximum length of life rather than the average. Further figures quoted by Harris show that in reality only a few otters reach these great ages. In London Zoo, for example, the average life span of 36 Eurasian otters prior to 1911 was three years four months and the longest lived was seven years three months at its death. From 1930 to 1960, of 19 individuals, only four lived for more than a year and the longest-lived otter survived a mere 28 months. Although Harris described these figures as depressing, they are probably a closer reflection of what happens to wild otters than the maximum life spans he meticulously recorded.

In most populations of wild animals only a tiny proportion of those born live out their full potential life span. In fact very often quite a high proportion of the population dies even before reaching maturity. Thereafter the proportion dying of disease, starvation, accident or predation is often fairly constant until the age at which senescence sets in and mortality increases. A convenient way of looking at this is to consider a theoretical group of a thousand animals and to estimate how many survive each age interval. Age intervals may be all the same length, a month or a year for example, or may correspond to significant stages in the animal's life such as birth to weaning, to independence or maturity, etc.

Using carcasses supplied by trappers in Oregon, Tabor and Wight (1977) were able to establish the ages of 113 female otters by examining growth lines in their canine teeth. From their data they assessed the mortality of otters as being 32 per cent in the first year of life, 54 per cent in the second and 27 per cent thereafter (Figure 6.7A). As different age classes of otters may not have the same susceptibility to trapping the figures must be regarded as an approximation but they are not unexceptional for an animal like the otter, being very similar to those estimated for the European badger and somewhat lower than the red fox. A higher mortality in the second year of life might be expected in a species where the young do not become independent until the end of their first year. Notice that these figures indicate that less than a quarter of female otters survive long enough to produce their first litter and that less than 1 per cent live for more than 13 years in the wild. Indeed, given Wayre's comments about the death of his otter Kate, one might imagine that there would be an increase in mortality by the tenth year of life and a corresponding reduction in the number of otters living beyond that age.

A second collection of otters, trapped in Ontario, corresponds reasonably well with the predictions of Tabor and Wight (Figure 6.7B) and although the number of otters in age class 1 is disproportionately low, there is no significant difference between the samples.

Thus, in the wild mortality is likely to be higher in the first two years of life than subsequently. Although the annual survival of adult otters is probably around 75 per cent, only one or two otters in a hundred will survive to ten years and only a few in every thousand to 15 years. As large animals tend to live longer than small ones, it is probable that a slightly higher proportion of giant and sea otters would survive to ten years, and a smaller proportion of Asian small-clawed otters, but the same general principles would apply to all species.

PARASITES AND DISEASE

Stephens (1957) was sent an otter which had been trapped in Cornwall after a goose had disappeared. As meat and a goose feather were found in the animal's stomach it seems likely that it was indeed the guilty party but a post-mortem examination revealed substantial extenuating circumstances. The unfortunate animal not only had advanced renal calculi (kidney stones), advanced tuberculosis of the lungs and possibly bronchitis, but also inflammation of the heart lining, damaged heart valves, a haemorrhage of the heart wall and a cyst on one ureter. One wonders how it managed to stagger into the trap.

Unfortunately, few wild otters other than sea otters have been subject to an examination as detailed as this one. Most of the large collections of otter bodies (particularly in North America) have been studied with a specific end in view — usually age determination and/or reproductive biology. As far as I know, no systematic study of otter corpses has been

Figure 6.7   Survival of American river otters. (A) shows the theoretical number of otters left alive at the start of each age class from an initial cohort of 1,000 animals when mortality is 32 per cent in the first year, 54 per cent in the second and 27 per cent in succeeding years. (B) shows the proportion of animals in each age class in a sample caught by fur trappers. Age class 0 = first year of life, 1 = second year of life, et seq.

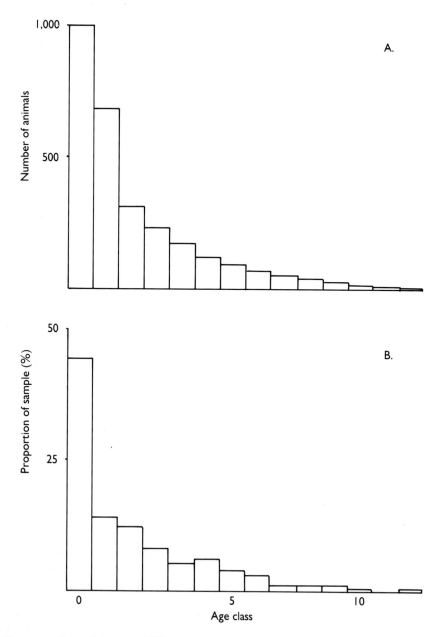

Sources: A — Tabor and Wight (1977); B — Stephenson (1977).

made by a pathologist or parasitologist. Fairley (1972) carried out a detailed macroscopic examination of the 32 otters he collected and he also sectioned the kidneys of 15 of these to search for signs of leptospirosis (see below). However, apart from minor damage to one liver he found no signs of disease or evidence of leptospirosis. Although Jensen (1964) did not systematically examine the 473 otters she received for disease or parasites, she did note that two animals were emaciated and had kidney stones, decayed teeth and an abscess on the neck while another two had severe cirrhosis of the liver.

Fairley also searched for intestinal parasites and found specimens in six otters, but he concluded that these were parasites of fish which had been ingested by the otters along with the prey. An analysis of faecal samples revealed 21 genera of parasites including five flukes, one tapeworm, 21 roundworms and 19 protozoa (Stephens, 1957). Unfortunately, there is no way of knowing which of these were resident in the otters and which had passed through having been incidentally ingested during a meal. Mönnig (1950) listed only two species of helminth worms found in otters, *Euparyphium melis*, a fluke and the fearsome *Dioctophyme renalis*, a huge nematode that attacks the kidneys of several species of carnivore in addition to man, pig, horse and cattle and which may grow to over a metre long.

A small number of the otters tracked by Erlinge were parasitised by tapeworms which he believed to be a species of *Diphyllobothrium*. Since the species known from Europe do not normally parasitise mammals it is probable that another genus was involved. On the other hand, it has been suggested that a species of *Diphyllobothrium* in North America may use otters as a host although there is not enough information available to confirm this (C.R. Kennedy, pers. comm.). Another tapeworm, identified in 6 per cent of otter scats from Montana, is known as *Ligula intestinalis* (Greer, 1955) but this normally only parasitises fish and fish-eating birds. The birds are infected when they eat diseased fish and although the otter undoubtedly ingests the worm it is probable that most are destroyed by mastication so that few if any would reach the otter's gut intact but would simply pass straight through and be expelled with the faeces (C.R. Kennedy, pers. comm.).

Since the bulk of otters received by most investigators are skinned before being sent in, the opportunities for studying ectoparasites have been very limited. Harris believed that ectoparasites were very uncommon while Stephens maintained that otters frequently carry ticks. No doubt the truth lies somewhere in between.

One dead female otter I received was covered in ticks but she was in very poor condition. She had been shot by a game keeper because she was very thin and appeared to be blind in both eyes. Blindness in otters has been commented on by a number of people and of 118 otters whose circumstances of death I knew, four were believed to be blind. J. Williams (pers. comm.) set out to collect information on this by looking through old books and asking otter hunters who had been active much earlier this century. Despite this all of the 21 records he obtained were since 1957. In most cases the otters were blind in both eyes but in two otters, only one eye appeared to be affected. As none of these otters was examined in detail there is no way of knowing what the causes were. It has been suggested, however, that some herbicides could cause blindness. If an otter were to pass through vegetation which had been recently sprayed, it is quite possible that the eyes could be contaminated although what the effects would be is unknown. One thing that is clear is that blindness does not necessarily incapacitate otters since one of the specimens reported to Williams was considered to be in good condition despite having apparently lost the sight of both eyes.

Blindness has also been discovered in some sea otters although only ever in one eye in the wild (Kenyon, 1969). A captive sea otter, Suzie, developed blindness in both eyes over a period of four years, but despite this she survived a further two years and was able to find her way round her enclosure and locate food without difficulty.

The disease encountered most frequently in wild and captive sea otters was enteritis but this seemed normally to be a secondary infection brought on by stress. Kenyon concluded that a bacterium of the *Clostridium* group was responsible and that although it was found in the guts of healthy otters, it only became active when the animals were debilitated through starvation, cold or exhaustion.

Over a dozen species of internal parasites have been found in sea otters but most of these appear to be normally harmless and seem to be shared with the other marine mammals found locally such as fur seals and sea lions. Most of the otters examined by Kenyon and his colleagues were either parasite-free or carried only a light load. Two potentially pathogenic species were recorded and these were present in several otters, occasionally in very large numbers. *Microphallus pirum* is a trematode which can cause enteritis when abundant because it is covered with sharp spines which damage the gut lining. *Terranova decipiens* is a nematode worm and although the adults seem to be harmless, the larvae can penetrate the wall of the sea otter's intestine and invade other organs. The perforations resulting from this can lead to peritonitis and the subsequent death of the host.

Sea otters seem to be genuinely free of external parasites except for the occasional stray louse, although Kenyon *et al.* (1965) found that about 3 per cent of the otters on Amchitka had light infestations of a mite (*Halarachne miroungae*) which lives in the nasal passages and is, technically at least, external.

Captive animals are subject to a wider range of ills than their wild relatives and diseases which are common in zoos are not necessarily of any significance outside. The care of captive animals has improved markedly in recent years and the very fact that captive animals may live longer than wild ones may predispose them to certain types of disease which are rare or unknown in free-living populations. Duplaix-Hall (1975) gave a comprehensive list of diseases diagnosed in captive river otters and stressed the frequency of pneumonia which developed when otters' coats were allowed to deteriorate.

Wayre's otters do not suffer greatly from disease although he found that bite wounds were likely to become septic if not treated and dental abscesses also occurred occasionally and required prompt treatment. The only transmitted disease Wayre (1979) considered particularly important was a form of leptospirosis known as Weil's disease. The splendidly-named bacterium *Leptospira icterohaemorrhagiae* is carried by rats and causes jaundice. Otters are very susceptible to this and likely to die without warning so Wayre used small gauge wire mesh to exclude rats from his otter enclosures and set traps around them.

MORTALITY

The chances of finding otters that have died of natural causes are very low except in the case of the sea otter. Moribund sea otters frequently come ashore just before death and as their corpses float, those that die at sea are often washed up on the beach. Kenyon was, therefore, able to make counts of dead otters and to carry out examinations of corpses which had not decomposed too far.

Most mortality occurred in the late winter and Kenyon recognised two main groups of dead animals, those whose death was due to injury in rough seas and those which were emaciated and showed signs of enteritis, probably bought on by starvation. Although the exact ages of these otters could not be determined (their teeth do not have growth lines) Kenyon found that those in the second category consisted mainly of large juveniles, approaching sub-adulthood and old animals with well-worn teeth and grizzled fur. A high proportion of these otters had defective teeth which would have made it very difficult for them to tackle hard-shelled food. In many of the adults the teeth were worn down to the gums and some juveniles suffered from malocclusion so that the back teeth would not close together properly.

On Amchitka, where Kenyon was working, the sea otter population was very dense and this had led to a reduction in the food supply, particularly of the more favoured soft-bodied species. The hard-shelled but more easily found food formed the bulk of the diet, particularly in the case of less fit animals such as juvenile and old otters. Malocclusion is apparently not abnormal in young sea otters when the molars erupt at about one year of age and during this time the young are normally still dependent on the mother who is able to provide them with suitable food. On Amchitka the weather is frequently very bad in the late winter and because of the food shortage some females do not have sufficient fat reserves to enable them to continue feeding a large juvenile at the expense of their own food intake. If this happens the mother may abandon the pup before it is capable of fending for itself so that she may survive even if it does not. Females with smaller young seem better able to manage but Kenyon estimated that as many as 50 per cent of the young sea otters failed to make the transition to independence in this area, many of them through starvation.

In the northern part of their range, considerable numbers of sea otters may die during the formation of sea ice. In fact the northern limit of sea otter distribution is probably determined by the extent of ice formation in winter (Kenyon, 1969). Otters can tolerate the ice and severe weather provided that there are open leads where they can feed.

In 1971 and 1972, sea ice extended well beyond its normal limits on the Alaskan peninsula and had a profound effect on the sea otter population. In 1971 it advanced rapidly and many otters were trapped and forced onto the ice or land where they died of malnutrition or related diseases. In 1972, although the ice was more dense and lasted longer, it advanced more slowly and the otters were able to swim in advance of it. Eventually they were concentrated at the tip of the peninsula, beyond the edge of the ice and when it retreated, they dispersed back towards their original ranges. Mortality in 1972 seemed to be low but in 1971 200 dead sea otters were seen during surveys which only covered a small part of the area (Schneider and Faro, 1975).

Another form of mortality that falls mainly on the young pups on Amchitka is predation by bald eagles. The intensity of this is not known exactly but since most of it takes place when the eagles are feeding young, a count of prey remains in eagle nests gives an indication of its extent. In 1972 a fairly detailed survey was carried out when half the known bald eagle nests were examined and the remains of 56 sea otter cubs found (Sherrod et al., 1975). At that time the population of sea otters on Amchitka was in the region of 7,000 and Kenyon has estimated that dependent young form 15 per cent of the total population. If only half the cubs eaten by bald eagles were found this would indicate that bald eagles take about 10 per cent of the otter pups born each year, or about one-fifth of the total juvenile mortality. Sea otters would seem to be an important source of food for the eagles since sea otter pups were one of the largest prey items available to them and they formed 21 per cent of the prey items identified.

Another possible predator of sea otters, probably mainly adults, is the white shark, which had attacked at least 60 of 657 sea otters examined by Morejohn et al. (1975). Each of these otters had characteristic lacerations and many had fragments of shark teeth embedded in their flesh or bones but curiously none had been partly eaten. No one has ever found sea otter remains in a white shark's gut although whole grey seals and chunks of elephant seal as well as other species have been recorded. Do white sharks attack sea otters and then spit them out? If so, about 9 per cent of the mortality in California seems to be due to such attacks. If some are eaten the full impact of predation is evidently higher.

In the last century the most important mortality factor for sea otters was undoubtedly persecution for their fur (see Table 7.5) and for many other species, human predation was, and in some cases still is, a major cause of mortality. The connection between overexploitation and declines in the populations of some species is clear (see Chapter 7) but even in these we do not know what proportion of the total populations was being removed each year or what other mortality factors affected them. Otters killed at the hand of man are more easily counted than those dying a natural death, even if indirect methods, such as monitoring the export of skins, have to be used. No doubt similar mechanisms to those outlined for sea otters on Amchitka regulated the populations of other unexploited species. Starvation would have particularly affected the youngest and oldest members of the population while disease and accidents would have been less selective in their impact.

Virtually all the otter deaths that have been systematically recorded were at the hand of man. In the 1970s I tried to collect data on otter mortality in Britain and received information on 165 otters of which more than three-quarters had been killed deliberately or inadvertently by man (Table 6.2).

Since the proportion of otters in each category is greatly affected by the

Table 6.2 Mortality records for otters in Britain and East Germany

	Britain (%)	East Germany (%)
Killed on roads	34	11
Killed deliberately	37	33
Found dead	16	14
Caught in fish traps	10	36
Killed by dogs	2	4
Other causes	1	2
Number of otters	165	486

Note: Other causes include electrocution and drowning under ice.

Sources: Britain, personal records; Germany, Stubbe (1977).

likelihood of discovery of a body or the report of an incident, it is not surprising that road casualties and otters which had been shot figured prominently and otters found dead were less frequently reported.

In a similar, though more extensive survey carried out in East Germany, Stubbe (1977) found a much higher proportion of otters killed in fish traps and although the proportion killed deliberately was about the same, road deaths formed a lower proportion of the total.

Occasionally I received reports of several otters killed at the same place, sometimes over a very short period. For example, 22 otters were shot near Lochailort in 1969. Trapping, snaring and shooting of otters in these remote areas took place over a long period although it is now illegal. In general, the otters seemed able to withstand the cull although local populations may have been depleted, at least in the short term.

Jefferies *et al.* (1984) obtained records of 84 otters which were killed in Britain in traps set for fish, crabs and lobsters between 1975 and 1983. They believed that this was a gross underestimate of the total number killed. Many were killed in areas where otters are common; for example, in 18 months, 23 were killed in fyke nets (Figure 6.8) set for eels in freshwater lochs in the Outer Hebrides. In the same area between 1978 and 1981, a further 22 were drowned in lobster pots. Reports were also received from areas where otters are scarce, such as Norfolk, where it was believed that six otters drowned in fyke nets during one season recently. This is particularly disturbing since it has been estimated that the population of otters in Norfolk in the mid-1970s was between 30 and 40 animals (Macdonald and Mason, 1976).

On a smaller scale, though equally serious, was the report of five road deaths in seven years beside the River Glaven in Norfolk, a tiny river only 13 km from source to sea. In addition to these, and during the same period, two further otters were shot on the river and two more were killed on the road within 15 km of the Glaven. The effect of mortality on that scale in such a small area may be much greater than larger numbers of deaths occurring where otters are more common.

Figure 6.8   Fyke net

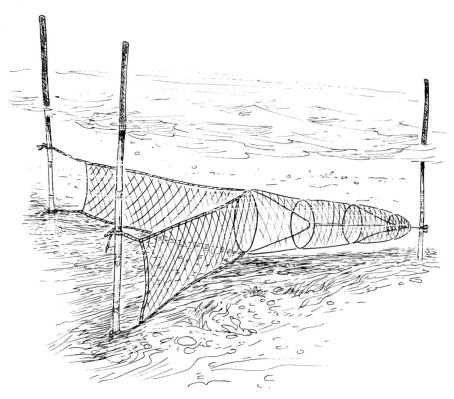

A further mass mortality occurred in Shetland near the oil terminal at Sullom Voe when a minimum of 14 otters died during an oil spill in 1978. This caused considerable concern at the time, not because of the number of otters killed but because a larger future spill could have a catastrophic effect on the population of coastal otters in the islands.

The last few paragraphs may have given the impression that most otter mortality, in Britain at least, is due to man's activities. This may be so, although as explained earlier, the number of otters dying of natural causes is impossible to assess. It is important to realise that although man may cause a substantial proportion of otter mortality, he does not need to do so in order to 'control' the population. Although sea otters, now protected from man and subject to few natural predators, have increased in numbers, they only do so until they reach the carrying capacity of the environment. Left to themselves they would never have dropped below it. Once this level is reached again, natural mortality factors such as those operating at Amchitka come into play, particularly poor survival of the young. Starvation and disease among the adult population may also play a part in ensuring that the population remains reasonably stable. Thus, although man can reduce otter populations, they will not increase uncontrollably if he leaves them alone.

The two ways in which man has had the greatest impact on otter populations throughout the world are by overexploiting them, usually for their fur, and by destroying or degrading their habitat. These factors are explained in more detail in the next chapter which explores the relationships between man and otters most of which, until very recently, have been to the detriment of the otters.

7 Otters and man

The public image of otters has undergone a complete reversal during the course of the twentieth century. Once regarded as voracious predatory vermin, otters are now seen by most people as attractive and interesting animals whose decline, and in some places extinction, is greatly regretted. Books like Williamson's *Tarka the Otter*, Maxwell's *Ring of Bright Water*, magazine articles and television programmes have been so effective in transforming public opinion that it is now unusual to find someone who is genuinely antagonistic to otters, at least in Britain. Indeed, many nations now offer otters some form of legal protection and there are a number of organisations devoted to furthering the welfare of otters.

It is ironic that despite these changes, otter populations are under much greater threat today than they were when otters were regarded as unmitigated pests. Public interest seems to increase in proportion to the threats and yet the threats themselves are on the whole the results of the activities of a civilised society.

PERSECUTION OF OTTERS

Organised persecution of the otter has a long history. In Britain for example, the earliest pack of otter hounds is recorded from the thirteenth century and by 1566 the otter was officially designated as a pest in the 'Acte for the Preservation of Grayne' which empowered parish constables and churchwardens to offer a bounty on otters and other supposed vermin. No doubt this resulted from the otters' interest in the well-stocked fish ponds which were then used as a living larder by the more affluent members of society. Otters were probably also attracted to traps set for eels, salmon, and so on, in which they could wreak considerable havoc. In 1544 Sir Henry Savile wrote to his brother enquiring after 'a man that can kill otters very well' whom he wished to employ to reduce the otters on his estate which were causing 'exceeding much harm at divers places' (Howes, 1976). Similar attitudes undoubtedly prevailed throughout Europe but North American otters were relatively free from harassment until the sixteenth century although small numbers were killed for their fur by the indigenous population.

Little is recorded from earlier centuries but some interesting information has come from parish records in south Yorkshire (Howes, 1976). For example, in 1619, a dead otter attracted sixpence (2.5 p) in bounty in Doncaster, 50 per cent more than a polecat and three times the rate for a weasel. Enterprising bounty hunters probably took their otters to the parishes of Arksey, Worksop, Worsborough or Wortley where the price on an otter's head was one shilling (5 p). The attractions of this bounty meant that in any parish small numbers of otters would be brought in each year. Although the average for the parish of Arksey was only one per year, Howes calculated that if this was typical of south

Yorkshire between 35 and 40 might be caught each year in the area (some 1,200 km^2). This is in fact a very high total for such a small area (see Table 7.4) and if the extrapolation is valid, could well be a significant factor in reducing otter populations locally or at least keeping them at a low level.

Historically, trapping and hunting with dogs were the only effective means of killing otters. Thus in the sixteenth century the Norwich Assembly decreed that fishermen on the River Yare should keep a dog for hunting otters and should carry out two or three hunts per year 'upon pain to forfeit ten shillings' (50 p) (King et al., 1976). Early firearms were too unreliable, and probably too dangerous, to use in game preservation but by the end of the eighteenth century they had developed sufficiently to be effective for hunting and this may have been a significant extra pressure on the otter in Britain. William Guest suggested that by 1800 otters had become extinct on the River Don near Doncaster as a result of the 'vigilance of the expert gunner' (Howes, 1976). No doubt otters in other parts of Europe faced similar pressures.

In Britain persecution of predators has been carried out mainly by keepers for game preservation. Shooting as a sport has traditionally been restricted to edible species such as grouse, pheasant, deer, etc. and otters have never been systematically trapped or shot for their fur. The persecution of polecats (*Mustela putorius*), pine marten (*Martes martes*) and wild cats (*Felix sylvestris*) led to the extinction of each of these in most of Britain. They became restricted to small areas in Wales (polecat) and Scotland (pine marten and wild cat) although all three are now slowly expanding their ranges (Langley and Yalden, 1977). At the beginning of the twentieth century when populations of the other three species were at their most restricted, otters were probably uncommon though more or less ubiquitous (Harrison Matthews, 1952). The otter population was undoubtedly under pressure from keepers and had been reduced in numbers but it was not eliminated in most parts of Britain although local extinctions may have occurred. For example, on one island off the west coast of Scotland, otters were exterminated by keepers (E.M. Andrews, pers. comm.). By the end of the Second World War, numbers had recovered and the otter was comparatively common throughout the country (Stephens, 1957). This coincided with a massive reduction in the amount of keepering. The numbers of game keepers increased in the last 30 years of the nineteenth century but declined from 22,500 in 1901 to 6,000 by 1951 (Potts, 1980).

In many European countries, particularly in the north, otters are considered as game and the numbers killed are recorded for statistical purposes. It is not always clear from the records whether otters were trapped or shot or whether the motive was principally profit or to protect fish and other game but the result is that, in a few countries, it has been possible to use the returns as an index of otter populations. When catches declined, conservation measures were taken.

This is well demonstrated in Sweden and the annual cull from 1939 to 1969 is shown in Figure 7.1 From 1938 to 1941 otters were protected, except at fish-rearing ponds, but thereafter the number killed increased rapidly to a maximum of around 1,500 per year. Then the numbers caught began to decrease and in 1958 otters were protected in the

Figure 7.1   Number of otters killed in Sweden during each hunting season from 1939 to 1969

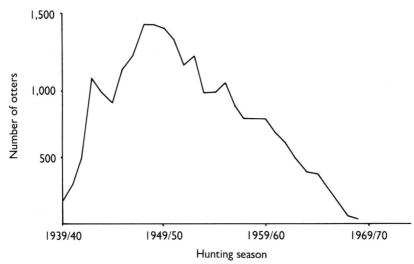

Source: Erlinge (1972a).

northern districts of Sweden. Despite this the catch continued to fall in other parts of the country and conservation measures were progressively introduced until by 1968 otters were protected throughout Sweden. Elsewhere, reliable data on the numbers of otters killed are difficult to find. A few examples are shown in Table 7.1 from which one can see that there is a great deal of variation from one country to another both in the extent of records and in the numbers of otters killed. In recent years in

Table 7.1   The annual kill of Eurasian otters in various countries during the twentieth century

	1930s	1940s	1950s	1960s	1970s
Sweden	?	1,000	1,000	300	*
Norway	?	?	?	?	600
Denmark	?	260	220	170	*
Britain	400	?	200	100	10
Russia	?	5,600	8,000	7,800	4,500

Notes: a. Data for most countries come from official returns through the fur trade. For Britain the records of the otterhounds have been used.
b. * indicates legal protection for otters.

Sources: Sweden, Erlinge (1972a); Norway, Heggberget and Myrberget (1979); Denmark, Jensen (1964); Russia, Kucherenko (1976); Britain, personal records.

Europe, appreciable numbers of otters have only been killed in Norway and Turkey. The figures for Britain are not strictly comparable as they only refer to otters killed for sport by hounds, the number trapped or shot is unknown. On the other hand the detailed records kept by the otter hunters in Britain do make it possible to calculate the catch per unit effort and this has been invaluable in unravelling the timing of the otters' decline (see below). Table 7.1 also shows that in each area for which long-term records are available (Sweden, Denmark and Britain) there was a decline in the numbers of otters killed.

Otters as Fur Bearers

River Otters. Otters have probably been killed for their fur ever since man first learnt to stitch the skins of small animals together and discovered that otter fur was amongst the densest and most luxuriant. The earliest historical records date back to Ireland in 1408 when John, son of Dermod, was charged 164 otter skins for arrears of rent by King Henry IV. The value of skins has varied considerably and not always in line with changes in the value of money. It rose from three shillings (15 p) in the late fifteenth century to a guinea (105 p) in the mid-1750s (Howes, 1976) but by the early 1900s, was down to between ten and fifteen shillings (50−75 p) (King *et al.*, 1976). During the 1960s and 1970s the price seems to have been of the order of £10−£15. This was sufficient to make otter shooting and trapping worthwhile on a casual basis in those parts of Britain where otters were still very common, such as the Scottish islands. Reports from there suggest that otter skins formed a welcome if occasional source of additional income to some of the inhabitants. However, the number killed purely for their skins has always been quite small and sport and game protection have always been the main reasons for killing otters in Britain.

Elsewhere profit was perhaps the main reason, particularly in states where the fur trade was important. This is particularly the case in Russia and also in North America, where river otters formed a small but significant proportion of the organised fur trade from its inception in the sixteenth century. In both countries the fur trade was fostered for political reasons, the traders and trappers were important pioneers extending the frontiers and developing economic links with the native populations.

The otter's part in this was small. Beavers, bison and muskrat dominated the American trade, sable and fox the Russian, but of the various small fur bearers trapped in America, otters were one of the more valuable. Table 7.2 gives an indication of the relative importance of different species although there are no figures which might indicate the yearly totals. It is quite clear that otters formed a relatively small part of the total catch.

The value of skins varied and Table 7.3 shows the market values of skins held by the trading post at Astoria on the west coast of America during the 1812/13 season. Beavers, bison and river otters are at the upper end of the market while at the lower end come the less desirable furs such as mink, muskrat, raccoon and possum all of which were worth less than 50 cents a skin.

Table 7.2   Numbers of skins from trading posts in the Upper Missouri region

Bison	125,000
Beaver	11,000
Muskrat	11,000
Fox[a]	4,600
River otter	200

Notes: a. Red foxes (*Vulpes vulpes*) and grey foxes (*Urocyon cineroargenteus*).
b. Records are incomplete and include various trading posts between 1828 and 1843. Figures indicate proportions not total numbers killed.
Source: Wishart (1979)

The only estimate I can find for the annual catch comes from the Rocky Mountain area where the American Fur Company and the Rocky Mountain Fur Company competed for business in the early 1830s (Wishart, 1979). At that time, approximately 30,000 beavers per year were caught in an area of about 800,000 km². If otter captures here were in similar proportions to those in the Upper Missouri region (Table 7.2) this would indicate a cull of around 400–500 otters. Even if the proportion of otters was twice as high in the Rocky Mountains, a thousand otters a year in an area five times the size of England and Wales does not seem excessive in comparison, for example, with the annual kill by the British otter hunts (Table 7.1).

Otter trapping continued in North America into the twentieth century and, in some states at least, at a level which affected the status of otters. In Michigan in the 1920s, otter numbers became so low that there was concern that they might become extinct and they were completely

Table 7.3   Values of pelts in North America during the early nineteenth century

Species	Value ($)
Sea otter	25–60
Grizzly bear	10
River otter	5
Beaver	3–6
Bison	3–6
Lynx	2
Mink	0.25–0.40
Muskrat	0.20–0.40

Source: Wishart (1979).

protected from 1925 to 1940 (Lagler and Ostenson, 1942), while in Montana otters were protected from 1949 (Greer, 1955). As in Europe, game laws were introduced and various states used these in order to introduce quotas or closed seasons and, ultimately, to prohibit trapping altogether. In some states, however, otter trapping continued and two of the most productive states after the Second World War were North Carolina and Louisiana. In North Carolina between 800 and 1,300 otters were trapped each year between 1949 and 1953 (Wilson, 1954).

In Michigan, after 15 years of protection, trapping restarted as complaints were made by fishermen and beaver trappers about the adverse effects of the increasing otter population. Trapping was allowed during the open season for beavers for two years in certain counties in North Michigan but all otter carcasses had to be handed in to the Department of Conservation when the pelts were sealed. This made it possible to obtain material for a study of the otter's diet (to investigate the claims of fishermen and beaver trappers) and ensured that a reasonably accurate picture of the number of otters killed could be obtained. Two hundred and sixty six otters were killed in the first year and 173 in the second.

In some states otter trapping continued right through the 1970s. In Arkansas, for example, 400 otters were trapped in the 1979/80 season. However by this time the river otter had been added to the list of species in Appendix 2 of the Convention on International Trade in Endangered Species, which meant that export of otter skins had to be regulated. This stimulated research into the abundance of otters and their biology although it did not proscribe trapping for fur. Trapping of otters also continued in Russia where between 1940 and 1970 an average of 6,000 otters were killed each year. The highest rate of capture occurred between 1951 and 1956 when an average of 8,800 otters were harvested annually (Kucherenko, 1976).

Table 7.4 illustrates the level of exploitation of otters in some of the places where they have been systematically trapped or killed. The figures should be interpreted with care as the extreme values are based on rather tenuous data and they cover a wide range of latitudes, dates and habitats. Only in Sweden, Britain and Russia is there any evidence that these yields were sustained over several years and ultimately declines occurred in all three of these areas. Nevertheless, it would seem that otter populations which are not under pressure from other sources have withstood culls of up to 10 otters per 1,000 km^2 per year.

Sea Otters. Perhaps the most remarkable information in Table 7.3 is the value of sea otter skins, up to ten times greater than bison, beaver and river otters. Novikov (1962) describes the sea otter's pelt as one of the most valuable furs known and Phillips (1961) is almost lyrical in his description:

> The gorgeous beauty of sea-otter skins — jet-black, smooth, short-haired loveliness gleaming underneath with silver ...

As a result of possessing this desirable commodity the sea otter has suffered more at the hands and guns of the fur trade than any other

Table 7.4 Estimate of the intensity of cull of river otters by hunters and trappers

Area	Date	Otters killed per 1,000 km²/year	Reason
1 South-west England	1920–40	7	C
2 South Yorkshire (UK)	17C.	30	C
3 Sweden	1940–60	2	F & C
4 Denmark	1941–67	5	F & C
5 Amur-Ussuri (USSR)	1945–65	9	C
6 Michigan	1940/1	7.5	F
7 North Carolina	1949–53	8.5	F
8 Rocky Mountains (USA)	18C.	0.5–1	F
9 Peruvian Amazon	1960–70	7	F

Note: F = fur trade; C = control.

Sources: 1 Pring, 1958; 2 Howes, 1976; 3 Erlinge, 1972a; 4 Jensen, 1964; 5 Kucherenko, 1976; 6 Lagler and Ostenson, 1942; 7 Wilson, 1954; 8 Wishart, 1979; 9 Smith, 1981.

species of otter. By the beginning of this century it had been brought close to extinction throughout its range, surviving in a mere dozen isolated areas.

Persecution of the sea otter was not a new phenomenon in the nineteenth century although it reached a peak then. Archaeological remains show that sea otter pelts have been worn, and their flesh eaten, for millennia. In California the remains of skeletons and burnt bones have been found in middens dating back 3,000 years (Davis, 1977). There is no evidence to suggest that the aboriginal Californians depleted sea otter stocks but the Aleuts in the northern Pacific had a much more serious impact on sea otter populations, at least on Amchitka Island where midden remains dating back 2,500 years have been excavated. To interpret these Simenstad et al. (1978) made use of the fact that they knew what effect sea otter populations had on the sublittoral communities (see Chapter 4). The sizes of sea urchin remains together with the proportions of other coastal prey in the Aleuts diet indicated that sea otters must have been rather scarce in the areas in which they hunted. Since sea otter remains were also present though in small numbers, they concluded that the Aleuts had hunted the nearby sea otters so much that the population had been substantially reduced and that the offshore community had altered until it became similar to that found in areas where sea otters are sparse or absent today.

Although pressure from the Aleuts may have been intense, it was probably very localised because when the fur traders from Russia, America and Europe discovered the sea otter populations in the eighteenth century there were plenty of otters for them to catch. The ruthless manner in which otters were hunted down is a textbook example of bad management of wild animal populations. Time after time, as new colonies of sea otters were found, the hunters would move in and reduce the population to a vestige or to extinction, often over a very short time indeed. For example, shortly after the Pribilof Islands were first discovered two sailors moved in and within a year had killed 5,000 animals. In their second year of hunting they only managed to kill a further 1,000 and within six years there were no sea otters left (Harris, 1968).

Lensinck (1960) estimated that in the 126 years that Alaska was occupied by the Russians over 800,000 sea otters were killed there by hunters of various nations. Despite this, when Alaska and the Aleutians were bought by America in 1867, there were still enough sea otters left to make hunting them worthwhile. Costa (1978) concluded that in the 40 years after the purchase of Alaska, the value of sea otter skins taken from the territory far exceeded the price of $7,200,000 paid for it. Since over 100,000 sea otters are known to have been killed in that time this is probably no exaggeration, suggesting an average price of about $70 per skin which is not excessive for the period.

The annual catches of sea otters in Alaska were, not surprisingly, much higher at the beginning of the nineteenth century than later (Table 7.5) but even as early as 1821 there was some concern about stocks and the Russian-American Company tried to introduce conservation measures. These were not universally accepted but trade was much lower over the following years until the territory changed hands in 1867. From then until the end of the century there was an increase in the efforts to catch otters and captures rose from c. 3,000 per annum at the end of the 1860s to about 5,000 per annum in the 1880s. The results of this intense exploitation can be seen both in the reduction of catches and the soaring values of pelts during the 1890s. During the 1920s blackmarket prices in the region of $2,000 to $3,000 are quoted although skins confiscated by the United States government and sold at public auction fetched much lower prices ranging up to $450 for high quality pelts in favoured colours.

When in 1911 the Fur Seal Treaty was signed giving protection to sea otters as well as fur seals, only a few were left. Estimates suggest that

Table 7.5 Approximate annual culls of sea otters in Alaska and the prevailing value of the pelts

Date	Cull	Value ($)
1790–1810	10,000–15,000	20–100
1830–1865	1,000–2,000	15–60
1867–1890	3,000–5,000	30–170
1891–1900	600	285–1,125
1910	34	1,700

Sources: Cull, Lensinck (1960); values, Harris (1968).

Figure 7.2   The range of the sea otter before intensive exploitation began and at the time when hunting ceased

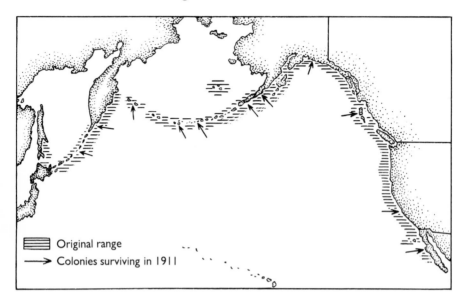

Original range
Colonies surviving in 1911

there were probably only 500 to 1,000 animals, scattered in eleven isolated sub-populations across the northern Pacific from the Kiril Islands between Russia and Japan in the west to Benito Island, Mexico in the south-east (Figure 7.2). Even these did not all survive, the populations in Benito Island and Queen Charlotte Island, Alaska becoming extinct in the 1920s, the saddest point in a long and sorry tale.

Other Otters. Needless to say, the other species of otters have also been exploited although none so badly as the sea otter. Even so, populations of some other species have been significantly reduced because of the fur trade, notably those of the giant otter of South America. This species, like the sea otter, has a more valuable fur than the smaller river otters and was therefore a more desirable quarry. Figures for otter exports provided by the Peruvian Ministry of Agriculture (Brack-Egg, 1978) are summarised in Figure 7.3 and illustrate this point clearly as well as the inevitable result of such exploitation.

At first more than two-thirds of the skins exported were from the larger species but during the 1950s the number of river otters killed increased at a much greater rate than the giant otters. Even this increase seems to have been too much, for while the number of river otters exported doubled again during the 1960s the catches of giant otters decreased until in 1969 only 47 were sold. The export of skins was prohibited after 1970 and in that year there was a last minute clearing of cupboards which caused a small rise. Despite the fact that up to 1970 between 6,000 and 10,000 river otters were killed each year with no apparent impact this species was also protected from 1973.

These figures do not of course include illegally exported skins or skins exported via Colombia so they can only be used as a guide to relative

Figure 7.3   Annual totals of otter skins exported from Peru

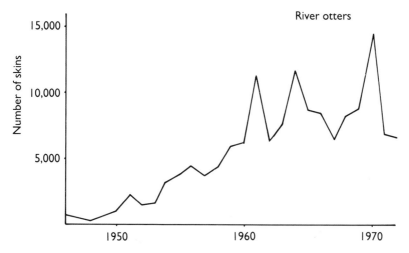

Source: Brack-Egg (1978).

numbers and changes in proportions. In Colombia itself, Donadio (1978) estimated that the official figures were probably equalled by the number of smuggled skins. Here too the giant otters seem to have been over-exploited, although not as soon as in Peru. In 1965 the official number of giant otter skins exported was 1,032, five times as many as the same year in Peru. Nevertheless, by the early 1970s the numbers were well down — 311 in 1970, 85 in 1971 and between 20 and 30 in 1972. Over the same period, river otter skins increased from about 1,200 to between 6,000 and 7,000. Colombia also protected its giant otters although not until 1975. By the mid-1970s otters were protected in most South American countries although inevitably illegal trading continued.

The plight of the sea cat is typical of the fate of otters in many parts of the world. The skin of each otter is worth about three months' wages to a Chilean unskilled labourer and Brownell (1978) pointed out that:

In Peruvian waters these otters are often shot by fishermen because of the alleged damage they do to the stocks of freshwater prawns. In addition they are probably taken incidental to fishing operations in Peru and Chile. In Chile the species is hunted by fishermen especially south of Isla Chiloe for their skins.

Otter Hunting for Sport

In Britain the otter is one of several species of mammal that has traditionally been hunted with hounds. Although this may have originated in attempts to control otters it has long been considered a field sport and during the nineteenth and twentieth centuries sport has been the dominant motive for otter hunting.

Otter hunting has not always been considered respectable but some of the earliest records refer to royal hunts including those of King John (thirteenth century), Edward II (fourteenth) and Henry VII (sixteenth) (King *et al.*, 1976). In a booklet describing the history of the Buckinghamshire Otterhounds, it is said that the Buckingham County Museum has a charter by Henry II authorising the establishment of a pack of royal 'otter dogges' and a royal pack of hounds was kept up until Hanoverian times (Ivester-Lloyd, undated). However, otter hunting does not seem to have been regarded as the highest form of sport even then, the early monarchs preferred to hunt more 'noble' quarry such as deer.

Otter hunting first became fashionable in the Elizabethan era and again in the eighteenth century (Howes, 1976) but it was not until the nineteenth century that anything resembling the modern sport was developed and it was probably in the 1880s that the true 'otter hound' first became established as a breed. Originating as a cross between a rough-coated French hound and a blood-hound (Ivester Lloyd, 1978), these large shaggy dogs are noted for their endurance and remarkable scenting abilities (Figure 7.4). Ironically, the decline of the otter and its extinction in parts of England could well lead to the extinction of the hound specifically bred to hunt it, although efforts have been made to

Figure 7.4   Otter hound

maintain the breed for showing.

If the end of the nineteenth century ushered in what might be termed the modern sport of otter hunting, it also ushered out some of the less savoury techniques employed by earlier practitioners. At one time nets were used to entangle otters and dreadful barbed spears used to impale them. Ivester Lloyd believed that 'present day sportsmen would have considered early otter hunting methods unsporting, to put it mildly', and there is no doubt that only during the twentieth century did otter hunting develop into a true field sport.

Finding an otter required considerable skill on the part of the huntsman as well as his hounds. Much of this 'houndwork' could be readily seen because working in the water impeded the progress of the hounds and this was one of the major attractions of the sport. On a typical day's hunting the first task was usually to find the scent of an otter, the hounds searching the banks for the otter's scent trail, known as its 'drag'. Once found, the hounds followed the drag in the hope of catching up with the otter. Much of the skill of the huntsman lay in ensuring that the hounds were not hunting in the wrong direction, away from the otter, and in refinding the trail when it was temporarily lost. Needless to say, on some occasions the trail was permanently lost and the hunt was unable to register a 'find'. About half the drag trails led to an otter, sometimes in its holt or another retreat, sometimes already on the move. If the huntsman thought that the otter was hiding he would try to make it bolt, usually by using terriers but sometimes by digging the animal out.

Once the otter had been put to flight, it was allowed time to get away before the hounds were allowed to follow ('given law'). The hunt proper then ensued with the otter being chased, both in the water and on land, by the hounds with the help of the hunt followers. Despite the apparently overwhelming odds against otters, they frequently escaped and in the period immediately before the otter's decline only about half the otters found were killed.

Although it might seem that the principal aim of an otter hunt is to kill otters, hunt followers also enjoyed watching the skill of the huntsman and his hounds and the excitement of the chase. Nevertheless, the huntsmen were undoubtedly under pressure to demonstrate their skill and effectiveness and this was best shown by a good tally of otters killed during each season. In addition, anticipation of a possible kill added to the excitement of the chase for some people and, up to the mid-1960s, a kill was usually regarded as the most satisfactory conclusion to a day's hunting. Descriptions of hunting, particularly those from the nineteenth century, often describe the chase in great detail and sometimes the actual kill with some relish. On the other hand many people who went hunting did not look forward to the kill but went merely in the hope of seeing an otter.

There is no doubt that all hunt supporters had a positive interest in otters and a measure of respect as well, as the following extract from *Records of the Dartmoor Otter Hounds 1740–1940* by G.R. Mott shows:

The hero of the day was found some way up the Doccombe Brook lying rough, and hounds soon put him to ground in the rocks above. They were taken well away and out of hearing of the terrier during bolting operations and the otter, with ample 'law', made upstream. At the top edge of the wood hounds turned him, and with a chorus that will not readily be forgotten raced him one and a half miles down to the junction, the dense cover enabling their pilot to gain the main river. Instead of making downwards to gain the security of the weirpool, he turned up, and the pace was exceptionally hot as the pack screamed after him. To our astonishment he shortly scaled the precipitous slopes on the right bank and gained the brook, possibly hoping to reach the rocks. This time he had a close shave as he once more joined the river. Again he set his mask upwards, and before long came the only check of the day as he lay down in the bracken. Hounds were glued to him as they hit him off again, and a terrific burst followed up towards Clifford Bridge till they closed in on this 20lb dog otter some 600 yards below the bridge. Time: Two hours twenty-five minutes.

Hunt Records. Many otter hunts kept detailed diaries which are of considerable value, containing a record of hunting success from year to year in different areas as well as information on where otters were found and the weights of otters that were killed. Needless to say, such information is scattered and difficult to collate but a fruitful source has been the *Yearbook of Otterhunting* for the years 1950–66 which was used to establish the date of the otter's decline (see below).

Hunt records were first used as an index of otter populations by a committee which was set up to determine whether or not the otter population of Britain had declined (Hewer, 1969). Information was obtained from a number of interested individuals and organisations but only the otter hunts could provide quantitative data. Using records from 1900, 1937, 1947, 1957 and 1967 it was demonstrated that despite a fairly constant level of hunting success up to 1957, there was a distinct decline between 1957 and 1967 in many areas. The committee concluded that this indicated a decline in otter population over that period but were unable to draw any firm conclusions about the causes of the decline. Five years later a second report covered the hunting seasons for the years 1968 to 1971 (Hewer, 1974). This was less conclusive and some people suggested that data from the hunts were unreliable. It was at about this time that the first detailed surveys of otters were started.

There are three main problems with the interpretation of recent hunting records: (1) changes in hunting practice; (2) selection of hunting areas; (3) a decrease in the frequency of hunting.

1. When it became clear that otter numbers were declining in Britain the hunts progressively decreased the proportion of otters found that they killed until by 1975 only a half-dozen or so were being killed each year, compared with over 200 per year in the mid-1950s (Figure 7.5). This change in technique means that records from the mid-1960s on are not strictly comparable with those from earlier decades.
2. If in one hunt area the otters declined on different rivers at different rates, by concentrating their hunting on the most favourable areas, a hunt could maintain a constant level of success while the otter population declined around it. This need not be done in an effort to deceive but it is

Figure 7.5   Proportion of otters found by otter hounds in Britain that were subsequently killed

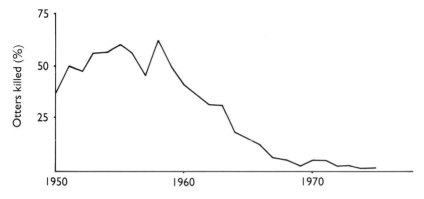

Source: Chanin and Jefferies (1978).

natural that a huntsman would endeavour to give a good season's hunting to his supporters and, by reducing his hunting effort on those rivers with no otters, do so inadvertently.

3. Most hunts spent fewer days hunting in the 1970s than in previous decades. In the 1950s and 1960s the average season consisted of about 50 days hunting but this declined to only 33 days over the period 1970 to 1975 and was only 24 days in 1976. There was also a decrease in the number of hunts from 13 in the mid-1950s to nine in 1972. This gives greater scope for the sort of selectivity mentioned above and also means that small chance fluctuations in hunting success will have a much greater effect on the apparent success rate.

The records were a very valuable source of information on hunting success before and immediately after the decline. They alerted people to the fact that a decline had taken place and later helped to ascertain the cause (see below). However, as the 1960s progressed their value as indicators of changes in otter populations was much reduced.

Otter Hunts and Conservation. The contrast between the hunter's desire to kill otters and their evident respect for the animal was mentioned earlier. Another apparent contradiction is that on the one hand the hunts considered that they carried out the function of controlling otters and on the other, they regarded themselves as conservers and preservers of the animal.

In fact, it is unlikely that the hunters regulated the numbers of their prey, at least during the twentieth century. Following the reduction in pressure from keepering the otter population seems to have increased until it was limited by the amount of suitable habitat available. Indeed one might suggest that the otters limited the number of hunts since, as the otter population declined, some of the hunts died out because there was insufficient 'prey' for them.

On the other hand, there is probably some truth in the assertion that the hunts helped to ensure that populations of otters did not fall too low, at least in the nineteenth century. Unlike the polecat, pine marten and wild cat which were persecuted to extinction in many areas, the otter survived, despite the fact that it was regarded by many as vermin. Just as some farmers will tolerate the presence of a few foxes on their farm in order to have the pleasure of hunting them, I am sure that the otter hunts were able to persuade some landowners and river keepers to leave the 'control' of otters to the hunters rather than deal with it themselves. During the 1960s and 1970s the hunts also took positive steps to reduce the number of otters killed when they realised that there had been a serious decline in numbers.

It is clear that the hunts took a responsible attitude towards the exploitation of otters and also co-operated with scientists in providing information about their hunting success. In view of this, it is unfortunate that during the late 1970s there should have been some disagreement between the hunts and other people concerned with otter conservation. Although both groups had the same aim disagreement was almost inevitable when people concerned with animal welfare took up the cause of otter conservation. This resulted in the hunts feeling that conserving the otter meant banning otter hunting. It is even possible that the support of the anti-hunting fraternity handicapped efforts to achieve legislative protection for the otter by uniting the field sports supporters.

Legally protecting the otter made it almost inevitable that otter hunting would have to cease, at least in England and Wales. For many this was a sad end to a tradition stretching back through the centuries. The hunts accepted the state of affairs and did not, as some feared, turn to hunting previously undisturbed otters in Scotland. A number of hunts disbanded but others reorganised themselves as mink hunts and these continue to meet on some of the rivers they once hunted for otters.

THE DECLINE OF THE EURASIAN OTTER

The overexploitation of sea otters led to the decline and near extinction of this species but the decline of the Eurasian otter, although due to man, was not the result of his desire for otter fur or to protect stocks of fish. Although the Eurasian otter still has the widest distribution of all otters and occurs throughout Europe, it has declined substantially in many countries during this century and in some countries only vestigial populations remain.

In Britain, thanks to the meticulous records kept by the otter hunts, it has been possible to follow the course of the decline and to pinpoint some of the factors involved. Elsewhere in Europe detailed information is only available from those countries where government licensing organisations keep records of the game killed by sportsmen and hunters. Nevertheless in most European countries there is clear evidence that a decline has occurred — otters are no longer to be found in areas they previously inhabited — but the timing of these declines and the underlying causes are less clear.

The Otter in Britain

Not surprisingly, it was the otter hunters who first noticed a decline in otter numbers in Britain and the first public statement of their concern was made in an article entitled 'Where are the otters?' by Ivester Lloyd (1962). The analysis of hunting records published a few years later showed that a decline had indeed occurred between 1957 and 1967 but because the records between these dates were not examined it was not possible to determine the cause. When in 1977 the 'Joint Otter Group' published a report on the otter in Britain no further information was available and the report listed ten pressures on otters which might have been the cause of the decline. These were: disturbance by humans; hunting; riparian clearance; pollution; disease; road casualties; severe winters; the increasing mink population; the impact of fisheries; killing for pelts.

In the same year, I obtained a number of copies of the *Yearbook of Otterhunting* from two people interested in otter hunting. Neither had a complete set but, when I looked at the two collections, I found that between them I had all the copies from 1950 to 1966. In addition, details for the years 1967 to 1971 were available (Hewer, 1974) giving a total of 21 years of complete records for all the hunts. I was also lent a copy of *Records of the Culmstock Otterhounds* (Pring, 1958) which included records for that hunt from 1907 to 1957. An analysis of these clarified our understanding of the decline and showed which factors were most likely to be important (Chanin and Jefferies, 1978).

The number of days spent hunting by packs of hounds varied from place to place and year to year, so hunting success was calculated as the number of finds per hundred days hunting. This can conveniently be described as percentage success and is determined by dividing the number of finds by the number of days spent hunting and multiplying by one hundred.

Figure 7.6 illustrates the typical fluctuations in hunting success for two

Figure 7.6   The hunting success of the Dartmoor and Culmstock Otterhounds before the otter population declined

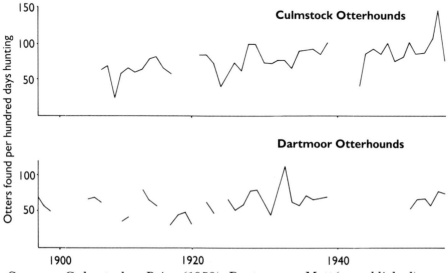

Sources: Culmstock — Pring (1958); Dartmoor — Mott (unpublished).

hunts in south-west England over the period 1897 to 1956. The data for the Culmstock Hunt are more complete and show a significant correlation between the date and the hunting success. Although there is considerable variation from year to year, there is an underlying trend over the 50-year period. During this time the average hunting success was 76 per cent but there was a tendency for it to increase. The results for the Dartmoor Hunt are more fragmentary and do not show a significant increase but they do show that the hunting success varied in a similar way although the average was slightly lower at 62 per cent.

It is easy to see from these graphs that the hunting success varied a great deal from year to year and no one would seriously suggest that this indicates changes in otter populations. It does, however, highlight the problems which arise when figures from only a few isolated years are available. Sometimes it is possible to explain particularly extreme values. For example, the two lowest points on the graph for the Culmstock Otterhounds are from years when the weather was extremely bad, a long drought in the first case and floods in the second. The very low figure for the same hunt in 1946 is probably because there was very little hunting during the war and in the first season afterwards the hounds (as well as the huntsmen) were out of practice. On the other hand it is noticeable that after a poor year (or even a run of poor years such as 1917 to 1920 for the Dartmoor Otterhounds) the success rate soon climbs back to the average or above.

This is in stark contrast to the situation from 1957 onwards, when the success rate dropped more or less simultaneously in the seven hunts operating in southern Britain and had not returned to previous levels 14 years later. The rapidity and extent of the decline varied somewhat; worst hit was the Pembroke and Carmarthen Otterhounds which averaged 78 per cent from 1950 to 1955 and only 23 per cent from 1966 to 1971. The Culmstock fared rather better but it is remarkable that in each of the hunt areas the decline started at about the same time — in 1957 or 1958 (Figure 7.7).

Four hunts were also active in northern Britain during the 1950s and 1960s where the decline was much less clear cut. In fact the Border Counties Otterhounds in north Wales were as successful at the end of the period as they were at the beginning.

The Cause of the Initial Decline. These figures indicate that whatever caused the decline must have occurred more or less simultaneously throughout southern Britain but not have affected the north so severely. After considering all the factors which might have caused the decline, we concluded that the one which fitted the pattern best was pollution and in particular the use of pesticides belonging to the organochlorine group (similar to DDT). Dieldrin and related products such as aldrin, endrin and heptachlor were introduced in 1955 for a wide range of uses including sheep dipping, seed dressing and mothproofing. In 1956 populations of peregrine falcons and sparrowhawks suddenly began to decrease and within a few years, huge numbers of dead seed-eating birds were found in areas which had recently been sown with grain dressed with these compounds. Dead birds of prey of many species were also found and when analysed their bodies were shown to contain very high

Figure 7.7   Hunting success of six of the packs of otter hounds in southern Britain during the otter's decline

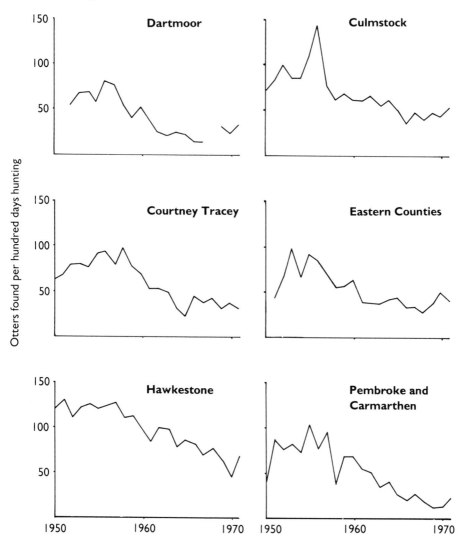

Source: Chanin and Jefferies (1978).

doses of the pesticides. The bodies of many foxes and badgers were also found and many of these contained high concentrations of pesticides. Much of this mortality was attributed to the use of dieldrin and its relatives. The seed-eating birds died from eating the grain and the predators died because they ate poisoned prey.

Some of these chemicals are very persistent as well as highly toxic and they take a very long time to break down. They can be washed through the soil into streams and rivers where they are picked up by plankton and invertebrates before being passed along the food chain through fish to otters and other fish-eating predators. Of 31 dead otters examined and analysed between 1963 and 1973, 25 had measurable quantities of dieldrin in their bodies.

The effects of these pesticides are of two kinds — lethal, causing rapid death, and sub-lethal where the dose is insufficient to kill the animal but can have serious effects on its physiology. In particular it has been shown that some pesticides can affect the breeding ability of many species. Although we do not know which was most important, both lethal and sub-lethal poisoning probably played their part in the otter's downfall. It seems very likely that, as with foxes, badgers and birds of prey, a certain number of otters were killed outright although there is no way of knowing whether this had a significant effect on the population levels. However, a reduction in the breeding rate would not only make it more difficult for the population to recover but could also, over a period of years, lead to a continuing decline in the population as otters dying, from natural or unnatural causes, were not replaced. A few dead otters were found at the time but the earliest post-mortems were not carried out until 1963 and the cause of death of otters found before then were not determined. Hunters reported that otters seemed to have ceased to breed during the late 1950s and early 1960s although they may have started again by 1969 (Cranbrook, 1977).

As the decline started 20 years before the information leading to its elucidation was gathered together it is impossible to prove that dieldrin was responsible although the evidence is very convincing. The use of dieldrin as a seed dressing for spring sown cereals was stopped by voluntary agreement in 1962, and most other uses ceased in 1965 and 1966. By the 1970s dieldrin was only used as a dressing for autumn and winter sown cereals and in the woollen industry for mothproofing so the amounts finding their way into the streams were considerably less than in the ten years following its introduction. In a recent survey Hider *et al.* (1982) collected over 500 fish for analysis throughout Britain and could only detect dieldrin in 19 of them, of which only nine had quantities high enough for concern. One would expect therefore that, like the peregrine, the otter should be making a comeback and returning to its original population levels but it is not doing so. Why?

Otter Surveys. In order to answer that question, we first need to ask what happened to the otter population after the initial decline. The position up to the mid-1960s is clear enough but for reasons outlined above, the hunting records are more difficult to interpret after the decline because of changes in hunting intensity and practice so other methods had to be used to monitor the otter population. The method chosen was a series of surveys, carried out first with the aid of volunteers and later by full-time trained surveyors.

The first large-scale survey was carried out by volunteers and although it did not achieve a complete or even a uniform coverage of the country, it did indicate that in some areas, particularly in central England, signs of otters were very hard to find. An intensive local survey carried out in Norfolk in 1974/5 showed how serious the situation had become in that county (Macdonald and Mason, 1976). They visited a total of 233 sites and found signs of otters at only 32 of these, from which they estimated that the population of otters in the county was only 17 pairs. They also calculated that the carrying capacity of the rivers they surveyed was between 52 and 77 pairs. Although some people had doubts about the basis on which the actual and potential number of otters in the county were calculated, the study showed unambiguously that the otter population in Norfolk had undergone a severe decline.

Following these preliminary reports, four large-scale national surveys were carried out in the British Isles between 1977 and 1981 using full-time researchers. In each survey a series of sites was selected along rivers and streams, spaced between 5 km and 8 km apart. At each site up to 600 m of bank was searched and the presence or absence of otter signs recorded together with information on the type of river and its surrounds. Scotland and Wales were almost completely covered but in England and Ireland sample surveys were carried out. The surveyors divided each country into a checkerboard of 50 km squares and carried out surveys in alternate squares, looking at about 100 sites in each. Although the fact that no signs of otters are found at one site does not necessarily mean that no otters ever go there, by searching large numbers of sites one can get a good impression of the overall abundance of otters in an area.

Table 7.6   Otter surveys in Britain and Ireland. A summary of the searching effort and the results

Area	No. of surveyors	Date	Sites visited	Sites positive (%)
Wales	3	1977−8	1,030	20
England	1	1977−9	2,940	6
Scotland	2	1977−9	4,636	73
Ireland	2	1980−1	2,323	92

Note: Positive sites are those at which signs of otters were found.

Sources: Wales, Crawford et al. (1979); England, Lenton et al. (1980); Scotland, Green and Green (1980); Ireland, Chapman and Chapman (1982).

Table 7.6 shows how serious the decline had become in England, particularly in comparison with Ireland where signs of otters were found practically everywhere the surveyors looked. There is evidently a general relationship between high human populations and low otter densities which is also borne out by Figure 7.8 where the regional differences in mainland Britain are illustrated. Notice that it is in the heavily populated and industrialised areas of Scotland and Wales that otters are scarce and in England the only area where signs were reasonably common was the South-West. Apart from the Welsh border, north Norfolk and parts of Northumberland, otters seem to be very scarce or absent throughout England and in the central part of the country they are probably extinct.

Returning now to the situation in England in the 1960s, the hunt records show that although there had been substantial declines, otters

Figure 7.8   Results of otter surveys in mainland Britain between 1977 and 1978. Note that in England only half of the 50 km × 50 km squares were surveyed

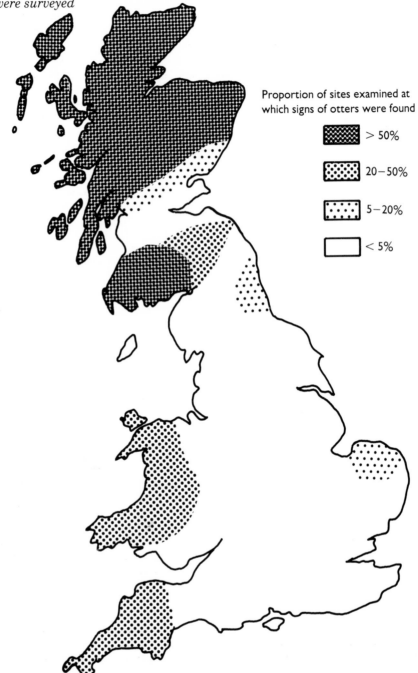

Proportion of sites examined at
which signs of otters were found

> 50%

20–50%

5–20%

< 5%

Sources: England — Lenton, Chanin and Jefferies (1980); Scotland — Green and Green (1980); Wales — Crawford et al. (1979).

were still being found in all the hunt areas, albeit in reduced numbers. For example, the Buckinghamshire Otterhounds covered an area which now seems to be devoid of otters and yet between 1962 and 1965 they found about 15 otters per year (28 per cent) and even from 1968 to 1971 they were still able to find an average of four otters per year (21 per cent). In other words, by the time controls on the use of dieldrin were introduced the population had not been wiped out but it was much reduced. The Dartmoor Otterhounds and the Pembroke and Carmarthen Otterhounds on the other hand suffered the most severe declines in hunting success (reduced by 63 per cent and 77 per cent respectively) and yet at the end of the 1970s the otter populations in these areas seemed to be thriving.

This indicates that although there was a widespread decline in numbers of otters throughout much of England and Wales in the 1950s and 1960s, following the reductions in the use of dieldrin and related pesticides, otter populations began to recover in some areas (Wales and the South-West) but continued to decline elsewhere. There are three possible reasons for this:

1. The populations were so low and fragmented after the initial decline that in some areas they were below the level at which a recovery could have taken place. Perhaps because males and females did not encounter each other sufficiently frequently to ensure that breeding occurred.
2. Despite the controls on the use of dieldrin and allied compounds, levels in the aquatic environment remained sufficiently high to continue to affect otters, perhaps by reducing the breeding potential.
3. Further environmental changes came about which led to additional pressures on the otter thereby preventing a recovery.

These possibilities are not mutually exclusive but finding direct evidence for any of them is likely to be difficult if not impossible. The first suggestion seems rather unlikely since one would expect the populations in south-west England and Wales to have continued to decline as they were worst hit by the initial decline.

Similar arguments might be applied in the case of the second explanation although there are factors which lend support to it. In both Wales and south-west England the main use of dieldrin is likely to have been in sheep dipping rather than seed dressing and it is possible that in central England the level of pesticide in the environment did not decline as quickly because of the continued application of winter dressed cereals. In addition, there is evidence of continuing pollution by pesticides in some areas. An otter that recently died in Norfolk was found to have high concentrations of pesticides of several types in its tissues although the origins are unknown. In an unfortunate incident in Devon, a bulldozer inadvertently broke into a dump of dieldrin and caused considerable leakage. Despite efforts by the Water Authority to minimise the damage, significant levels of dieldrin were subsequently found in fish and also in otter spraints collected downstream (E.M. Andrews, pers. comm.).

Further Pressures on Otters. Another factor causing concern is pollution by heavy metals, particularly mercury, cadmium and lead. In a survey of heavy metals in fish collected throughout Britain, Mason *et al.* (1982) found disturbingly high concentrations of these elements in many specimens. At the majority of sites, levels of mercury and lead were sufficiently high to put the health of otters at risk. They pointed out that lead and cadmium in combination can cause inhibition of sperm production in mammals which could presumably lead to sterility. Fish from 13 per cent of the sites had both these metals at unacceptably high concentrations.

Other environmental changes that have occurred include the spread of feral mink, increases in the recreational use of waterways and the clearance of river banks by waterway engineers.

The relationship between mink and otters was discussed in detail in Chapter 4. It is a curious coincidence that mink first began to breed in the wild in Britain at exactly the same time as the otter began to decline in numbers and hardly surprising perhaps that the two facts have been linked. All the same, it is quite clear that mink have not driven otters from their ancestral haunts for mink are only now spreading into some of the areas in central and eastern England where otters are most scarce and in the South-West, where mink have been established the longest, otters are still flourishing.

Over the last 30 years the number of people taking part in recreational activities on or beside water has increased enormously and there is no question that disturbance to the otter's habitat has been immense. What is less clear is how much effect this has had on the otters. In a recent study of factors correlated with the distribution of otters in Wales, Macdonald and Mason (1983a) used three indices of human disturbance to the stretches of river they investigated: the numbers of fishermen, population density in adjacent parishes and the density of campsites. None of these was significantly correlated with the density of otter signs. Macdonald (1983) has also pointed out that otter holts have been recorded in towns and that in Shetland one female otter reared cubs in a holt under a breakwater despite the fact that it was used three times daily by ferries. Macdonald had also found that otters on the west coast of Scotland were not prevented from hunting by disturbance from fishermen and tourists. She suggested that the importance of human disturbance had been exaggerated and that although otters are somewhat retiring, providing they can find a secure retreat during the day time, a certain amount of disturbance can be tolerated.

Further evidence for this was obtained by Green *et al.* (1984) particularly for a male which was observed travelling through a town in daylight and often slipped past fishermen and bankside walkers without being seen. They also found that otters avoided dogs and reacted adversely to their presence even when the dogs had not noticed them.

Of the 15 factors investigated by Macdonald and Mason, only three were significantly associated with the density of otter signs and they were the number of potential holt sites, the number of mature ash trees (*Fraxinus excelsior*) and the number of mature sycamore trees (*Acer pseudoplatanus*). In an earlier study on the River Teme, Macdonald *et al.* (1978) also concluded that ash and sycamore trees were important to otters since 18 of the 22 potential holts they found were under the roots of these two species, which between them formed only 10 per cent of the total number of mature trees. This suggests that in these areas at least the density of otters may be affected by the number of potential dens and that elsewhere den site availability may be an important factor in determining the suitability of habitat for otters. In a survey of otter dens throughout Wales, ash and sycamore trees were the most important sites and 38 per cent of dens were in the roots of these two species (Coghill, pers. comm.). The reason for this seems to be that both have shallow spreading root systems which make ideal roofs for otter holts.

Macdonald and Mason also pointed out that modern management of rivers is almost always to the detriment of such features. Mature trees, particularly those with spreading roots, leaning trunks and overhanging branches are frequently removed by river managers in case they fall into the river causing flooding and damage to bridges or other structures. Intensive management had taken place on many of the stretches of river searched by Macdonald and Mason, the worst excesses being recorded on a section of the River Severn where only three mature trees remained in the 5 km of bank surveyed. If, as seems likely, the availability of breeding sites is reduced by such management, the impact on the otter population may be imagined.

Sycamore and ash trees are not the only sites of actual or potential otter holts but many sites are likely to be removed during bank clearance and tidying up. Coghill's data are particularly revealing; he found that all the tree holts were within 10 m of the water's edge and three-quarters of them were in the roots of trees that leaned over the water — these would be particularly vulnerable to the engineers.

The extent of river management work in Britain is not recorded, at least in ecological terms, and although it is clear that a substantial amount of river 'improvement' has taken place in the last 15 years or so there is little chance of proving that this has caused the demise of the otter in so many counties. On balance, however, it would seem at the very least to be one of the most significant factors responsible.

Summary. The otter population of Britain has undergone a substantial decline over the last 30 years, particularly in England. An initial decline, probably caused by the use of toxic chemicals was followed in some areas by a partial recovery but throughout most of lowland Britain the population continued (and perhaps continues) to decline. Otters are already extinct in several counties in central England and very close to extinction in the South-East, much of East Anglia and parts of northern England. Although the populations in Scotland, Wales and the South-West seem reasonably secure, those in Norfolk and the extreme north of England are very vulnerable. There is little doubt that man is as responsible for the decline of otters in Britain, albeit inadvertently, as he was for the near extermination of the sea otter in the Pacific Ocean.

Western Europe

Elsewhere in Europe the status of otters varies as widely as in Britain although it seems unlikely that any country has a population as abundant and ubiquitous as Ireland. The information available is much less complete than for the British Isles and more difficult to summarise, not least because in some countries estimates are based on anecdotal evidence. Field surveys have been carried out in a few countries, particularly around the Mediterreanean by workers from the Vincent Wildlife Trust, and there is also information from game bag records, particularly from Scandinavia.

In order to try and summarise the data I have used four categories corresponding approximately to the situations of otters in England, Wales, Scotland and Ireland (Table 7.7). Apart from the results of field surveys and those based on game bag records (Norway, Denmark and Sweden), the information I have used is taken from a review of the status of otters in Europe undertaken by von Müffling (1977).

The overall impression is that, as in Britain, the population of otters is lowest in central areas and highest at the periphery. This is partly coincidental but Ireland, Scotland, Finland, Greece and Portugal do have in common a fairly low population density and a non-intensive farming industry.

The actual causes of these declines are as difficult to pin down as those in Britain, particularly as there is only information on the timing of the decline in those countries where game records are kept. Erlinge (1972a) suggested that in Sweden pollution of waterways was to blame but, rather than pesticides, he concluded that heavy metals were responsible. Green and Green (1981) and Elliot (1983) suggested that pollution may restrict the otter populations of France and Spain but were unable to determine what pollutants might be involved. In reports from Portugal and Greece, Macdonald and Mason (1982a, 1982b) emphasised that although otters have not seriously declined there yet, there is at least a potential threat from pesticides. Greece has recently joined the European Economic Community and Portugal has expressed interest in doing the same which could result in a substantial increase in the use of pesticides in order to increase farm productivity. In southern Italy, Macdonald and Mason (1983b) concluded that the outlook for otters was bleak since in addition to pollution and the removal of bankside vegetation the rivers suffer considerable disturbance from fishing, hunting and gravel extraction.

In the Netherlands excessive hunting and trapping probably caused the near extinction of otters by 1940. The population was then completely protected and partially recovered but other pressures such as pollution, land reclamation and fishermen's bownets now assume a greater importance in limiting the population (von Wijngaarden and van de Peppel, 1970). Fishing traps of various types have been considered to be a substantial cause of otter mortality elsewhere (see Chapter 6), especially in Germany, Sweden and Denmark although their overall importance is difficult to establish. Erlinge (1972a) considered that the use of bownets was a major factor in the decline of otters in his study area in southern Sweden. After fishermen began to leave them out through the whole winter instead of removing them as previously, several otters drowned, a whole family group on one occasion. Hodl-Rohn (1976) concluded that although fish traps were not the principal cause of the otters' decline in West Germany, the introduction of synthetic material in making the traps meant that otters were no longer able to escape from them and many were drowned.

Table 7.7 The status of the Eurasian otter in Europe

I. Otters extinct or very scarce over the greater part of the country

England	(6%)	Lenton et al. (1980)
France	(15%)	Green and Green (1981)
Italy	(8.5%)	Macdonald and Mason (1983b)
The Netherlands		van Wijngaarden and van de Peppel (1970)
Switzerland		von Müffling (1977)
West Germany		Hodl-Rohn (1976)
East Germany		Stubbe (1980)
Austria		von Müffling (1977)

II. Substantial declines but otters still abundant in some areas and present over most of the country

Wales	(20%)	Crawford et al. (1979)
Spain	(40%)	Elliott (1983)
Yugoslavia	(44%)	Liles and Jenkins (1984)
Denmark		Strandgaard and Asferg (1980)
Sweden		Erlinge (1972a)
Norway		Heggberget and Myrberget (1979)

III. Declines in some parts of the country only

Scotland	(73%)	Green and Green (1980)
Portugal	(70%)	Macdonald and Mason (1982a)
Greece	(62%)	Macdonald and Mason (1982b)

IV. Population abundant throughout the country

Ireland	(92%)	Chapman and Chapman (1982)

Notes: Where systematic surveys have been carried out the results are given (in parentheses) as a percentage of the total sites visited where signs were found.

Russia and Eastern Europe

Although von Müffling included reports from most East European countries except the USSR, they are very difficult to interpret and it seems that little systematic research has been carried out. It would appear that otter populations have declined in several countries but nowhere as badly as in the worst-hit countries in the West.

Some information on otters in Russia is available from a paper describing the status of otters in the Amur-Ussuri region on the eastern coast of Russia, to the north and east of the Chinese border (Kucherenko, 1976). Between 1945 and 1965 the number of otter skins bought by the state fur purveyors varied between 1,200 and 2,200 per year and averaged about a fifth of the total catch in Russia. From 1966, however, there was a catastrophic decrease until in 1972 only 170 skins were bought. The decline was attributed to 'anthropogenic factors' which simply means that, as in the West, man was directly or indirectly responsible. It is possible that the decrease in skins did not exactly reflect the decline in the number of otters since the author estimated that the actual population decreased to about a quarter of its original level. A substantial decline none the less. Detailed figures for other parts of Russia are not given but since the otters from the Amur-Ussuri region formed the same percentage of the total before and after 1966 it seems probable that otters declined in other parts of Russia also.

CONSERVATION OF OTTERS

In the 1970s and 1980s, conservation became an issue of significant international importance. Practically all nations pay at least lip service to the notion of conservation of their native fauna and flora and the majority make genuine efforts to prevent the destruction of wildlife, sometimes at the expense of development. Despite the fact that the political will exists to protect otters and to prevent or reverse declines in their populations, the number of cases where this has actually happened is very small indeed. In Europe, for example, otter populations continue to decline despite the fact that they have been protected in most countries for many years. Only in the Netherlands did the otter population recover after legal protection and even there the future prospects are not as good as they may have seemed ten years ago. In most cases the problem for conservationists is not whether to protect otters, but how to do so.

Usually there are four main methods available to conservationists: legislation, habitat protection and improvement, education and captive breeding. These are by no means mutually exclusive but the most effective combination will vary according to the circumstances.

Legislation

As pointed out earlier, the first legislation involving otters was concerned more with their destruction than their preservation and usually involved the payments of bounty on otters that had been killed. During the twentieth century most protective legislation was introduced as an integral part of game laws by countries which recognised the otter as a resource to be exploited and included it among those animals whose hunting was regulated. By introducing quotas and closed seasons these countries tried to manage otter populations in such a way as to sustain the yield of furs. They did not always succeed, but this was due more to extraneous changes in otter habitat than to the greed of the hunters. Ultimately most of the European countries found that despite their efforts otter populations continued to decline and they therefore extended the closed seasons right through the year to give total protection to otters.

OTTERS AND MAN

The protection of sea otters comes into a different category since by the time it was protected, exploitation had far exceeded anything that could conceivably be regarded as rational. In 1911 the governments of the United States, Great Britain, Russia and Japan signed the Fur Seal Treaty which included in its provisions an agreement to cease hunting sea otters. This was followed on 31 May 1913 by the signing of a 'Presidential Proclamation for the Preservation and Protection of Fur Seals and Sea Otters' by President Woodrow Wilson which enshrined the treaty in United States' law. For the first 50 years or so, this resulted in the complete cessation of hunting sea otters by the Americans although it has been suggested that the Japanese were less rigid in their adherence to the treaty. Confiscations by the United States government also indicate that some poaching took place on the east side of the Pacific. It was not until the 1960s that further organised killing of sea otters took place when a small experimental cull was carried out between 1962 and 1967 and 1,000 sea otters were killed. The skins were sold by the state of Alaska and the bodies used for research. During the late 1970s the states of Alaska and California sought permission to carry out further culls of sea otters, in Alaska because the population was thought to be large enough to withstand an annual cull and still continue its slow expansion and in California because of apparent conflict between sea otters and shell fisheries.

Britain has been extremely tardy in introducing legislation to protect mammals, whether hunted or not. Comprehensive bird protection was enacted in 1930 and many species of birds were given some form of legal protection in the nineteenth century. Until the Conservation of Wild Creatures and Wild Plants Act of 1975 only piecemeal legislation to protect deer, seals and badgers amongst the mammals had reached the statute books.

To some extent the hunting fraternity was self-regulatory and seems to have been able to ensure that most beasts of the chase were not overhunted. For example the closed seasons for species such as fox and deer are designed to prevent disturbance during the breeding season, a luxury not available to the otter with its non-seasonal breeding. The otter's respite was during the winter when inclement weather forced a halt to hunting. Needless to say, trapping and shooting took place at any time of year.

Although at first the 1975 Act only gave protection to bats amongst the mammals, many people felt that the otter should have been added to the list. A vigorous 'Save the Otter' campaign was mounted by Friends of the Earth with this as a principal objective (King et al., 1976). In 1976 the Joint Otter Group was set up by the government conservation agency, the Nature Conservancy Council, to consider the evidence on the status of otters in Britain and to recommend any conservation measures it thought necessary. The group concluded that the evidence pointed to a substantial and continuing decline in England and that some form of legal protection was desirable. In their report, O'Connor et al. (1977) pointed out that although they believed that the otter ought to be legally protected in England and Wales, the wording of the 1975 Act meant that it could not be added to the schedule of protected species until it had become so rare throughout Britain that its extinction was imminent. So long as a

161

substantial population remained in Scotland it seemed that otters in England and Wales could not be protected. Eventually the law was clarified and the Nature Conservancy Council recommended to the government that the otter should be added to the list. From 1 January 1978 it became illegal to catch or kill an otter or to attempt to do so in England and Wales.

The problems that were exposed by this confusion added to the dissatisfaction with this law and in 1982 it was replaced with the Wildlife and Countryside Act which not only confirmed the protection of otters in England but extended it to Scotland as well. In addition this act made provisions for the protection of habitats and made it an offence to disturb or destroy the dens of protected animals.

Where otters have been killed in substantial numbers by hunters and trappers, the benefits of legal protection are obvious but in Britain where by 1975 only a handful of otters were being killed each year by the hunts the advantages were not so clear. Although many people were in favour of legal protection there were a great many others who were not. Some of these were field sportsmen who felt that protecting the otter was intended to be an anti-hunting measure rather than a means of conserving otters, but there was also a strong feeling in the minds of many people that preventing the killing of otters was a cosmetic measure. The real threats to otters were habitat destruction, disturbance and pollution, none of which would be reduced by the legal protection of the otter. They also argued that once the otter was protected people would feel that nothing more would need to be done.

While it is true that legal protection alone could not 'save' the otter, these arguments overlook some important benefits of legislation. The controversy generated over otters in 1976 and 1977 brought the plight of the animal to the public's attention, and the fact that it was finally added to the schedule of protected species underlined the need for something to be done. This helped to arouse a great deal of public sympathy for otters which makes the task of conservation organisations a great deal easier when they try to conserve or improve otter habitat. When dealing with landowners or Water Authority engineers they have a powerful argument in their favour if they can show that certain types of management are harmful to the otter, a protected species. In addition, the Nature Conservancy Council has a special responsibility towards species which are protected including encouraging research into their ecology and monitoring their status and distribution. All these factors taken together mean that adding the otter to the protected list did far more good than simply to make catching and killing them illegal.

Habitat Protection and Improvement

While legal protection may be a useful, rather than essential, step towards the conservation of otters, far more important in many countries is the need to conserve and if possible increase suitable habitat. This problem is particularly acute in western Europe but it is not confined to that part of the world. In many developing nations the efforts being made to open up previously inaccessible areas for forestry, agriculture, and so on may seriously reduce otter habitat. In South America, for example, although hunting has been one of the main threats to otters, enormous hydro-electric schemes have been devised by a number of countries and these may have a drastic effect on the suitability of many rivers for otters.

On some continents it is possible, if the political will exists, to set aside large areas as National Parks or Reserves which may form substantial refuges for wildlife. The size of these can be difficult to comprehend in Britain, for example the Kafue National Park in Zambia is roughly the size of Wales. In Europe the high density of people in most countries makes it very difficult to find areas large enough to designate solely as nature reserves on that scale. In Britain, National Parks may be very large but they were established more for their landscape and amenity value than for wildlife conservation so farming, building and the extraction of minerals can take place in them. In addition most of them have been established in upland areas where the land has a lower agricultural value and, therefore, they contain little habitat of value to otters.

Nature reserves on the other hand are managed with conservation as a principal objective but they are usually small in relation to the size of an otter's home range. They may perform a useful function in providing a secure refuge for otters but unless the habitat outside the reserve is reasonably suitable, such an oasis has very little real value to the otter.

Since total protection of enough suitable habitat to ensure the survival of a viable population of otters is not practical in many parts of Britain the idea of creating havens for otters has been developed. This involves the protection of a number of small areas of suitable habitat spread throughout the ranges of several otters in areas where their habitat is threatened. Instead of setting up formal nature reserves voluntary agreements are made by riparian owners in consultation with Water Authority engineers to manage short stretches of waterway in sympathy with the otter's requirements. Nature reserves can be incorporated into such a scheme and may form useful nuclei near which other havens can be established but it is unnecessary to set up nature reserves specifically for otters.

Where landowners express an interest, advice is given and, if appropriate, the land designated as a haven. This has no legal force but the informal recognition of their interest is welcomed by many landowners.

In Norfolk, the Otter Trust has designated over 300 km of waterway as otter havens although about a quarter of this receives only partial protection. In other parts of Britain the Otter Haven Project of the Vincent Wildlife Trust has been setting up havens, working closely with local naturalists and conservation organisations. The policy of the Vincent Wildlife Trust is to concentrate on the better otter rivers since sparse or isolated groups of otters may not survive. This means that work is concentrated in Wales, the South-West and northern England. Populations in Scotland are at the moment considered sufficiently secure to be left while more urgent work is done in the south. An important aspect of the work is giving advice to riparian owners on management practices which are beneficial or at least not harmful to otters and liaising with Water Authority engineers over major improvement schemes. Advice may be given on which species of trees or shrubs to plant, which trees should not be cut down because they cover otter dens and where management will have little impact on the needs of the otter.

Practical management is also carried out by staff, often with the help of volunteers. This may involve the planting of trees and shrubs, fencing of banks to prevent grazing by cattle and sheep and the design and building of otter dens and resting places. In early experiments, artificial materials such as drain pipes leading to stone or brick built chambers were used, in the same way that the hunts did in the past. These have given way to an emphasis on natural materials such as heaps of rocks or tree roots and stumps as well as the stabilisation of naturally occurring stick piles.

It will be many years before the efficacy of these measures can be determined although efforts are being made to monitor the use of havens by otters. In the meantime, in Britain at least, they do seem to be the most effective method of assisting otters in those areas in which they still occur.

Education

Educating landowners, public authorities, industries and the general public is probably the most important task in conservation today. The otter is a prime example of a species which can only effectively be conserved by increasing people's awareness of its needs. No matter how many laws there are nor how many nature reserves, the otter will continue to decline unless the degradation of its habitat on a large scale can be halted or reversed. The only practical way to do that is to inform people of the consequences of their actions and persuade them to do something different.

Much of the work of the Otter Haven Project is educational, and they try particularly to influence those people who have the greatest impact on riparian habitats — landowners and waterway engineers. Sometimes persuasion is needed, perhaps to spend a little more money in order to carry out an operation in a way that is less harmful to otters. At other times it is necessary to show that there are other, and sometimes cheaper, methods of achieving their aims that are less damaging to the environment. For example, engineers are now beginning to realise that cutting down trees is not the answer to most of their drainage problems, and that sometimes it can cost more than leaving the trees in place. The shade cast by trees reduces the rate at which water weeds grow and once the trees are removed growth speeds up. The resulting excessive growth can lead to floods during summer storms and the usual cure is to carry out more frequent weed cutting or to use expensive herbicides.

In 1972 £2.5 million was spent on herbicides by Water Authorities, Drainage Boards and farmers (King and Potter, 1980). It has been calculated that it costs £25/km to treat a dyke with herbicides in comparison with £8–£15/km for mechanical methods and £33 by hand. Some authorities have applied herbicides three or four times per year and on occasions at double or triple the recommended dose (Newbold, 1975). No wonder that a study in the Netherlands showed that tree-lined streams cost half as much to maintain as those devoid of trees.

Trees have other useful functions. For example the roots of some species, particularly alder (*Alnus glutinosa*), can be very effective in stabilising banks against erosion and trees also provide a fruitful source of food. A substantial proportion of the food available to fish consists of invertebrates that have fallen into streams from bankside trees. Mason and Macdonald (1982) concluded that in some places the input of terrestrial invertebrates was as much as or greater than the production of bottom-living invertebrates in the stream. They also pointed out that most of the input occurred earlier in the year than the peak production within the stream and that at certain times more than 90 per cent of the diet of salmonids consisted of terrestrial species.

The Vincent Wildlife Trust has also emphasised that a simple and relatively inexpensive way to encourage the growth of bankside trees is to fence the river bank. In areas where the stocking density of cattle is high, regeneration of trees is prevented by grazing but the exclusion of stock by fencing can lead to a dense growth of herbs and shrubs as well as young trees, all of which benefit the otter.

Education is also important in the developing world. It may be more effective than ineffectual legislation at preventing Brazilian Indians from shooting giant otters, Chilean labourers from trapping river otters or Peruvian fishermen from destroying the sea cat. The problem in these countries is to find a way to get the message across, particularly when preventing the destruction of otters has an impact on the livelihood of the individuals concerned.

Captive Breeding

Many people maintain that the breeding of endangered species in captivity is an important aspect of conservation with the ultimate aim of supplementing diminished wild populations or re-introducing those that have become extinct. So far only a very small number of species have been returned to a truly wild state in sufficient numbers to re-establish a viable population, for example, the Hawaiian goose or ne-ne and the European bison.

Despite these examples it is too early to be sure that captive breeding will be a conservation tool of major significance. It is probably best considered as a stop-gap measure which may be used to preserve a species until the factors causing its decline have been determined and eliminated. Usually it is preferable to do this before the population becomes critically low.

In recent years it has become clear that it is possible to breed regularly some species of otter in captivity. In Britain, a collection of Eurasian otters maintained by the Otter Trust reared 30 cubs to independence between 1976 and 1981. Fifteen Asian small-clawed otter cubs have also been raised. American river otters have frequently bred in captivity but to date no other species has been the subject of a long-term breeding programme.

The success of the Otter Trust in raising Eurasian otters means that it is now in a position not only to maintain its own collection but also to send otters to other collections to help found breeding stock. It has also initiated a programme of re-introductions and in order to facilitate this has built special pre-release pens. In these large, semi-wild enclosures young otters are allowed to live an undisturbed life where they do not have an opportunity to become accustomed to human beings. An experimental release programme has been planned by the Nature

Conservancy Council and the Otter Trust to discover how successful re-introductions might be in East Anglia.

The first otters, a male and two females were released in July 1983, the male was fitted with a radio-transmitter which made it possible to follow his movements in the weeks following release. The transmitter remained on the otter for seven weeks and during this time he stayed close to the release point. The three otters were sighted together from time to time and evidently occasionally travelled as a group. The home range of the male extended to about 11 km of river by the time the transmitter fell off. Encouragingly, during this time his activity was very much like a normal wild otter. Subsequently a check was kept on the otters by searching for spraints which up to October were found over 19 km of river. In August 1984 the footprints of an otter cub were found in the area, showing that at least one of the females had bred successfully.

Two similar groups were released nearby in 1984 and further releases are planned for the following years (D.J. Jefferies, pers. comm.). The project is seen as a holding operation to help maintain a viable population of otters in the short term. In the long term it can only succeed if the factors causing the decline in the area can be eliminated.

If losses of otters through accidental drownings in fish traps are significant, adding to the population in this way will slow down or reverse the rate of decline. Meanwhile efforts are being made to reduce deaths of otters in fish traps by developing excluders to prevent them from entering. There is also concern about the levels of some environmental pollutants, particularly polychlorinated biphenyl compounds (commonly known as PCBs) in the area. If these are affecting otters only the removal of the sources of contamination will guarantee the future of the otter population but, in the short term, captive-bred otters which have not been exposed to pollution during rearing may have a better chance of breeding and rearing young than otters that were born in the wild.

Obviously a key to the success of re-introductions is rehabilitation of the habitat. If the measures taken to remove adverse factors are successful then the otter population should survive. If not, it will eventually become extinct as it has elsewhere in England. At the very least, the fact that some of the released otters have been fitted with radio transmitters means that some information on the habits of otters in lowland rivers will be obtained, albeit the habits of captive-bred animals.

CODA

This chapter has shown that until about 200 years ago the impact of man's predation on otter populations was relatively small and local. In the nineteenth and twentieth centuries exploitation increased markedly and some species were greatly reduced in numbers, the sea otter almost to extinction. During the twentieth century the control of trapping and fur trading has progressively reduced the threats from deliberate killing but at the same time more insidious threats have arisen as man has polluted and destroyed the habitat of otters.

In the 1960s nearly 20 species of otters were recognised. By 1980 the vagaries of classification had reduced that number to nine. The next reduction in numbers of species must come as a result of extinction and whether it happens or not depends very much on man's attitude to the natural world. If he is willing to acknowledge and respect the needs of the other species on this planet the otters will survive and, perhaps, prosper.

Bibliography

Alm, G. (1946) 'Reasons for the occurrence of stunted fish populations with special regard to the perch', *Lantbruksstyrelsen*, 24, 1–146

Ames, J.A. and Morejohn, G.V. (1980) 'Evidence of white shark, *Carcharodon carcharias*, attacks on sea otters', *Enhydra lutris. Calif. Fish Game*, 66, 196–209

Ansell, W.F.H. (in press) 'Notes on a tame otter (*Hydrictis maculicollis chobiensis*) in Zambia', *Black Lechwe*

Beckel-Kratz, A. (1977) 'Preliminary observations on the social behaviour of the North American otter *Lutra canadensis*', *Otters: Journal of the Otter Trust*, 1977, 28–32

Ben Shaul, D.M. (1962) 'The composition of the milk of wild animals', *Int. Zoo Yb.*, 4, 333–42

Best, A. (1962) 'The Canadian otter, *Lutra canadensis*, in captivity', *Int. Zoo Yb.*, 4, 42–4

Brack-Egg, A. (1978) 'Situación actual de las nutrias en el Peru' in N. Duplaix (ed.), *Otters: Proceedings of the First Meeting of the Otter Specialist Group*, IUCN, Morges, pp. 76–84

Brownell, R.L. (1978) 'Ecology and conservation of the marine otter *L. felina*' in N. Duplaix (ed.), *Otters: Proceedings of the First Meeting of the Otter Specialist Group*, IUCN, Morges, pp. 104–6

Cabello, C.C. (1978) 'La Nutria de Mar *L. felina* en la Isla de Chiloé' in N. Duplaix (ed.), *Otters: Proceedings of the First Meeting of the Otter Specialist Group*, IUCN, Morges, pp. 108–18

Calkins, D. and Lent, P.C. (1975) 'Territoriality and mating behaviour in Prince William Sound sea otters', *J. Mammal.*, 56, 528–9

Chanin, P.R.F. and Jefferies, D.J. (1978) 'The decline of the otter *Lutra lutra* in Britain: an analysis of hunting records and discussion of causes', *Biol. J. Linn. Soc.*, 10, 305–28

Chapman, P.J. and Chapman, L.L. (1982) *Otter Survey of Ireland 1980–81*, The Vincent Wildlife Trust, London

Clapham, R. (1922) *The Book of the Otter*, Heath Cranton, London

Collier, W.P. (1908) 'Notes on the otter (*Lutra vulgaris*)', *Zoologist*, (4) 12, 92–6

Cooper, J., Wieland, M. and Hine, A. (1977) 'Subtidal abalone populations in an area inhabited by sea otters', *Veliger*, 20, 163–7

Costa, D. (1978) 'The sea otter: its interactions with man', *Oceanus*, 21, 24–30

Cowen, R.K., Agegian, C.R. and Foster, M.S. (1982) 'The maintenance of community structure in a central Californian giant kelp forest', *J. Exp. Mar. Biol. Ecol.*, 64, 189–201

Cranbrook, Earl of (1977) 'The status of the otter (*L. lutra* L.) in Britain in 1977', *Biol. J. Linn. Soc.*, 9, 305–22

Crawford, A.K., Evans, D., Jones, A. and McNulty, J. (1979) *Otter Survey of Wales*, Society for the Promotion of Nature Conservation, Lincoln

Cuthbert, J.H. (1973) 'Some observations on scavenging of salmon *Salmo salar* carrion', *Western Nat.*, 2, 72–4

Davis, B.S. (1977) 'The southern sea otter revisited', *Pacific Discovery*, 30, 1–13

Davis, J.A. (1978) 'A classification of otters' in N. Duplaix (ed.), *Otters: Proceedings of the First Meeting of the Otter Specialist Group*, IUCN, Morges, pp. 14–33

Day, M.G. (1966) 'Identification of hair and feather remains in the guts and faeces of stoats and weasels', *J. Zool., Lond.*, 148, 201–17

Dobben, W.H. van (1952) 'The food of the cormorant in the Netherlands', *Ardea*, 40, 1–63

Donadio, A. (1978) 'Otter trade and legislation in Colombia', in N. Duplaix (ed.), *Otters: Proceedings of the First Meeting of the Otter Specialist Group*, IUCN, Morges, pp. 34–42

Donnelly, B.G. and Grobler, J.H. (1976) 'Notes on food and anvil using behaviour by the Cape clawless otter, *Aonyx cinerea*, in the Rhodes Matopos National Park, Rhodesia', *Arnoldia*, 7, 1–8

Dunstone, N. (1976) 'Vision in relation to sub-aquatic predatory behaviour in the mink (*Mustela vison* Schreber)', PhD thesis, University College of Wales, Aberystwyth

Duplaix, N. (1972) 'Otters of the world', *Animals*, 14, 438–42

—— (ed.) (1978) *Otters: Proceedings of the First Meeting of the Otter Specialist Group*, IUCN, Morges

—— (1980) 'Observations on the ecology and behaviour of the giant river otter *Pteronura brasiliensis* in Suriname', *Terre Vie*, 34, 495–620

Duplaix-Hall, N. (1975) 'River otters in captivity: a review' in R.D. Martin (ed.), *Breeding Endangered Species in Captivity*, Academic Press, London, pp. 315–27

Elliott, K.M. (1983) 'The otter (*Lutra lutra* L.) in Spain', *Mamm. Rev.*, 13, 25–34

Elmhirst, R. (1938) 'Food of the otter in the marine littoral zone', *Scott. Nat.*, 1938, 99–102

Erlinge, S. (1967a) 'Home range of the otter *Lutra lutra* L. in southern Sweden', *Oikos*, 18, 186–209

—— (1967b) 'Food habits of the fish otter (*Lutra lutra* L.) in south Swedish habitats', *Viltrevy*, 4, 371–443

—— (1968a) 'Territoriality of the otter *Lutra lutra* L.', *Oikos*, 19, 81–98

—— (1968b) 'Food studies on captive otters (*Lutra lutra*)', *Oikos*, 19, 259–70

—— (1969) 'Food habits of the otter (*Lutra lutra*) and the mink (*Mustela vison*) in a trout water in southern Sweden', *Oikos*, 20, 1–7

—— (1972a) 'The situation of the otter population in Sweden', *Viltrevy*, 8, 379–97

—— (1972b) 'Interspecific relations between otter (*Lutra lutra*) and mink (*Mustela vison*) in Sweden', *Oikos*, 23, 327–35

Estes, J.A. (1980) '*Enhydra lutris*', *Mammalian Species*, 133, 1–8

Estes, J.A. and Palmisano, J.F. (1974) 'Sea otter: their role in structuring nearshore communities', *Science*, 185, 1058–60

Estes, J.A. and Smith, N.S. (1973) 'Research on the sea otter, Amchitka Island, Alaska', *U.S. At. Energy Comm. Rept.*, AT (26–1), 520

Estes, J.A., Jameson, R.J. and Johnson, A.M. (1981) 'Food selection and some foraging tactics of sea otters' in J.A. Chapman and D. Pursley (eds.), *Proceedings of the Worldwide Furbearers Conference*, Frostburg, Md., pp. 606–41

Estes, J.A., Johnson, A.M. and Jameson, R.J. (1978) 'Research on the sea otter in Alaska' in N. Duplaix (ed.), *Otters: Proceedings of the First Meeting of the Otter Specialist Group*, IUCN, Morges, pp. 120–5

Ewer, R.F. (1973) *The Carnivores*, Weidenfeld and Nicolson, London

Fairley, J.S. (1972) 'Food of otters (*Lutra lutra*) from Co. Galway, Ireland and notes on aspects of their biology', *J. Zool., Lond.*, 166, 469–74

Fisher, E.M. (1939) 'Habits of the southern sea otter', *J. Mammal.*, 20, 21–36

Fitter, R.S.R. (1964) 'In danger of extinction in France', *Wld. Wildl. News*, 24, 5

Foott, J.O. (1970) 'Nose scars in female sea otters', *J. Mammal.*, 51, 621–2

Gilbert, F.F. and Nancekivell, E.G. (1982) 'Food habits of mink (*Mustela vison*) and otter (*Lutra canadensis*) in northeastern Alberta', *Can. J. Zool.*, 60, 1282–8

Gorman, M.L., Jenkins, D. and Harper, R.J. (1978) 'The anal scent sacs of the otter (*Lutra lutra*)', *J. Zool., Lond.*, 186, 463–74

Green, J. (1977) 'Sensory perception in hunting otters, *Lutra lutra* L.', *Otters: Journal of the Otter Trust*, 1977, 13–16

Green, J. and Green, R. (1980) *Otter Survey of Scotland 1977–1979*, Vincent Wildlife Trust, London

—— (1981) 'The otter (*Lutra lutra* L.) in western France', *Mamm. Rev.*, 11, 181–7

Green, J., Green, R. and Jefferies, D.J. (1984) 'A radio-tracking survey of otters *Lutra lutra* (L., 1758) on a Perthshire river system', *Lutra*, 27, 85–145

Greer, K.R. (1955) 'Yearly food habits of the river otter in the Thompson Lakes region, northwestern Montana as indicated by scat analyses', *Am. Midl. Nat.*, 54, 299–313

Grigor'ev, N.D. and Egorov, Y.E. (1969) ['On the biocenotic connections of the American mink with the river otter in the Bashkir S.S.R.'], *Sb Tr. Vses. Nauch-Issled Inst. Zhivotn. Syr'ya Pushniny*, 22, 26–32

Hall, K.R.L. and Schaller, G.B. (1964) 'Tool-using behavior of the California sea otter', *J. Mammal.*, 45, 287–98

Hamilton, W.J. and Eadie, W.R. (1964) 'Reproduction in the otter, *Lutra canadensis*', *J. Mammal.*, 45, 242–52

Harper, R.J. and Jenkins, D. (1981) 'Mating behaviour in the European otter (*Lutra lutra*)', *J. Zool., Lond.*, 195, 556–8

Harris, C.J. (1968) *Otters: a Study of the Recent Lutrinae*, Weidenfeld and Nicolson, London

Harrison Matthews, L. (1952) *British Mammals*, Collins, London

Heggberget, T.M. and Myrberget, S. (1979) 'Den norske bestand au oter 1971–1977', *Fauna*, 32, 89–95

Hewer, H.R. (1969) 'The otter in Britain', *Oryx*, 10, 16–22

—— (1974) 'The otter in Britain — a second report', *Oryx*, 12, 429–35

Hewson, R. (1973) 'Food and feeding habits of otters *Lutra lutra* at Loch Park, north-east Scotland', *J. Zool., Lond.*, 170, 159–62

Hider, R.C., Mason, C.F. and Bakaj, M.E. (1982) *Chlorinated Hydro-carbon Pesticides and Polychlorinated Biphenyls in Freshwater Fishes in the United Kingdom, 1980–81*, The Vincent Wildlife Trust, London

Hildebrand, M. (1954) 'Incisor tooth wear in the sea otter', *J. Mammal.*, 35, 595

Hillegaart, V., Sandgren, F. and Ostman, J. (1981) 'Behavioural changes in captive female otters (*Lutra lutra* L.) around parturition', paper presented to the Second River Otter Symposium, University of East Anglia

Hodl-Rohn, I. (1976) 'The status of the otter in the German Federal Republic', *Otters: Journal of the Otter Trust*, 1976 (no pagination)

Houk, J.L. and Geibel, J.J. (1974) 'Observation of underwater tool use by the sea otter, *Enhydra lutris*, Linnaeus', *Calif. Fish Game*, 60, 207–8

Howes, C.A. (1976) 'The decline of the otter in south Yorkshire and adjacent areas', *Naturalist, Hull*, 1976, 3–12

Ivester-Lloyd, J. (1962) 'Where are the otters?', *Gamekeeper and Countryside*, August 1962, 299–300

—— (1978) 'Otterhounds defined', *The Field*, 1 March 1978, 341

—— (undated) *The Buckinghamshire Otter Hunt*, G.W. May, London

Jefferies, D.J., Green, J. and Green, R. (1984) *Commercial Fish and Crustacean Traps: a Serious Cause of Otter Mortality in Britain and Europe*, The Vincent Wildlife Trust, London

Jenkins, D. (1980) 'Ecology of otters in northern Scotland. I. Otter (*Lutra lutra*) breeding and dispersion in mid-Deeside, Aberdeenshire, in 1974–79', *J. Anim. Ecol.*, 49, 713–35

Jenkins, D. and Burrows, G.D. (1980) 'Ecology of otters in northern Scotland. III. The use of faeces as indicators of otter (*Lutra lutra*) density and distribution', *J. Anim. Ecol.*, 49, 755–74

Jenkins, D. and Harper, R.J. (1982) 'Fertility in European otters (*Lutra lutra*)', *J. Zool., Lond.*, 197, 299–300

Jenkins, D., Walker, J.G.K. and McCowan, D. (1979) 'Analyses of otter (*Lutra lutra*) faeces from Deeside, N.E. Scotland', *J. Zool., Lond.*, 187, 235–44

Jensen, A. (1964) 'Odderen i Danmark', *Danske Vildtundersogelser*, 11, 1–48

Kenyon, K.W. (1969) 'The sea otter in the eastern Pacific Ocean', *N. Amer. Fauna*, 68, 1–352

Kenyon, K.W., Yunker, C.E. and Newell, I.M. (1965) 'Nasal mites (Halarachnidae) in the sea otter', *J. Parasitol.*, 51, 960

King, A. and Potter, A. (1980) *A Guide to Otter Conservation for Water Authorities*, The Vincent Wildlife Trust, London

King, A., Ottoway, J. and Potter, A. (1976) *The Declining Otter: a Guide to its Conservation*, Friends of the Earth, London

Knudsen, G.J. and Hale, J.B. (1968) 'Food habits of otters in the Great Lakes region', *J. Wildl. Mgmt.*, 32, 89–93

Kruuk, H. (1972) 'Surplus killing by carnivores', *J. Zool., Lond.*, 166, 233–44

Kruuk, H. and Hewson, R. (1978) 'Spacing and foraging of otters (*Lutra lutra*) in a marine habitat', *J. Zool., Lond.*, 185, 205–12

Kucherenko, S.A. (1976) ['The common otter (*Lutra lutra*) in the Amur-Ussuri district'], *Zool. J., Moscow*, 55, 904–11

BIBLIOGRAPHY

Lagler, K.F. and Ostenson, B.T. (1942) 'Early spring food of the otter in Michigan', *J. Wildl. Mgmt.*, 6, 244–54

Laidler, L. (1980) 'The giant otter *Pteronura brasiliensis* in Guyana', *Otters: Journal of the Otter Trust*, 1980, 26–8

Laidler, K. and Laidler, L. (1983) *The River Wolf*, Allen and Unwin, London

Langley, P.J.W. and Yalden, D.W. (1977) 'The decline of the rarer carnivores in Great Britain during the nineteenth century', *Mamm. Rev.*, 7, 95–116

Laws, W.A. (1978) 'Mink and otters in Herefordshire', unpubl. ms.

Le Cren, E.D. (1962) 'How many fish survive?', *River Bds. Ass. Yb.*, 1961, 57–65

Lensink, C.J. (1960) 'Status and distribution of sea otters in Alaska', *J. Mammal.*, 41, 172–82

Lenton, E.J., Chanin, P.R.F. and Jefferies, D.J. (1980) *Otter Survey of England 1977–79*, Nature Conservancy Council, London

Liers, E.E. (1951) 'Notes on the river otter (*Lutra canadensis*)', *J. Mammal.*, 32, 1–9

Liles, G. and Jenkins, L. (1984) 'A field survey for otters (*Lutra lutra*) in Yugoslavia', *J. Zool., Lond.*, 203, 282–4

Lloyd, H.G. (1980) *The Red Fox*, Batsford, London

Loughlin, T.R. (1980) 'Home range and territoriality of sea otters near Monterey, California', *J. Wildl. Mgmt.*, 44, 576–82

Lowrey, L.F. and Pearse, J.S. (1973) 'Abalones and sea urchins in an area inhabited by sea otters', *Mar. Biol.*, 23, 213–19

McClean, J.H. (1962) 'Sublittoral ecology of kelp beds of the open coast area near Carmel, California', *Biol. Bull.*, 122, 95–114

MacDonald, D.W. (1977) 'On food preference in the red fox', *Mamm. Rev.*, 7, 7–23

Macdonald, S.M. (1983) 'The status of the otter in the British Isles', *Mamm. Rev.*, 13, 11–23

Macdonald, S.M. and Mason, C.F. (1976) 'The status of the otter (*Lutra lutra* L.) in Norfolk', *Biol. Conserv.*, 9, 119–24

—— (1982a) 'The otter *Lutra lutra* in central Portugal', *Biol. Conserv.*, 22, 207–15

—— (1982b) 'Otters in Greece', *Oryx*, 16, 240–4

—— (1983a) 'Some factors affecting the distribution of otters', *Mamm. Rev.*, 13, 1–10

—— (1983b) 'The otter (*Lutra lutra*) in southern Italy', *Biol. Conserv.*, 25, 95–101

Macdonald, S.M., Mason, C.F. and Coghill, I.S. (1978) 'The otter and its conservation in the River Teme catchment', *J. Appl. Ecol.*, 15, 373–84

McFadden, Y.M.T. and Fairley, J.S. (1984) 'Food of otters *Lutra lutra* L. in an Irish limestone river system with special reference to the crayfish *Austropotamobius pallipes* (Lereboullet)', *J. Life Sciences R. Dubl. Soc.*, 5, 65–76

Mason, C.F. and Macdonald, S.M. (1980) 'The winter diet of otters (*Lutra lutra*) on a Scottish sea loch', *J. Zool., Lond.*, 192, 558–61

—— (1982) 'The input of terrestrial invertebrates from tree canopies to a stream', *Freshw. Biol.*, 12, 305–11

Mason, C.F., Macdonald,. S.M. and Aspden, V.J. (1982) *Metals in*

BIBLIOGRAPHY

Freshwater Fishes in the United Kingdom, 1980–1981, The Vincent Wildlife Trust, London

Maxwell, G. (1960) *Ring of Bright Water*, Longman, London

Melquist, W.E. and Hornocker, M.G. (1983) 'Ecology of river otters in Idaho', *Wildl. Monogr.*, 83, 1–60

Melquist, W.E., Whitman, J.S. and Hornocker, M.G. (1981) 'Resource partitioning and coexistence of sympatric mink and otter populations' in J.A. Chapman and D. Pursley (eds), *Proceedings of the Worldwide Furbearers Conference*, Frostburg, Md., pp. 187–220

Miles, H. (1984) *The Track of the Wild Otter*, Elm Tree, London

Mitchell-Jones, A.J., Jefferies, D.J., Twelves, J., Green, J. and Green, R. (1984) 'A practical system of tracking otters in Britain using radiotelemetry and 65-Zn', *Lutra*, 27, 71–84

Mönnig, H.O. (1950) *Veterinary Helminthology and Entomology*, Ballière, Tindall & Cox, London

Morejohn, G.V. (1969) 'Evidence of river otter feeding on freshwater mussels and range extension', *Calif. Fish Game*, 55, 83–5

Morejohn, G.V., Ames, J.A. and Lewis, D.B. (1975) 'Post mortem studies of sea otters, *Enhydra lutris*, in California', *California Dept. Fish Game, Mar. Tech. Rep.*, 30, 1–81

Morrison, P., Rosenmann, M. and Estes, J.A. (1974) 'Metabolism and thermoregulation in the sea otter', *Physiol. Zool.*, 47, 218–29

Mortimer, M.A.E. (1963) 'Notes on the biology and behaviour of the spotted-necked otter (*Lutra maculicollis*)', *Puku*, 1, 192–206

Mott, G.R. (undated) 'Records of the Dartmoor Otter Hounds 1740–1940', unpublished typescript

Müffling, S. von (1977) *Fischotter in Europa*, Loizenkirchen

Neal, E.G. (1977) *Badgers*, Blandford Press, Poole, Dorset

Newbold, C. (1975) 'Herbicides in aquatic ecosystems', *Biol. Conserv.*, 7, 97–118

Novikov, G.A. (1962) *Carnivorous Mammals of the Fauna of the U.S.S.R.*, Israel Prog. Sci. Translat., Jerusalem

O'Connor, F.B., Sands, T.S., Barwick, D., Chanin, P., Frazer, J.F.D., Jefferies, D.J., Jenkins, D. and Neal, E.G. (1977) *Report of the Joint NCC/SPNC Otter Group*, Nature Conservancy Council, London

Ostfeld, R.S. (1982) 'Foraging strategies and prey switching in the Californian sea otter', *Oecologia*, 53, 170–8

Owen, D.F. (1974) *What is Ecology?*, Oxford University Press, London

Phillips, P.C. (1961) *The Fur Trade*, 2 vols., University of Oklahoma Press, Norman, Oklahoma

Pitt, F. (1927) *Moses, My Otter*, Arrowsmith, London

Poole, T.B. and Dunstone, N. (1976) 'Underwater predatory behaviour of the American mink (*Mustela vison*)', *J. Zool., Lond.*, 178, 395–412

Potts, G.R. (1980) 'The effects of modern agriculture, nest predation and game management on the population ecology of partridges (*Perdix perdix* and *Alectoris rufa*)', *Adv. Ecol. Res.*, 11, 1–79

Pring, G. (1958) *Records of the Culmstock Otterhounds*, privately published, Exeter

Procter, J. (1963) 'A contribution to the natural history of the spotted-necked otter (*Lutra maculicollis* Lichtenstein) in Tanganyika', *E. Afr. Wildl. J.*, 1, 93–102

Radinsky, L.B. (1968) 'Evolution of somatic sensory specialisation in otter brains', *J. Comp. Neurology*, 134, 495–506

Ribic, C.A. (1982) 'Autumn movements and home range of sea otters in California', *J. Wildl. Mgmt.*, 46, 795–801

Rowe-Rowe, D.T. (1977a) 'Prey capture and feeding behaviour of South African otters', *Lammergeyer*, 23, 13–21

—— (1977b) 'Variations in the predatory behaviour of the clawless otter', *Lammergeyer*, 23, 22–7

—— (1977c) 'Food ecology of otters in Natal', *Oikos*, 28, 210–19

—— (1978) 'Biology of two otter species in South Africa' in N. Duplaix (ed.), *Otters: Proceedings of the First Meeting of the Otter Specialists Group*, IUCN, Morges, pp. 130–9

Sandegren, F.E., Chu, E.W. and Vandervere, J.E. (1973) 'Maternal behaviour in the California sea otter', *J. Mammal.*, 54, 668–79

Scheffer, V.B. (1953) 'Otters diving to a depth of sixty feet', *J. Mammal.*, 54, 255

Schneider, K.B. (1978) 'Sex and age segregation of sea otters', *Alaska Dept. Fish Game Final Report*, W-17-4 to W-17-8

Schneider, K.B. and Faro, J.B. (1975) 'Effects of sea ice on sea otters (*Enhydra lutris*)', *J. Mammal.*, 56, 91–101

Schusterman, R.J. and Barrett, B. (1973) 'Amphibious nature of visual acuity in the Asian "clawless" otter', *Nature*, 244, 518–19

Sheldon, W.G. and Toll, W.G. (1964) 'Feeding habits of the river otter in a reservoir in central Massachusetts', *J. Mammal.*, 45, 449–54

Shepheard, S. and Townshend, E.O. (1937) 'The otters of Norfolk', *Trans. Norfolk and Norwich Nat. Soc.*, 14, 138–42

Sherrod, S.K., Estes, J.A. and White, C.M. (1975) 'Depredation of sea otter pups by bald eagles at Amchitka Island, Alaska', *J. Mammal.*, 56, 701–3

Shimek, S.J. (1977) 'The underwater foraging habits of the sea otter (*Enhydra lutris*)', *Calif. Fish Game*, 63, 120–2

Shimek, S.J. and Monk, A. (1977) 'The daily activity of the sea otter off the Monterey peninsula, California', *J. Wildl. Mgmt.*, 41, 277–83

Simenstad, C.A., Estes, J.A. and Kenyon, K.W. (1978) 'Aleuts, sea otters and alternate stable-state communities', *Science*, 200, 403–11

Smith, N.J.H. (1981) 'Caimans, capybaras, otters, manatees and man in Amazonia', *Biol. Conserv.*, 19, 177–87

Stephens, M.N. (1957) *The Otter Report*, UFAW, London

Stephenson, A.B. (1977) 'Age determination and morphological variation of Ontario otters', *Can. J. Zool.*, 55, 1577–83

Strandgaard, H. and Asferg, T. (1980) 'The Danish game bag record II', *Dan. Rev. Game Biol.*, 11, 1–112

Stubbe, M. (1977) 'Der Fischotter *Lutra lutra* (L. 1758) in der D.D.R.', *Zoologischer Anzeiger*, 199, 265–85

—— (1980) 'Die Situation des Fischotters in der D.D.R.' in C. Reuther and A. Festetics (eds.), *Der Fischotter in Europa — Verbreitung, Bedrohung, Erhaltung*, Selbstverlag, Oderhaus and Gottingen, pp. 179–82

Tabor, J.E. (1974) 'Productivity, survival and population status of river otter in western Oregon', MS thesis, Oregon State University

Tabor, J.E. and Wight, H.M. (1977) 'Population status of river otter in western Oregon', *J. Wildl. Mgmt.*, 41, 692−9

Tarasoff, F.J. (1974) 'Anatomical adaptations in the river otter, sea otter and harp seal with reference to thermal regulation' in R.J. Harrison (ed.), *Functional Anatomy of Marine Mammals*, Vol. 2, Academic Press, New York, pp. 111−41

Tarasoff, F.J., Bisaillon, A., Pierard, J. and Whitt, A.P. (1972) 'Locomotory patterns and external morphology of the river otter, sea otter and harp seal (Mammalia)', *Can. J. Zool.*, 50, 915−27

Timmis, W.H. (1971) 'Observations on breeding the oriental short-clawed otter *Amblonyx cinerea* at Chester Zoo', *Int. Zoo Yb.*, 11, 109−11

Trowbridge, B.J. (1983) 'Olfactory communication in the European otter *Lutra l. lutra*', PhD thesis, University of Aberdeen

Vandervere, J.E. (1970) 'Reproduction in the southern sea otter', *Proc. Seventh Ann. Conf. Biol. Sonar and Diving Mammals, Stanford Res. Inst.*, pp. 221−7

—— (1983) 'Annual reproduction, dependency and gestation periods of one wild southern sea otter (*Enhydra lutris nereis*)', *Otters: Journal of the Otter Trust*, 1983, 28−30

Veen, J. (1975) 'Het voorkomem en enige gedragsverschijnselen van de visotter *Lutra lutra* L. in Noord-Holland', *Lutra*, 17, 21−37

Watson, H. (1978) *Coastal Otters in Shetland*, The Vincent Wildlife Trust, London

Wayre, P. (1976) *The River People*, Collins, London

—— (1979) *The Private Life of the Otter*, Batsford, London

—— (1980) 'Report of Council 1980 — Breeding', *Otters: Journal of the Otter Trust*, 1980, 6−8

—— (1981) 'Report of Council 1981 — Breeding', *Otters: Journal of the Otter Trust*, 1981, 6

Webb, J.B. (1975) 'Food of the otter (*Lutra lutra*) on the Somerset Levels', *J. Zool., Lond.*, 177, 486−91

—— (1976) *Otter Spraint Analysis*, Mammal Society, Reading

Weir, V. and Bannister, K.E. (1973) 'The food of the otter in the Blakeney area', *Trans. Norfolk and Norwich Nat. Soc.*, 22, 377−82

Wijngaarden, A. van and Peppel, J. van de (1970) 'De otter, *Lutra lutra* (L.) in Nederland', *Lutra*, 12, 3−70

Williamson, H. (1927) *Tarka the Otter*, Harmsworth, London

Wilson, K.A. (1954) 'The role of mink and otter as muskrat predators in northwest Carolina', *J. Wildl. Mgmt.*, 18, 199−207

Wise, M.H. (1978) 'The feeding ecology of otters and mink in Devon', PhD thesis, University of Exeter

—— (1980) 'The use of fish vertebrae in scats for estimating prey size of otters and mink', *J. Zool., Lond.*, 192, 25−31

Wise, M.H., Linn, I.J. and Kennedy, C.R. (1981) 'A comparison of the feeding biology of mink *Mustela vison* and otter *Lutra lutra*', *J. Zool., Lond.*, 195, 181−213

Wishart, D.J. (1979) *The Fur Trade of the American West*, Croom Helm, London

Woodward, D.W. (1980) *Selected vertebrate endangered species of the seacoast of the United States: Southern Sea Otter*, United States Fish and Wildlife Service, Washington, DC

BIBLIOGRAPHY

Yadav, R.N. (1967) 'Breeding the smooth-coated otter *Lutra perspicillata* in Jaipur Zoo', *Int. Zoo Yb.*, 7, 130–1

Yearbooks of Otterhunting (various editors), published by the Master of Otter Hounds Association, London

Zee, D. van der (1981) 'Prey of the Cape clawless otter (*Aonyx capensis*) in the Tsitsikama National Coastal Park, South Africa', *J. Zool., Lond.*, 194, 467–83

—— (1982) 'Density of Cape clawless otter *Aonyx capensis* in the Tsitsikama Coastal National Park', *S. Afr. J. Wildl. Res.*, 12, 8–13

Zeller, F. (1960) 'Notes on the giant otter *Pteronura brasiliensis* at Cologne zoo', *Int. Zoo Yb.*, 2, 81

Zyll de Jong, C.G. van (1972) 'A systematic review of the nearctic and neotropical river otters', *Royal Ontario Museum*, 80, 1–104

Index

INDEX

INDEX